Beaufighter

The Allies' Multi-Role Combat Aircraft

For Noel and Oliver

Beaufighter

The Allies' Multi-Role Combat Aircraft

Edward Rippeth

AIR WORLD

First published in Great Britain in 2026 by
Pen & Sword Airworld
An imprint of
Pen & Sword Books Ltd
Yorkshire - Philadelphia

ISBN 978 1 03614 469 2

A CIP catalogue record for this book is available from the British Library.

Typeset in INDIA by IMPEC eSolutions
Printed and bound in England by CPI Group (UK) Ltd, Croydon, CRO 4YY

The Publisher's authorised representative in the EU for product safety is Authorised Rep Compliance Ltd., Ground Floor, 71 Lower Baggot Street, Dublin D02 P593, Ireland.
www.arccompliance.com

For a complete list of Pen & Sword titles please contact

PEN & SWORD BOOKS LIMITED
47 Church Street, Barnsley, South Yorkshire, S70 2AS, England
E-mail: enquiries@pen-and-sword.co.uk
Website: www.pen-and-sword.co.uk

or

PEN AND SWORD BOOKS
1950 Lawrence Rd, Havertown, PA 19083, USA
E-mail: uspen-and-sword@casematepublishers.com
Website: www.penandswordbooks.com

FSC
www.fsc.org
MIX
Paper | Supporting responsible forestry
FSC® C013604

Contents

Acknowledgements		vii
Introduction		ix
Chapter 1	Conception *Bristol, Munich and the Air Ministry 1910-1938*	1
Chapter 2	Birth of the Beau *Development and War 1938-1940*	15
Chapter 3	Nightfighter *Nightfighter operations, the Blitz 1940-1941*	23
Chapter 4	Convoy Stooges *Guarding the Approaches 1941-43*	35
Chapter 5	Rogue Warriors in the Sky *Ground attack operations, North Africa 1941-42*	45
Chapter 6	Mediterranean Night Terror *Nightfighters in Malta 1942*	58
Chapter 7	Night Defender and Night Intruder *Home Defence and Bomber Command 1941-43*	69
Chapter 8	Il Flagello Di Dio *Mediterranean shipping strikes 1942-43*	85
Chapter 9	Aussie Battler *New Guinea and Timor operations with RAAF*	102
Chapter 10	The Bloody Flax *Daylight operations, Mediterranean* *October 1942 to July 1943*	121

Chapter 11 Mud, Gubbins and Glory 134
Nightfighting operations, Torch to Tunis 1942–May 1943

Chapter 12 Beaufighter Trauma 145
Long-range Instep Patrols, Bay of Biscay 1942-44

Chapter 13 Whispering Death 154
India and Burma campaign 1943-45

Chapter 14 Nightfighter Paradise 169
Nightfighter operations, Pantelleria and Sicily, May to August 1943

Chapter 15 Strike Wings 177
Anti-shipping operations, English Channel & North Sea 1942-45

Chapter 16 The Gates of Hell 190
Long-range Aegean Operations 1943–44

Chapter 17 Italian Denouement 201
All Beaufighter units, Italy and the Balkans 1943-45

Epilogue 213

Appendix 1: Beaufighter Squadrons of the Second World War 216

Appendix 2: Gazetteer of Outstanding Beaufighter Aircrew 221

Appendix 3: Coastal Command Strike Wings 224

Appendix 4: South-East Asia 901 Fighter Bomber Wing Summary 225

Appendix 5: Specifications and Performance Summaries of Operational Beaufighter Marks 226

Endnotes 227

Index 245

Acknowledgements

The journey of discovery which this book represents could not have happened without the wonderful contributions of a range of people. First of all, the team at Pen and Sword, from the sage advice and trust of John Grehan, who picked up my original proposal, the superb photo sourcing by Martin Mace, and the wonderful patience and considerable editorial skills of Kenneth Patterson and Amy Jordan in crafting the book you see now. I have been so lucky to have had the passionate support and input from Jim Turner of the RAAF 30 Squadron Association, full of wonderful anecdotes about Australia's adopted aircraft. I am also very grateful for Graham Pitchfork for allowing me to use quotations gleaned from the priceless interviews he conducted of Beaufighter crews in his excellent book *Beaufighter Boys* (pub. Grub Street) and to Greenhill Books, who provided permission on behalf of the Estate of Jon Braham, to extensively quote from this great ace's biography (*Scramble*, pub. Greenhill Books). Also thanks to Joe Coles, publisher of the superb *Hush-Kit* aviation substack, whose encouragement and support enabled me to take the step from voracious reader with an itch to write, to published author. And finally, my huge thanks to Judith, Sophie, Imogen and Oliver for their patience while their husband and Dad buried himself quietly for hours on end in a pile of national archives and texts in producing this work.

Introduction

The 14 October 2025 saw the passing of one of Australia's last Beaufighter airmen, David 'Bruce' Robertson, a hero of 30 Squadron and the pivotal New Guinea fighter bomber campaign. There are no flying Beaufighters, although a couple of aircraft are in restoration, and the Beaufighter is noticeably almost entirely absent from the rich legacy of classic Second World War movies. History books on the great campaigns of the Second World War rarely mention it all. Yet the Beaufighter flew some of the most dangerous and exhilarating missions of the war, bringing mayhem and destruction in every theatre of the war.

This book is intended to correct this omission, this sense of the RAF's forgotten aircraft, and to retrospectively and properly pay tribute to Robertson and the legions of heroic Beaufighter crew, many killed in action, almost all now dead. But it needs to do more. The 'so what?' question needs to be addressed. The operations carried out by these brave crews were not peripheral to the war, they were central and made a substantial impact – far more than is commonly understood. This book explores this impact and links the Beaufighter's considerable achievements to the wider course of the war.

The sheer breadth of the Beaufighter's operations demands an unconventional structure. Because in 1942, the Beaufighter was suddenly fighting everywhere at the same time – nightfighting over British cities, shipping strikes in the Med, convoy patrols over the North Sea, ground attack in New Guinea, long-range air combat over Biscay, nightfighting in Malta and North Africa, and even the very first missions over Burma. In every one of these campaigns, the Beaufighter arrived on the losing side, and ended up winning. It was right in the thick of things at every critical turning point, repeatedly jabbing at soft spots in the Axis war machine with real consequences, to the point where it might even be regarded as the aircraft that changed the course of the war.

Nightfighter, anti-shipping strike aircraft, long-range fighter and ground attack fighter bomber – it redefined every role it took on. It became the first true weapons platform, and multi-role combat aircraft – providing the model for legendary aircraft like the de Havilland Mosquito, the F4 Phantom and the Panavia Tornado. This despite the fact it was a hastily designed lash-up, a modestly performing oversized 'heavy fighter', and might easily have been parked with the Westland Whirlwind in obscurity. Instead, the lash-up proved of historic importance in winning the greatest war of all.

This is the story of the Beaufighter and how it helped win the war in so many roles and theatres. It's also the story of the Royal and Commonwealth Air Forces learning to fight in a war in darkness, desert, jungle and ocean. It is also the story of radar fighter direction, where the latest technology needed to be allied to the right airframe to work effectively. But most of all it's the story of tiny units of incredibly brave men, who were finally equipped with the aircraft to take the war to the enemy and hit them where it hurt most.

Chapter 1

Conception

Bristol, Munich and the Air Ministry 1910-1938

There are heavy fighters, and there's the Beaufighter. It was by any conventional reckoning far too big to be a fighter, and only its creators could call it beautiful. Unlike the Spitfire or the Mosquito, there was little romance in its creation. Just steadfast professionalism and pragmatism at a time when anxiety and confusion reigned. This epically versatile, brutally functional aircraft was the offspring of possibly the greatest centre of industrial innovation the world has ever seen. Because the Beaufighter belongs in a long line of Bristol's industrial creation going back to the great Isambard Kingdom Brunel.

The Bristol Aeroplane Company Ltd was founded in the city bearing its name in 1910, the brainchild of the businessman Sir George White. British aviation's other pioneers, men like Tommy Sopwith and Geoffrey de Havilland, started out as brave young men who built machines for themselves to fly, which led to orders to make planes for others, as designers and manufacturers. Sir George was very different – he was already forty-nine and a very wealthy businessman when the Wright brothers made the first powered flight at Kittyhawk, North Carolina. It's not even clear that Sir George ever flew. He was a businessman, and a great Bristolian, years before he dabbled in flying machines, winning his baronetcy in 1904 for public service in his philanthropic support for Bristol's zoo and hospital.

Sir George was in many ways the heir to Isambard Kingdom Brunel, the brilliant engineer and transport pioneer who had built his incredible legacy in Victorian Bristol – the Great Western Railway, the Clifton suspension bridge, the *Great Western* and *Great Britain* steamships, the latter a gorgeously preserved reminder of the city's historic past amid the cafes, shops and restaurants of Bristol's recent Harbourside development. Among his many business interests, White would become a shareholder in Brunel's Great Western Steamship company. White would also be the driving force behind bringing new forms of public transport to his beloved home city, an interest started when he was a young solicitor in 1874, when he joined the Bristol Tramways company. At the time, the company was running horse-drawn trams and cabs, but under White the network was greatly expanded, and then transformed when White and his engineer Robert Clifton Robinson introduced electric trams to the city. He also set his sights much wider, investing in tram networks in Dublin, Gloucester, Middlesbrough and West London. Evidently, trams were not enough for White, and in 1906, he set about introducing a fleet of double-decker motor buses, which led to his building of a motor construction plant in 1913 – and subsequent car manufacturing. Bristol is probably the only city in the world which was a major manufacturer of locomotives, ships, aircraft and motor vehicles – and even today, Filton in northern Bristol remains a major manufacturing arm of British Aerospace.

Unlike Brunel, White was not an engineer and was never an inventor – what he had was an intuitive sense of what the future looked like and a keen legal and financial understanding of what it took to make it happen. So perhaps it shouldn't be too much of a surprise that when George, on a trip to France, saw Wilbur Wright demonstrating one of his aircraft in 1909, he immediately saw the possibilities of flight as a commercial enterprise. Despite the misgivings of numerous business colleagues and partners who thought him mad, on 19 February 1910, George put down £25,000 for his new company, the British and Colonial Aeroplane Company.[1] He also reserved what was his preferred company name, the Bristol Aeroplane Company, to be adopted later. Always a canny lawyer, White feared not being able to attain a trademark using the great city's name while the company lacked credibility as a start-up. There were good grounds for caution. He bought his first aircraft from the French company Zodiac. The problem was it didn't fly, and worse than that, didn't fly in front of a lot of supporters and investors. Typically undeterred, White sued and got his money back, and his new aeronautics engineer, George Challenger, 'borrowed' another French design (Henri Farman) and put a Gnome engine into it. The Bristol Boxkite[2] was born, the first of a long line of Bristol aircraft.

At this point, White was consumed by ideas, also starting a successful flying school,[3] with his son learning to fly, as well as being involved in a top-secret plan to build a flying boat with a well-connected naval officer, Dennistoun Burney (later a Conservative MP).[4] While this proved a total failure, it did involve hiring Frank Barnwell, a Scotsman who had built with his brother the first powered aeroplane in Scotland in 1909, and a graduate of Glasgow University. Barnwell proved to be a brilliant and visionary designer, producing the Bristol Scout, a light, highly manoeuvrable single-seat biplane which pre-dated the Nieuports and Sopwiths which would pivot the air war back to the allies in late 1916. If they had been used in numbers, the Scouts could easily have dealt with what became known as the 'Fokker Scourge' of late 1915 and early 1916.

The scourge were the new Fokker E.I. Eindecker monoplanes, which arguably defined the idea of the fighter – a machine designed purely to shoot down enemy planes; not for the reconnaissance purpose allotted to the new-fangled flying machines by the armies of each side. The Eindecker carried a revolutionary innovation – a machine gun which could fire forward safely through the rotating propellor blades, using an interruptor gear. Unfortunately, the suffocating directive from the RFC's top brass ensured that the Royal Aircraft Establishment's BE2, a slow, reliable and stable two-man reconnaissance plane, was prioritised above all – the aircraft was there to serve the intelligence needs of the army, nothing else. If the Fokker Scourge served one purpose, it was to force a change of thinking within the Army and the Royal Flying Corps. It provoked a campaign which reached Parliament led by Noel Pemberton Billing (later founder of Supermarine) to break the RAE's stranglehold on air supply and proved a need for fighters that could win air superiority to allow successful army reconnaissance.

One man observing this close-to was Captain Frank Barnwell, who had left Bristol and served for over a year with the Royal Flying Corps with 12 Squadron. He returned to Bristol in late 1915 and took to the drawing board. He also hired an assistant designer in early 1916, the Bristol-born and educated Leslie Frise, who was working with a rival aircraft manufacturer, Boulton Paul. It would be an inspired choice.

Following the mounting losses of the BE2C, the RFC had put out a requirement for a new reconnaissance aircraft which was able to defend itself. Bristol's rivals were the Royal Aircraft Factory and Armstong-Whitworth, whose RE8 and FK8 essentially replicated the BE2 with a bit more speed from a more powerful engine. They were no more immune from increasingly powerful new generation Albatrosses and Pfalzes than the BE2 had been to the Eindeckers. What Barnwell and his new assistant Frise produced was a game-changer for the Royal Flying Corps and also provided a waymarker for the Beaufighter twenty-five years later – the Bristol F2B 'Fighter'. After the Bristol Scout and Eindecker had defined the scout or fighter as a lightweight, fast and highly manoeuvrable aircraft, Barnwell had produced something different. The Bristol F2B was a big, powerful two-man muscle machine which not only could fulfil the role of reconnaissance plane, but had greater top speed than most German fighters, and it had a very useful and under-appreciated attribute – it was almost unmatched in a dive.[5] In the terminology of a later war, the Bristol Fighter was the perfect 'boom and zoom' fighter, where pilots could use height advantage to make a diving pass on enemy aircraft.

What pilots of this new aerial beast shouldn't do was fritter away its power and energy advantage and get involved in a turning dogfight with more nimble fighters, which is precisely what happened on its particularly unfortunate debut. Led by their new commander, the famed Zeppelin-killer William Leefe Robinson, the Fighters of 48 Squadron adopted the standard defensive circle when attacked by Jasta 11's Albatrosses led by Manfred von Richthofen. What was a desperate survival tactic for the BE2c wholly negated the Fighter's great attributes and four of the six Fighters were shot down, including Leefe Robinson, who became a prisoner.[6] After this shocking introduction, aircrew learned how to use this highly effective aircraft properly, with 11 Squadron's Andrew McKeever (a Canadian) its leading exponent with thirty-one victories. A second notable Bristol Fighter ace was New Zealander Keith Park, 12 Squadron's top scorer with twenty victories, who of course would go on to even greater things.

The F2B wasn't particularly heavily armed – with a forward-firing Vickers and a Scarff-ring-mounted Lewis machine gun (sometimes two) for the observer. This was the same as the RE8 and other reconnaissance types. But its speed and power was of a different order, a fact not lost on the War Office, who decided in July 1917 to equip all fighter-reconnaissance and corps-reconnaissance squadrons with the new aircraft. By early 1918, RFC orders reached 2,200 and meant Bristol had to expand its manufacturing premises, particularly when orders also flowed in from the nascent US Army air corps. Bristol oversaw some very successful sub-contracting of the manufacturing of aircraft, but orders soon outstripped Rolls-Royce's capacity to supply the Fighter's Falcon engines. In the United States, attempts to fit the locally made Liberty engine (which was powerful but very heavy) led to several accidents, one of which caused the death of Bristol's test pilot, Joseph Hammond. Hammond's replacement as chief test pilot, Cyril Uwins, was appointed the day after Hammond's accident. Uwins would be employed at Bristol for over four decades, including a key role in developing the Beaufighter, and ended up Deputy Chairman of the company in 1957.

Unfortunately, Sir George White wouldn't live to see the Fighter's success – he died suddenly at home in October 1916, aged sixty-three. His son Stanley took over as head of the Bristol Aeroplane Company, which was now firmly established as a key supplier to the Royal Flying Corps, with its factories in Filton and Brislington. With the success of the Bristol Fighter lasting well into the 1920s with RAF service in India and the Middle East, Bristol would at least be well placed for the disarmament and the downturn in orders which faced the plethora of new aviation companies following the Armistice.

After the war, Barnwell and Frise continued to work on a variety of aircraft types, even while RAF orders melted away. One further element fell into place, which was Bristol's takeover of Cosmos Engineering, a small engine manufacturer run by one Roy Fedden, another Bristol-born and educated engineer, who would quickly become a key figure at Bristol. Following an apprenticeship, Fedden had started his career with the Brazil Straker car company, who built his car design the Shamrock in 1907.[7] During the war, the company took on aircraft engine repairs, and as the war approached its close, Fedden and draughtsman Leonard Butler had perfected two powerful aircraft engine designs, the Mercury and Jupiter. Neither arrived in time to be used in the war, but the Air Ministry was impressed enough to urge Bristol to take over the small company, which was facing bankruptcy after the war's end. Hence in 1920, Bristol became the only aircraft manufacturer in Britain who produced their own engines.

The next few years saw a huge retrenchment in the military, which affected the Royal Air Force in particular. At the same time, the civil aviation industry was finding its feet. Bigger aircraft could be built which could carry passengers and bigger freight loads. And of course, aircraft were finding ways of capturing and inspiring the public – from aerobatics displays to breathtaking journeys to air races and contests. Yet, for the whole of the 1920s, Bristol focussed on military aircraft, with a succession of designs which varied from the massive three-wing four engine Braemar, to the compact, all-metal fighter, the Bristol Bulldog,[8] an excellent Bristol Jupiter-powered biplane which achieved widespread adoption with the RAF, and also served with a number of other air forces. The Bulldog is perhaps best known for being the aircraft type in which Douglas Bader crashed and lost his legs.

The end of the war also saw a change in the naming conventions for Bristol planes, which had hitherto been prosaic and 'Ronseal', Scout and Fighter being prime examples. Bristol adopted alliterative naming for its aircraft, which seemingly involved a number of random visits to the dictionary to find nouns beginning with 'B' – the Twenties saw the Bristol Brownie, the Bobby, the Boarhound, the Badger, the Beaver, the Brandon, the Bullet, the Bullfinch, the Bulldog, the Bullpup, the Bloodhound (later reused for a missile), the Berkeley and the Badminton. At one stage Bristol produced the Bludgeon, a name deemed so unsuitable for an aircraft it had to be dropped in favour of the inoffensive but uninspiring Bagshot. In the end, the aircraft cursed with these two names would have more names than actual aircraft built – it was one of a number of prototypes not taken to production. It could have been worse, as on an early flight test, Cyril Uwins was one of the very first aviators to survive the lethal phenomenon of 'control reversal' (ailerons responding in the opposite way to control input) due to severe flexing of the wings, and while he got it down safely, the Bludgeon / Bagshot model went no further.[9]

The arrival of the 1930s would see a global depression, followed by the slide towards a second global war. Aviation continued to be a source of entertainment and endeavour – following on from Charles Lindbergh's solo Atlantic flight in 1927, Amy Johnson and Amelia Earhardt became superstars with their great flights of 1930 and 1932. However, in a sign of the times, the 1931 Schneider Trophy competition for the fastest seaplane was only held following a last-minute bequest, and only the British Supermarine S6 (winner in 1927 and 1929) was able to compete. This walkover meant Supermarine won the trophy permanently, and of course this set in train another inspiring fighter story. The Supermarine S6 would later be the first to officially break 400 mph, in the hands of George Stainforth, who crops up later in the Beaufighter's story.

The other aspect in all these exciting records was that aircraft performance and technology was bounding forward rapidly – and with the likes of Giulio Douhet and Billy Mitchell theorising about the dominant place of air warfare in the future, the British Air Ministry and senior staff in the Royal Air Force were forced into a perpetual process of informed guesswork as to what aircraft might be required in a war. This resulted in the issuing of a bewildering series of specifications which British manufacturers were invited to tender for. Between 1930 and the end of 1939, the Air Ministry issued 194 such directives,[10] the decade starting with a directive for a new torpedo bomber (M1/30) and ending with a spec for an experimental plane powered by Frank Whittle's new jet propulsion engines (E28/39). In that time, some interesting designs came to nothing, like the Supermarine B12/36, a four-engine bomber with swept wings allegedly capable of 360 mph. Others were clunkers that made it through the process, not least the hopeless Blackburn Roc, which took the dubious premise of a turret fighter and made it even slower to meet Fleet Air Arm requirements. Still, the Air Ministry system did at least produce the Spitfire, the Hurricane and the Vickers Wellington. Interestingly, one aircraft manufacturer which started the Second World War without having won a single Air Ministry specification for a newly designed aircraft was de Havilland.

The Bristol Beaufighter had another route. Its story started with a boast by the ebullient *Daily Mail* proprietor, Lord Rothermere, at a staff luncheon discussion about civil aviation, that he would build the 'fastest commercial aeroplane in Europe'.[11] Rothermere's interest had been piqued by America's new 200 mph airliners, the Boeing 247 and Douglas DC-1. Rothermere looked at streamlined American monoplane airliners with stressed metal fuselages and retractable undercarriage and couldn't help but contrast them with the mass of wings, struts and wire that were the RAF's front-line biplane fighters like the Hawker Hart and Bristol Bulldog. Meanwhile, also mindful of the US aircraft, Barnwell had been working on a plan for a twin-engined monoplane – Type 135 – and Bristol were considering whether to embark on building the prototype as a private venture. Roy Fedden had strong connections with US manufacturers and he had seen up close the great strides forward they were making on several visits to the United States.[12] So Rothermere, with Bristol, was preaching to the converted.

As luck would have it, the *Bristol Evening World* editor Robert T. Lewis was able to brief Rothermere on Barnwell's detailed plans for Type 135. He wanted his new airliner to embarrass the RAF, and at another lunch meeting with Stanley White, Frank Barnwell and Roy Fedden at Stratton House in London, a deal was struck for Bristol to build this super new airliner, at a cost of £18,500. The new aircraft, redesignated the Bristol Type 142, was ready for its first flight at Filton on 12 April 1935, and had its airworthiness tests at Martlesham in June. Here, the aircraft that Rothermere named 'Britain First' was clocked at a speed of 307 mph, over 50mph faster than the prototype of the RAF's new fighter, the Gloster Gladiator. Rothermere had made his point, and presented the prototype to the Air Ministry and its commercial registration was soon after removed as it became used for RAF testing flights. The Air Ministry then swiftly issued Specification 28/35 and an order for 150 of the bomber variant after which coupled with orders from the air forces of Finland and Turkey, put paid to any ambitions the Bristol team may have harboured for civil aviation.

Frank Barnwell would make some key changes to the Type 142 in producing the Type 142M – which would be named the 'Blenheim'. The low wing of the 142 was raised 16 inches to mid-wing to allow an internal bomb bay below the wing spars, Barnwell noting '… which should if anything be an aerodynamic advantage'.[13] The new bomber had a glazed nose (forming the distinctive Mark I wedge shape), a bomb-aimer's position and a forward machine gun was added just below the cockpit, with another machine gun in a fully enclosed dorsal turret. The Blenheim was revolutionary for Bristol, and it required a transformation in its manufacturing processes. The factory workforce was no longer dealing with assembling and covering frame-based aircraft, but with a stress-skinned metal monocoque. An Armament Section was set up, specialising in building power-operated turrets, but also hydraulic engineering parts – undercarriage retraction gear and engine-driven pumps. And already, in the broad round-edged wings, the distinctive curve-edged triangle for a tail and the curved engine cowlings, the DNA of the Beaufighter can be clearly seen.

A key element to the new aircraft was its engines, which needed to exceed 500 horsepower. Roy Fedden was in the process of developing a new radial engine, the Bristol Aquila 1, based on the original sleeve-valved Bristol engine, the Mercury. In the end an upgraded Mercury engine would be used for the Type 142, and subsequently the Bristol Blenheim. Fedden was convinced the sleeve valves were the way to go with a great race on for more power, and all his subsequent engines would use them. The sleeve valve was a concentric, fitted valve which sat within each cylinder bore controlling fuel input and exhaust output, as opposed to the more common 'poppet' valve (essentially a spring and plug within the cylinder). Notably, US manufacturers like Pratt & Whitney and Wright stayed with the poppet valves, and were competitive in the Second World War. An aspect of the sleeve valves would feed into the Beaufighter myth – the engine was much quieter.

1935 had seen the first obvious signs of the drift to war. Hitler's new Nazi regime had marched into the Rhineland, and Mussolini into Abyssinia, with the League of Nations watching impotently. This triggered the National Government's Chancellor Neville Chamberlain to finally open the Treasury coffers for rebuilding of the Royal Air Force – with the Blenheim high up on the purchase list. In the words of Bristol's great chronicler, C.H. Barnes: 'Few industries have ever experienced such a sudden boom as that which began for aircraft manufacturers of Great Britain in the summer of 1935.'[14] And Bristol was right at the heart of the boom, building a new engine works on Gloucester Road to add to the main Filton Works, and boosting employment to over 8,000 workers on sites that covered a combined 732 hectares in the city by 1939.[15] Over the next few years, further shadow factories were built in and around Bristol, and at Weston-super-Mare.

Bristol also targeted two new Air Ministry Specifications – M15/35 and 24/35, for a land-based general reconnaissance/torpedo bomber. The former was the eighth spec for a torpedo bomber since the start of the decade, which had thus far reaped a succession of biplane torpedo bombers – the Blackburn Baffin and Shark, the Vickers Vildebeest, the Fairey Gordon and to a naval spec, the Fairey Swordfish. Barnwell and Frise decided it was time for a modern monoplane torpedo bomber. It's easy to assume that this represented a necessary and long-awaited step forward from obsolete biplanes, but the switch to a modern monoplane meant trade-offs. It was found during the Second World War that the Fleet Air Arm's biplanes (Swordfish and Albacore) had significantly better accuracy than monoplanes – a result of a much lower stall speed. Even the closed cockpit, perhaps the epitome of modernity, would probably cause greater crew mortality rates on torpedo bombers, where being shot down at low altitude was an occupational hazard.

This specification resulted in Bristol Type 152, the Beaufort, clearly the heir to the Blenheim, but a much stockier aircraft with a longer and deeper front fuselage, and the longer glazed nose similar to the Blenheim Mark IV (aka Bolingbroke).[16] The Beaufort first flew in October 1938 and was heavier and slightly slower than the Blenheim, despite having Fedden's latest Bristol engine model, the Taurus, which would break the 1,000 horsepower barrier. While it retained the sleeve valves, this was a more complex engine than the Bristol Mercury, with fourteen cylinders comprised of two rings of seven cylinders. The Taurus engine still required hand-crafted sleeve valves, and there lay the rub. It was time-consuming to build, meaning manufacture of the new engines was slow, and imperfections were common. Not only that, but the Taurus engine would be plagued by overheating problems which slowed development and weren't ever resolved satisfactorily.[17]

On 2 August 1938, Frank Barnwell was killed in an accident involving a light aircraft he had made, without seeing the Beaufort fly. Barnwell's loss rocked the Bristol Aeroplane Company at a moment when his leadership and direction was more needed than ever. At the end of September, British Prime Minister Neville Chamberlain went to Munich to try and negotiate a peaceful solution to Hitler's threatened invasion of the Sudetenland. War was avoided by sacrificing the Czechs, and Chamberlain's 'Peace in our time' would become synonymous with appeasement. However, Chamberlain's apparent surrender had bought Britain time, and an adrenaline shot for the Air Ministry in its rebuilding of the RAF. War was very clearly likely to happen and sooner than expected, and once again, orders were ratcheted up – the Ministry of Air Production's new Plan 'L'.

As the dust settled following Munich, there was a rapid reassessment of current aircraft production and while Hurricanes, Wellingtons, Blenheims and even some Spitfires were flowing off the production lines, there was a major gap in the RAF's front-line squadrons. There was no heavy, long-range fighter, nor any immediate prospect of any being ready in the event of an imminent war.

There had been two Air Ministry specs, F37/35, for a fighter armed with cannon, and F11/37[18] for a heavy twin-engined fighter. Importantly, what neither specification anticipated was the need for a fighter which could carry bulky AI radar and a radar operator. This was excusable for the early F37/35, but a primitive airborne radar set had already been flown in a Handley Page Heyford[19] and should have been a consideration when drawing up F11/37. F37/35 had resulted in the Westland Whirlwind, and the Whirlwind prototype flew just two weeks after Munich. The Whirlwind tested well, but the project was delayed following a decision to use more powerful Rolls-Royce Peregrine engines, which were still in development. The Whirlwind was a light, streamlined aircraft manned by just the pilot, and while its performance was very promising as a fighter, its range was poor. It was also too small for a second crewman or any kind of bulky internal machinery. For F11/37, a much bigger plane, the Boulton Paul Type 92, was chosen to develop to prototype. The problem with the Type 92 was it was designed for two planned engines, the super-powered Napier Sabre and the

Rolls-Royce Vulture, which would not be ready until late 1941. In the event, just one half-size prototype was produced before the project was cancelled. Bristol had actually tendered unsuccessfully for both specifications with rather idiosyncratic designs. This included the bizarre Bristol Type 153A, which had its fuselage nose faired into the leading edge of the wing, set well behind the two engines. It never made it off the drawing board.[20]

However, following Munich, the team at Bristol pulled a rabbit out of the hat. Prior to Barnwell's untimely death, the Bristol team had been discussing the possibility of a 'Beaufort Fighter', the Bristol Type 156, and early sketches were underway at the time of Munich. They say 'success has many fathers', and interestingly, Leslie Frise and Ray Fedden both laid claim to the idea.

Leslie Frise's words:

> 'Just before the war we recognised the obvious and urgent need for long-range fighter of decisive striking power… I got the idea of using as many parts of the Beaufort, and actually, by putting in the larger Hercules engines, and latering part of the body to take cannons and fighting equipment, was able to produce the required fighter in six months.'[21]

Fedden on the other hand, remarked:

> 'I was always of the opinion the conception of the Beaufighter with the introduction of Hercules engines, originated in the Engine Division and was pressed home strongly at Filton House for some time before any drawings were started.'[22]

That Fedden's engine team may have actually conceived the Beaufighter shouldn't be a surprise, as Frank Dixon's wry description of the great man rather echoes the aircraft itself: 'Fedden had bulk, and a commanding presence, immense dedication and drive, and a grasp of detail which made it impossible for his juniors to escape his devastating criticism.'[23] Fedden enjoyed having group photos of himself and his team, inevitably with him standing or sitting at the centre, a tall, broad man in a dark suit, hair brushed back from a widow's peak. Every inch the godfather.

The Bristol team proposed using the bulk of the Beaufort airframe – the wings, the tail section and the undercarriage – and the existing Beaufort production jigs at Filton would be used. The key difference was in the fuselage and engines. The Beaufort's glazed nose was replaced by a short, solid nose with four Hispano cannon fitted in the floor of the fuselage. The new aircraft would get Fedden's new Bristol Hercules engines, promising a big boost in power over the Taurus. With the Beaufort prototype having its successful first flight before the Air Ministry in recent memory, the proposal was made on 23 December to Air Marshal Wilfred Freeman, Air Member for Research and Development. There were concerns about the Beaufort Fighter's manoeuvrability, but Freeman immediately signed off an order for four prototypes to be built.

There was some salesmanship in the promises from Fedden and Frise of course – the Bristol Hercules, a bigger 14-cylinder engine would certainly have potential to be much more powerful than the Taurus, but as yet, Fedden hadn't worked out how he could build it in quantity. The sleeve valves were the problem. With the Aquino, Mercury and Taurus, these had to be manually crafted, which greatly added to the manufacturing time – and of course meant the valves were subject to imperfections when exact duplication was required. With war approaching, in which Bristol aero engines would be needed to power thousands of aircraft, this was potentially disastrous – in 1939 Bristol were supplying fifty two per cent of all RAF engines,[24] and important aircraft types were dependent on the Hercules being available in numbers. It would only be mid-1939 that Fedden had the answer, based on machine-tooled centrifugal lathes, delaying mass production until well into 1940.

So the Beaufighter was conceived. As it transpired, the aircraft would prove to be the first great nightfighter, yet curiously this was not an initial consideration. By late 1938, early AI radar sets had flown in an old Heyford, and more recently Avro Ansons and a Fairey Battle, yet without stimulating Air Ministry interest in a fighter plane that could carry AI radar. The head of Fighter Command, Lord Dowding, would admit the single spur for the long-range fighter panic was the prospect of tangling with the Luftwaffe's Messerschmitt Bf110 'Zerstorer', a sleek, heavily armed twin-engined fighter which had already been in service a year. So the Beaufort Fighter got the nod. Fortunately, it just happened that the Beaufighter was the perfect design to carry both an AI box and an operator.

Chapter 2

Birth of the Beau

Development and War 1938-1940

On 17 July 1939, at an airfield near Filton, the veteran Bristol test-pilot Cyril Uwins climbed into the new Bristol 156. In March, the 'Beaufort Fighter' had been given a new name – the Beaufighter. Its unpainted metal fuselage and wings gleamed in the sunshine of the early summer in south-west England, the roundels and serial number being the only concessions to its assigned military role – it carried no cannon or machine guns. It had taken just six months to produce following the signing of the Air Ministry contract, taking the relatively small number of 2,100 drawings to complete this first prototype, serial number R2052, as much was still shared with the recently flown Beaufort. RAF observers noted its size and some were concerned about its manoeuvrability and speed, but the Air Ministry had already ordered 300 two weeks earlier.[1]

The lightning progress to building this world-beater wasn't sustained, making a mockery of the Air Ministry's F17/39 requirement for 300 aircraft 'straight off the drawing board'.[2] In the end over 4,000 further drawings were required and the Beaufighter's arrival with squadrons missed key events in 1940. The new Mark I would have new Hercules III engines, generating 1,290 horsepower each, requiring huge propellers, which had a diameter of 12 feet 9 inches. To achieve ground clearance, the engines had to be mounted centrally in the wing, not underslung like the Beaufort. It also meant stronger and longer Lockheed undercarriage legs were used. Various other changes were required, with elevator control stiffened and the distinctive Beaufort tailfin slightly enlarged.

The result was an uncompromisingly big, brutal, magnificent aircraft which exuded power. It was much bigger than rival heavy fighters – its empty weight of nearly seven tonnes just about matched the maximum take-off weight of its rival, the Bf110, while its wing area of forty-six square metres was almost forty-five per cent greater than Japanese rival, the Kawasaki Ki-45 (code-named 'Nick').[3] The Beaufighter's appearance is dominated by the two massive engine nacelles encasing the fourteen-cylinder radial engines, extending in front of the short, rounded nose, and which entirely hide the forward fuselage when viewed from the side. As an aircraft it has the look of a muscle-bound bruiser with broad chest and outsize biceps (the engines) dwarfing the head (the cockpit). In contrast the Beaufort, which has the large, glazed nose jutting out well beyond the cockpit, and also well ahead of the smaller Taurus engines, looks a bit weedy. For many Beaufighter crewmen, like John Cunningham's great radar operator 'Jimmy' Rawlings, it was love at first sight:

> 'I pulled the hatch open, dropped down on the ground, and walked around to the front of the aircraft. It was good, whichever way you looked at it, sturdy and aggressive, although perhaps a bit heavy. But the two gigantic Hercules engines with which she was powered, air cooled and close cowled, with their huge propellers, sweeping through a wide arc, could surely lift anything. From the tip of that forked aerial at the nose [the AI dipole aerial] to her shapely rudder she was a beauty. I knew that somehow, as a gunner, powder monkey, operator or stowaway, it did not matter which, I just had to fly in her.'[4]

The fuselage and wings were covered in stressed metal panels, fixed in place by flush-head rivets, to help streamlining. The Beau's line of work would often involve flying at ultra-low level, where all manner of obstacles could get in the way – towers, trees, telegraph poles or ships' masts. There were several incidents on several occasions where aircraft survived having sections of the outer wing being sheared off, rather than crumpling the wing with fatal results; Beaufighters simply continued to fly, making it back to base with crew unhurt and a lengthy repair job for the mechanics. On the other hand, the much thicker inner wing had such huge tensile strength that 27 Squadron pilot Brian Harkness (operating over Burma) somehow hit a teak tree stump between fuselage and engine and still made it home.[5] The former Beaufort pilot and aviation author Roy Conyers Nesbitt also identified another strength when ditching – 'its stressed skin acted like skin on the water' compared with the de Havilland Mosquito's wooden ply which, 'with little tensile strength, could easily rip off on contact,' leading to rapid sinking and less chance for the crew to escape.[6]

The Beaufighter carried two crewmen: the pilot, and what was originally called the observer, who took on a number of vital roles – wireless/radio operator, navigator, and initially changing the ammunition drums for the four great 20-millimetre cannon, which stretched along the floor of the Beaufighter, or attempting to unblock jams. However, the second crew member would also prove essential for another task – operating the AI radar system. The early AI radar was a bulky item in its own right, but it also needed a second crew member to monitor and interpret the flow of radio pulses on the cathode ray screen. The Beaufighter's capacity for this meant it was a perfect fit for the evolving role of the nightfighter, which Dowding was soon to realise.[7]

The pilot had a roomy cockpit and a 'logical and relatively uncluttered' instrument panel, with superb forward visibility over the short nose, through one of the deepest glass windscreens of any aircraft. This better visibility greatly aided flying at low level – tree top height – which would prove a highly valuable capability. The screen was also bullet proof, along with armour plate behind the instrument panel, under both seats and along the rear wing spar to protect the fuel tanks. In short, this was a plane designed to be placed in peril. However, the gun sight's unfortunate positioning led to what became known as the 'Beaufighter scar', because during heavy landings the pilot's forehead often struck the sight when thrown forward.

The second crewman sat on a swivel seat underneath a Perspex cupola, about fourteen feet away from the pilot. The cupola allowed navigation by the stars and afforded a view of where the aircraft had been, but to see forward meant walking along the fuselage to join the pilot, through an armoured door. The crew's estrangement meant the radio intercom was essential for communication. Many of the later Coastal Command and ground attack Beaus also carried a machine gun, usually a Vickers K, to help fend off following fighters. Beaufighter crews who later switched to Mosquitos generally preferred the more sociable side-by-side seating, although they also valued the much easier escape options in the roomier Beau. Both crewmen were close to escape hatches – in the case of the pilot, he had a collapsible back of seat which meant he could quickly lift himself and swing back to the hatch. An easy exit was rarely possible when shot down during low level missions, although the Beau's toughness also meant crash-landings were very survivable.

The Beaufighter's Bristol Hercules engines would be repeatedly upgraded through the course of the aircraft's career. The prototype sported an early version of a classic engine that would be the second most manufactured British engine of the war (behind the Rolls-Royce Merlin), with 57,400 built and used in aircraft like the Short Stirling, Vickers Wellington and Handley Page Halifax. In 1939, the Hercules I was developing little over 1,000 horsepower, but this would increase by over eighty per cent through over eighty iterations of the Hercules over the next four years. They were noticeably bigger engines than the Beaufort's Bristol Taurus, weighing 890 kilogrammes, about 300kg more than the Taurus, and displacing thirty-eight litres compared to the Taurus' twenty-five litres. The prototype included an early version of the Bristol Hercules 'power egg' – the cowling, rear slats and engine cover – with the distinctive curved air intake for the supercharger placed on top of the cowling, absent on the Taurus-engined Beaufort, but a distinguishing feature of all Hercules powered aircraft. The Hercules supercharger gave the aircraft excellent speed at sea level (306mph for the Mark IF), which would prove to be very useful in several of its roles.

The creation of 'power eggs' would play a major role in RAF success, even beyond the Beaufighter. In 1938, the Rolls-Royce engineer (and former Air Ministry official) L.F.R. Fell was made chairman of the Interchangeable Power Plant Committee,[8] which sought to standardise engine fittings and bulkheads to allow different engines to be fitted to multiple-engined aircraft. In the case of the Beaufighter, this had an extraordinary unintended consequence. The first batch of Beaufighters had Hercules power eggs, but thanks to Fell's work, a Merlin power egg was also developed for the

Beaufighter. In 1941, the Avro Manchester bomber with its Rolls-Royce Vulture engines (essentially two combined Peregrine engines) proved shockingly unreliable, leading to heavy operational losses. At the same time, the Merlin-engined Beaufighter Mark IIF had markedly worse handling characteristics and reliability than the Mark IF. Using the Beaufighter power eggs, the Avro Manchester was converted into the four-engined Lancaster, saving months of redevelopment. This ultimately helped release more Bristol Hercules engines for Beaufighters, as the brilliant Lancaster quickly supplanted the Hercules-powered Short Stirling, meaning the Merlin-engined Beaufighter model ultimately was short-lived.

As an aircraft to fly, the Beaufighter was regarded as a beast, particularly among pilots flying it for the first time. The great power and forward front of gravity meant a lot of torque and a tendency to veer or swing left on take-off, while ground-looping was a hazard on landing. Another issue was sudden roll-over if one engine failed. For more experienced pilots, it was a beast that could be tamed, nightfighter ace Jeremy Howard-Williams commenting, 'In fact, apart from its fore and aft instability, the Beaufighter was one of the nicest planes to fly ever built.'[9]

Attempts were made to make the Beau more stable, including fitting a Mark IF with a double tail and rudder (as per Bf110), although Bristol settled on a 12-degree dihedral tailplane as the main solution, with most Mark VIs built with this arrangement, despite the cost in manoeuvrability. With the later 'Torbeau', the torpedo-carrying version needed stability above all else at low altitude, so it also had a long dorsal fin extending forwards from the tail.

The Beaufighter's size, its thick wings and tubby fuselage, did come with a penalty. The Mark IF had a maximum speed estimated at 323 miles per hour.[10] The Merlin version would make 335 mph, but after that, despite the spiralling horsepower from the later Hercules upgrades, the top speed remained stubbornly in the 320 to 330 mph range (the 'Torbeau' Mark X had two Hercules XX engines of 1,735 horsepower apiece, about 500 horsepower greater than the Mark I). This in part reflected the shifting roles of the Beaufighter in the war – while initially a long-range and nightfighter, by the end of the war it was assuming more strike and ground attack roles, but lack of speed was also an Achilles heel. It meant the Beaufighter was vulnerable to faster shore-based single-engined fighters, notably the Bf109F and the Focke-Wulf Fw190, and on a handful of occasions suffered heavy losses.

And of course, the Beaufighter was armed to the teeth. The standard Beaufighter armament was four 20-millimetre Hispano cannon with six 7.7mm Browning machine guns in an asymmetrical arrangement in the wings – four in the starboard wing, two in the port. The first prototypes and production versions lacked the machine guns, and it was found that recoil from firing the four cannon caused the nose to dip. One measure to resolve this problem was to build in a hefty four-gun turret to replace all but two cannon (the Beaufighter Mark V), although predictably their performance was appalling and thankfully only two were built. The Hispano cannon were not without other difficulties – the original Hispano HS404 was designed by the Swiss-French company Hispano-Suiza as a lightweight cannon which could be fired through the propeller hub of a fighter. The British Government bought a licence to build the renamed Hispano Mark I, and these were earmarked for the Westland Whirlwind and Bristol Beaufighter. At this stage, the cannon were fed by drums of sixty explosive shells, weighing in at 257 grams apiece. While highly destructive, a drum could be fired off in about six seconds, and during nightfighter operations, changing ammunition drums in the dark and often in a violently manoeuvring aircraft was difficult to say the least. As a result, British manufacturer Martin Baker developed a belt feed for the cannon, which was introduced later in 1941, and later marks carried 240 cannon rounds per gun.

However, this heavy armament was unprecedented at the time – a Beaufighter's weight of fire totalled a huge 12.1 kilograms per second, more than twice the weight of fire of the Bf110.[11] It meant the Beaufighter as a weapons platform would prove to be highly effective in myriad roles, and crucially, anticipated a critical need that would arise in almost every theatre of war. This need would become glaringly obvious in the days following 10 May 1940, as events took a dark turn away from Bristol's Filton works, where the RAF's first delivery of Beaufighters remained tantalisingly a few weeks away.

By 12 May, the Blitzkrieg was in full swing, with German Panzer columns reaching the banks of the Meuse River in Belgium. The Royal Air Force had deployed the Advanced Air Striking Force, consisting of twelve squadrons of Fairey Battles and Bristol Blenheims, both light bombers thrust into a tactical role which involved low level attacks on bridges and motorised and armoured columns. The result was a series of massacres by anti-aircraft fire and an umbrella of lethal Bf109 fighters. Of nine Belgian Air Force Battles that set out to bomb the Albert Canal, six were shot down. When later the RAF despatched eight, seven were shot down. Yet the crews, knowing what they faced in their hopeless machines, still took off and attacked with incredible courage, best exemplified by 12 Squadron's Flying Officer Donald 'Judy' Garland and his crew, who pressed home his attack in his fatally damaged aircraft and managed to destroy a span of the Weldwezelt bridge. Garland and his observer Thomas Grey were both awarded the Victoria Cross posthumously,[12] their gunner, L.R. Reynolds, overlooked. Further attempts were made to attack advancing columns of troops and armoured vehicles. On 14 May 1940 forty of seventy-one attacking Battles and Blenheims were shot down.[13] Leading war historian Alastair Horne commented:

> 'For the RAF on the Meuse that day was an unimaginable hell, a real Valley of Death from which few returned.'[14]

This was in stark contrast to the brutal efficiency of the Luftwaffe's Stukas. Meanwhile, the German advance continued unabated. What remained of the AADF soon afterwards switched to night operations, where losses were low but tactical impact was negligible, while the British Expeditionary Force faced its existential moment at Dunkirk.

The aircraft employed to stem the Wehrmacht's great advance, the Fairey Battle and the Bristol Blenheim, were pitifully equipped to do so. Both were easy prey for the much faster new Bf109Es, with just a single defensive machine gun. Both aircraft were even more inadequate when pressed into low level attacks – each aircraft featured just a single forward, small calibre

(7.7-millimetre) machine gun. Brave men were expected to fly into a crucible of fire and shell armed with a peashooter. While their bombs could cause damage if they hit targets, they seldom did when aircraft were under such heavy enemy fire. A Beaufighter packed a weight of fire forty-eight times greater than either the Battle or Blenheim.[15] It could have made a huge difference, but they weren't ready for France, and when eventually they were, it would be to face a very different emergency.

Chapter 3

Nightfighter

Nightfighter operations, the Blitz 1940–1941

London, 7 September 1940

On this day, for the first time in the war, London came under sustained attack, firstly by day, and with blazes still raging, a further wave of 318 Luftwaffe bombers attacked by night. In the resultant destruction, hundreds of innocent civilians died, and vast numbers of houses and warehouses were set ablaze. The Blitz had begun. In the context of the Battle of Britain, this day has come to be regarded as the moment the Germans lost the battle, by giving up the aerial onslaught against the RAF and its fighter stations. Lost in this narrative is the fact that for the RAF, so gloriously successful by day, the blitz that night represented total failure, ultimately with far-reaching political fall-out. Not a single German bomber was lost to nightfighters. Nor were any lost to anti-aircraft guns or barrage balloons or any aspect of the defensive effort. The British civilian population faced a brutal onslaught unprecedented in the nation's storied history, one which would eventually cost the lives of over 45,000 people, with seemingly no effective defences.

The reason for this failure was that two critical elements – airborne intercept radar (AI), and a plane to carry the AI, were not ready for effective operation. The drive through the 1930s, led by Henry Tizard and Robert Watson-Watt, to develop radio detection systems had undoubtedly reaped a rich reward. Initially funded to the tune of £10,000 by the RAF at the behest of a far-sighted senior RAF officer, Hugh Dowding,[1] 'CH' (Chain home) had been built, and all those coastal radar stations were in place for

Dowding and the country to cash in hugely on the investment, providing the guidance and control system for RAF fighter squadrons to win the Battle of Britain in the summer of 1940. However, two further radar deployments, AI and ASV (Air-to-surface vessel radar), had been left behind, and were still in an embryonic state. As also was the Bristol Beaufighter – operations-ready Beaus had still to reach front-line squadrons. A great champion of AI, Hugh Dowding had (if not immediately) identified the Beau from Bristol's design plans as the ideal AI-equipped nightfighter. Yet 'Stuffy' Dowding, the brilliant and visionary air chief who won the Battle of Britain, would be manoeuvred out of his position (along with 11 Group's inspirational leader Keith Park) by Sholto Douglas, Leigh Mallory and others, in part because he was seen to be single-minded in his approach to AI-equipped nightfighters, when other options were urgently needed to fill the gap. Dowding's replacement, Douglas, who was also heavily involved in pre-war AI development, shared his predecessor's stubbornness, which was great in pressing on with radar-guided defence, but he also stuck with wildly misconceived ideas, such as aerial mines and the later Turbinlite, for far too long. In his ramping up of Cat's Eye fighters (non-AI fighters guided by ground radar and searchlights), Douglas was vindicated.

The first operational AI Mark III had been in use since May 1940. It wasn't a great device, the problem being that it lost contact when a plane flew within one kilometre of the target, while echoes bouncing back from a target tended to be masked by pulses (radio signals sent from the plane). However, it was put into service initially with the specially established Fighter Interception Unit (FIU), who fitted AI to Bristol Blenheims with the aim of putting AI into practice in actual operations. Unfortunately, the Beaufighter's lighter, underpowered and under-armed stablemate singularly failed to meet AI pioneer Taffy Bowen's one vital performance criteria:[2] an AI-carrying nightfighter had to be twenty to twenty-five per cent faster than the bombers it was intercepting. The Blenheim was capable of 279mph top speed at altitude, scarcely any faster than the raiding Dornier Do17s, Heinkel He111s and Junkers Ju88s, all capable of over 270 mph.[3] But needs must. The Beaufighters weren't ready. The AI wasn't universally welcomed when it arrived with the existing Blenheim nightfighter squadrons. According to

29 Squadron's Jon Braham, it rarely worked and was generally distrusted[4] by the undertrained radar operators, who in the main had been hastily converted from their original role of observer/radio operator and air gunner.

The first great nocturnal air battle of the war had revealed another critical flaw of the Blenheim – it was way too lightly armed, even with the new 'fighter pack' of four 7.7 mm Browning machine guns stuck to the underside of the forward fuselage. Thus, on 18 June, several Bristol Blenheim fighters, not yet AI-equipped, intercepted a formation of bombers on an evening with clear night skies and an almost full moon. In a sustained air battle, three Heinkels were eventually shot down, but two of the Blenheims were also hit by defensive fire[5] and lost, with three crew killed – sadly one of the pilots killed was 29 Squadron's John Barnwell,[6] son of Bristol's great designer. While unusually good night-time visibility allowed the Blenheims to stay engaged and perform repeated attacks to eventually finish off the bombers with machine-gun fire, it also exposed them to defensive fire. A much greater weight of fire was required to cause instant, catastrophic damage, ideally in a single pass – because once alerted by gunfire, a still intact bomber could fire back at his assailant or make evasive manoeuvres in the dark.

The FIU's AI-equipped Blenheims had their first fleeting encounters with German aircraft in June 1940. Their first successful AI interception occurred on 22 June, with Glyn Ashfield destroying a Dornier Do17 with the loss of all its crew.[7] But such victories would continue to be as rare as hen's teeth and were notably absent on several of the biggest days of the September blitz. Until AI could be properly developed, most nightfighters flew without, and relied on 'Cats Eye' interception tactics, that is they were scrambled in response to CH plots and looked out for bombers lit up by searchlights. As a Cat's Eye interceptor didn't require space for a radar operator and radar, it at least allowed a much wider pool of fighter types to be employed. Flight Lieutenant Jon 'Bob' Braham scored his first and only victory in a Blenheim like this.[8] Other Cats Eye squadrons included two equipped with the Boulton Paul Defiant, 141 and 264 squadrons. The cumbersome turret fighters had been badly mauled in the early weeks of the Battle of Britain and both squadrons had been reassigned to night defence operations. There were also three Hurricane squadrons, which included 85 Squadron, commanded by Battle of Britain ace Peter Townsend, later of Princess Margaret fame. Eventually, both the Defiant and the Hurricane would prove quite effective in their allotted nocturnal role. This is more than can be said for the Handley Page Harrow, a washed-up 1930s bomber, which was employed by the newly created 420 Flight. The Harrow could barely manage 200 mph, but its role was as a tug to pull LAMs (long aerial mines attached to cables) into the path of German bombers. The idea was eventually abandoned, although it seems to have accounted for at least two bombers,[9] making it more effective than the later, even more wasteful Turbinlite project (see Chapter 7).

It was against this backdrop that, finally, the Bristol Beaufighter started to arrive with operational squadrons, in more of a trickle than a flood, with the limited production having also to serve Coastal Command's impatient demands. On 25 August, the first production Beaufighter arrived at Tangmere for trials with the Fighter Interception Unit. On 2 September 1940, four squadrons (25, 29, 219 and 600) each received one Beaufighter, to help pilots get started on the conversion from Blenheims. The full re-equipping and conversion training process would end up taking several months to complete. The night of 17/18 September 1940 would see Beaufighters of 29 Squadron fly their first operational night patrol, without encountering anything. The Beaufighter's first victory would be five weeks later, on 25 October, when 219 Squadron's Flight Sergeant Hodgkinson shot down a Dornier Do17, although without the benefit of AI. The upgrade from Blenheim to Beau coincided with the arrival of the AI Mark IV radar set, which resolved some of the problems of the Mark III.

A further crucial element in the defences was also addressed – Mark III and Mark IV radars were still proving ineffective without ground control guidance to vector the fighter into the vicinity of the enemy aircraft. In this regard, the radar plots of the coastal Chain Home radar stations simply weren't precise enough for night interceptions.[10] Basically, they could place a group of aircraft to within three to five miles. This wasn't a problem during the Battle of Britain, when the battle was in daylight and the German formations were easily visible from several miles on bright summer days. By night, this meant that AI-guided fighters were being directed into a huge black void, where the chances of getting a contact were still small, due to the range limits of the AI. The solution was to set up dozens of inland GCI (ground control interception) stations using shorter range radar sets with revolving antennae, capable of more precise on-screen fixes over 360 degrees. However, the first of these, at Durrington in Sussex, would only become operational in December, and it wouldn't be until well into January that the first batch of a dozen GCI sets were in place.[11]

Of course, in the real time that GCI stations, Beaufighter squadrons, crews and radar sets were being brought together towards operational effectiveness, the Luftwaffe blitz continued, and the RAF's nightfighters continued to make little impact. On 14/15 November, Coventry was targeted by 515 Luftwaffe bombers. The Germans had also been innovating, with the raid led by a group of thirteen target-marking Heinkels, guided by the X-Gerat radio beams. The main raiding force carried air bursting mines and heavy incendiary loads, and the result was that a large part of the city was devastated and at least 568 civilians killed.[12] Not a single plane was shot down by nightfighters, with the city's AA defences accounting for the one Luftwaffe bomber lost. Nazi Propaganda chief Josef Goebbels would revel in the destruction, tastelessly coining the phrase 'coventriert' ('to coventrate') to describe the process of turning a city to rubble. Coventry marked a crushing low, with RAF nightfighters clearly incapable of stopping such a force or inflicting significant losses. The month of November 1940 saw Luftwaffe bombers fly 5,495 sorties, of which RAF nightfighters shot down just two aircraft.[13] However, one of these victories would represent an important turning point.

Three days after Coventry saw an AI-equipped Beaufighter score its first victory, in the hands of Squadron Leader John Cunningham of 604 Squadron. It was a special moment, as his squadron colleague Rory Chisholm remarked, 'The news was electrifying. For me it meant that the bombers we were sent to chase were really there…'.

Cunningham would become one of the great Beaufighter aces, and 604 would become the first truly effective night fighting unit of the war. The squadron had been established in 1930 and used a variety of biplane types from the DH9 to the Hawker Demon before being allocated a nightfighter role in 1939, when they equipped with Bristol Blenheims, which were soon equipped with AI Mark III radar.[14] It meant a very quiet Battle of Britain, as the squadron's pilots failed to score a single victory. Cunningham had enlisted in the RAF in 1936 as an 18-year-old and joined 604 Squadron, which was then an auxiliary squadron made up of part-timers and reservists. Described by a colleague as having 'cherubic countenance – rosy cheeks, fair curling hair, and engaging smile',[15] he had also managed to land a rather special day job – he joined the de Havilland company, soon winning a role as a test pilot (he returned after the war as Chief Test Pilot). He would even crash a plane with Sir Geoffrey on board, the pair baling out. With its focus on night attacks, Cunningham and 604 effectively had to sit out the great air battles of the Battle of Britain, but he would be rewarded with promotion to squadron leader in September 1940.

As well as his undoubted leadership and piloting skills, Cunningham brought great technical nous to his job, and he would soon prove to be an articulate spokesman whose opinions were sought by senior brass. He demanded and got Beaufighter gunsights redesigned. He also developed a lengthy and productive partnership with his radio operator, 38-year-old Jimmy Rawlings, who had been his air gunner during his first Hawker Demon days with 604, and who Cunningham drafted in as radar operator after his third victory. Cunningham would very quickly develop effective nightfighter tactics – the key being to approach steadily from below to avoid being seen, holding fire until the bomber was well within his sights. One of his later 604 arrivals, Jeremy Howard-Williams, described another aspect of Cunningham's leadership style – he literally took his new pilots under his wing. 'John Cunningham's object in taking up all new pilots was to show them the Beaufighter was nothing to be frightened of. Many new aircraft which enter service are the subject of alarmist rumours… a demonstration of precision flying by the CO was the surest way of instilling confidence in inexperienced pilots.'[16]

Cunningham would become the Beaufighter's first great exponent and champion. That Cunningham and Rawlings brought something special to 604 Squadron would become clear not just in their own performance, but in that of his squadron, which would achieve almost twice the number of victories of any other nightfighter squadron up to the end of the Blitz in June 1941. The squadron would produce a cadre of superb nightfighter pilots, including aces Rory Chisholm, Edward Crew, Ian Joll and Keith Geddes, a Cambridge rugby blue who would later captain Scotland. But it took time. After Cunningham opened the scoring for 604 on 19/20 November, it would take five more weeks for the squadron to get a second (Cunningham again – he'd also get the squadron's third).[17]

The nightfighting infrastructure – GCI network, establishing communication protocols, aircrew training, and above all, actual Beaufighter aircraft – was coming together slowly, but it would be winter, accompanied by a skyrocketing decline in serviceability of the Luftwaffe's bombing force, that provided British cities the main respite, with just 1,225 bomber sorties[18] in February – scarcely a fifth of the November effort. Such statistics of course hid a number of things. Firstly, that the Luftwaffe continued to carry out highly proficient and damaging raids, notably achieving the 'Second Great Fire of London' in an attack which destroyed much of London's historic centre, and a three-day February onslaught against Swansea, targeted due to its docks and proximity to a major oil refinery. Secondly, that while Luftwaffe losses remained tiny, nightfighter efficiency in achieving interceptions and victories was improving for AI-equipped Beaufighters, but also 'Cats Eye' Hurricanes and Defiants, whose efficiency also rose greatly with GCI guidance. Whereas in January, 198[19] nightfighter sorties were required to bring down a single Luftwaffe bomber, by March this was down to twenty-four, and among AI-equipped nightfighters (mainly Beaufighters, but also Blenheims and Douglas Havocs), this was reduced to just eighteen sorties per kill, a level which would be maintained until the end of the Blitz in June.[20]

Things seemed to click into place over two consecutive nights, between 12 and 14 March, when nightfighters shot down fifteen bombers attempting to raid Liverpool and Birkenhead. Beaufighters claimed ten of these, including John Cunningham's fourth victory and Bob Braham's first Beaufighter score. Braham's description of the victory gives a perfect illustration of the intense teamwork involved with the new system – and the importance of the trio, GCI-radar operator-pilot:

'[Radar operator Sergeant] Ross and I were scrambled and vectored towards the coast near Skegness. We levelled out at 15,000 feet and with throttles wide open headed east. The GCI controller directed us towards the enemy, keeping up a running commentary. "He's four miles dead ahead." "You should get contact in a minute." I asked Ross if he had picked anything up. "Nothing yet." Tension was mounting. On a night like this [clear and moonlit] we should see him nearly half a mile away. To gain surprise we had to plan our approach to make it difficult to spot us as we came in for the kill. The controller's voice was now becoming more urgent. "Three miles, a little to port and above." "No contact." Then Ross came through over the intercom. "Contact, 4,000 yards and 20 degrees above. Gently port." This was it. I pressed the transmitter and shouted, "Contact" to the GCI controller. "Good luck, Bob, go in and get him."

'Now Ross had taken over the commentary where the GCI controller had left off... "Where do you want him, Bob?" "Dead ahead about 100 feet above me." This positioning should give us advantage. His gunners would be searching the sky, but anything coming from below was a dark, moving object against a dark background.'

'Further instructions followed from Ross:

"Harder port, ease it, now steady, range 2,000 yards and he is about 200 feet above... Steady, Bob, hold that height. He is just about 100 feet above at 1,000 yards." 'I can't see him yet.' "OK, throttle back a bit. Range now 900 yards, hold that course." 'What was that? As I stared, I thought I saw something moving. I blinked. My eyes were watering with the strain. Yes, there he was, a black object moving ahead of me and above, still far too far to make out what sort of aircraft he was.'

At about 400 yards, Braham opened fire, seeing strikes on the Dornier – but the guns soon jammed, meaning Ross had to detach himself from his oxygen feed and try to clear the jam in the four cannons. This didn't seem to work and Braham considered ramming the bomber. Surprisingly, the Dornier didn't take evasive action or return fire, and Braham tried one last time: 'I pressed the button, hoping against hope that the guns would fire. The Beau bucked as they roared away and, in a blinding sheet of flame, the Dornier 17 blew up in my face'.[21]

April would prove even more successful for the RAF's nightfighters. They amassed fifty-eight victories,[22] thirty-one by Beaufighters, and remarkably, 604 Squadron achieved twenty-three of these – in no small part to Graham Budd, who destroyed three bombers on the night of 10/11 April, for once stealing the limelight from John Cunningham, who was becoming something of a national hero. Lord Woolton, the Minister for Food, and in charge of trying to motivate the growing of home-grown produce, introduced a campaign ascribing Cunningham's success to his apparently brilliant night vision which came from eating carrots.[23] The Air Ministry fully approved of such propaganda – it was a way to hide the radar advances behind Cunningham's success. The newly nicknamed 'Cat's Eyes' Cunningham would emulate Budd on the night of 18/19 April, destroying three Heinkel He111s and taking his score to eleven.

This sudden uptick in losses occurred just as the Luftwaffe's bombers were needed on multiple fronts, with units despatched piecemeal to the Balkans, Greece and North Africa. Preparations for Barbarossa were ratcheting up. The Luftwaffe responded by deploying night intruder fighters (usually Dornier Do17s or Junkers Ju88s), flying 205 sorties in April.[24] The German intruders targeted the RAF's airfields and generally had more success catching RAF bombers returning from missions – however, they did shoot down three nightfighters, two Cat's Eye Hurricanes and one Spitfire, but no Beaufighters. The bombers' defensive fire tended to cause more problems – while their individual machine guns generally caused superficial damage to the sturdily-built Beaufighter, there were occasions where the pilot was hit and wounded or engines struck which led to the crew abandoning the aircraft. Accidents in the dark also remained the key hazard – including friendly fire, with a 600 Squadron Beau being shot down by a 604 Squadron Beau on 9 May. Fortunately, the crew baled out safely.

May saw the Blitz reach a crescendo of destruction. By this time, there was very little pretence about hitting targets of military importance, and bombers carried loads almost entirely comprised of incendiary bombs. The month opened with a three-day onslaught on Liverpool which killed 1,900 people, but 10/11 May saw the biggest raid of all – a huge attack on London, in which the Luftwaffe flew 571 sorties and inflicted the highest nightly death toll of the war, with 1,436 civilians killed.[25] But the cost to the Luftwaffe also reached a new peak – in the ten days of May leading up to the great London raid, the RAF claimed ninety-four bombers shot down, with their biggest nightly haul of twenty-five on 10/11 May. The Luftwaffe also ramped up its night intruder effort on this night with sixty-three sorties – with little result. Just one RAF fighter, a Hurricane, was lost on the night, most likely to defensive fire from a Heinkel. Across this ten-day period, Beaufighters were notably outscored by Cat's Eyes fighters, with Boulton Paul Defiants claiming thirty bombers against twenty-seven by the Beau. Shorter nights and clearer weather may have contributed, but one reason was simply that there were many more single-engined nightfighters. It should also be said that overclaiming was generally much more common in the Defiants and Hurricanes, and this particular month saw a notable mismatch between RAF claims and Luftwaffe losses. Whatever, the kills per sortie ratio remained firmly in the favour of the Beau. It was also sound evidence that the GCI network worked for both AI and Cat's Eye fighters. Sholto Douglas was proven correct to pursue a supplementary Cat's Eye strategy while Beau numbers were still building up. Large numbers of Hurricanes, Defiants and even Spitfires and their crews were available and underused for daytime defensive duties at a time when Beaufighter numbers were still relatively small.

The London raid on 10/11 May would also be the moment that Goering chose to cut his losses and effectively end the Blitz campaign. Clearly Barbarossa plans were uppermost in this decision, and the whole of Kesselring's Luftflotte 2 was despatched to the east for the launch of the invasion in June. Within a few weeks, just 203 bombers were left in the west. Was the decision hastened by the nightfighters and in particular the Beaufighter? There is certainly a slight frustration in Sholto Douglas's reported remarks that 'if the enemy had not chosen to pull out in the middle of May, Fighter Command would have inflicted such casualties that continuance of the night offensive would have been impossible'.[26] Douglas might have been exaggerating a little, but he deserves credit for completing the job his more illustrious predecessor had started – the complex, interconnected defence system with the AI-equipped Beaufighter at the apex, particularly considering where things were in November 1940 when he took over. For the rest of 1941 and 1942, Cat's Eye squadrons would gradually convert to Beaufighters. In the debit column, Douglas still found time for resource-wasting distractions, as we'll see.

So the Luftwaffe gave up their attempt to pound Britain into submission, and would never come close to matching the campaign. The Luftwaffe was not halted because it was defeated, yet it was possibly more important than that. The Beaufighter (and Cat's Eye accomplices) had inflicted lasting and permanent strategic damage on the Nazi war effort. In May 1941, with the war suddenly expanding on new fronts and a huge invasion plan in the offing, the Luftwaffe had a bomber fleet of just 1,511 aircraft[27] – exactly 200 fewer bombers than a year earlier. Goering had allowed the Luftwaffe's Blitz campaign to drift and become an extended, useless campaign of terror and destruction, which suddenly saw RAF nightfighters bite back hard, meaning the Luftwaffe's attempts to rebuild their bomber forces had been wasted. The Luftwaffe had blindly pursued a strategic bombing campaign which left it short of the aircraft and crews it needed in the east and, incidentally, to support its Mediterranean and North African campaigning. The other side of this was the chaos and dilatory underperformance in German aircraft production, and this came to a head with Nazi High Command's first major crisis once Barbarossa was underway, when the lack of bombers to support the huge but not decisive ground gains became acute. The crisis culminated in the suicide of the Luftwaffe's General of Procurement and Supply, Ernst Udet, in November 1941. Despite the efforts of his successor Erhard Milch, who attempted to quadruple production, the Luftwaffe would never have enough aircraft to meet the needs on multiple fronts. Not for the last time, the Beaufighter had tugged at a loose thread in the Nazi war machine.

Confirmed kills by nightfighter types Aug 1940 to Jun 1941

	No. Squadrons	Kills
Bristol Beaufighter	5	105
Boulton Paul Defiant	6	50
Hawker Hurricane	7*	41
Supermarine Spitfire	7*	15
Bristol Blenheim	3	15
Douglas Havoc	4	14
Handley Page Harrow LAM	420 Flight	2

*Includes only squadrons who registered confirmed night victories

Chapter 4

Convoy Stooges

Guarding the Approaches 1941–43

9 February 1941, North Atlantic east of Lisbon

On 8 February 1941, twenty-one ships of British Convoy HG53, loaded with ore and oranges from West Africa, departed from Gibraltar, with a small escort of a single destroyer and an armed sloop. Two weeks later, just twelve arrived in Liverpool. The convoy had been assaulted within hours of departure, when the U-boat U-37 struck, sinking two freighters. At dawn the following day, five huge Focke-Wulf Fw200 Condors from the Luftwaffe's specialist anti-shipping wing, *Kampfgeschwader 40*, took off from their base near Bordeaux and mounted an attack on the convoy of staggering potency. Attacking from a height of 150 feet, the Condors machine-gunned the merchantmen before dropping their deadly bombloads, six of which were hit by 550-pound bombs, destroying five of them. Anti-aircraft defences in the convoy were minimal, and only one Condor was damaged in the attack, crash-landing in Portugal. Another of the merchantmen was sunk later by the tracking U-37, with the German cruiser *Admiral Hipper* finishing off a ninth, despite arriving late having mauled another convoy. The massacre of HG53 came towards the end of a horrendous six months for British shipping, in which U-boats and the Luftwaffe had repeatedly decimated convoys, with the Condors alone accounting for 331,122 gross tonnage.[1] For the Germans, it was a free-for-all, which U-boat captains nicknamed the 'Happy time'.

Seemingly helpless in all the sinkings and general carnage was RAF Coastal Command. Created in 1936, in part to placate the RAF for the loss of control of the Fleet Air Arm, it had a relatively clear purpose – to protect the Royal Navy and British merchant marine from the enemy surface fleet, U-boats and aircraft. It was simply not in a fit state to achieve this purpose. In the panicked rearmament leading up to war, it got the hand-me-downs, leading to A.V. Alexander, First Lord of the Admiralty, to describe the Command as the 'Cinderella Service'.[2] While it had the manpower and an increasing number of squadrons, Coastal Command started the war with elderly Vickers Vildebeest biplane torpedo bombers, lightweight and inoffensive Avro Ansons for anti-sub patrols and US-built Lockheed Hudsons, a decent, lashed-up airliner which ended being used for a range of Coastal Command roles, including even escort fighter. However, all those Air Ministry specs did finally deliver Coastal Command's new torpedo bomber – the Bristol Beaufort arriving in the late spring of 1940, although still suffering from technical problems which would see the first squadron grounded for months – and the excellent Short Sunderland, a heavy long-range reconnaissance and anti-submarine flying boat. The third new aircraft was, of course, the hastily conceived afterthought provoked by the Munich crisis, the new long-range maritime fighter, the Bristol Beaufighter. Unfortunately, the Beaufighter was rightly prized by Fighter Command as its main nightfighter to tackle the immediate crisis of the Blitz, so once they finally started to trickle off the production line in September 1940, Coastal Command once again would get very short shrift.

By mid-1940, Coastal Command had three long-range fighter squadrons, 235, 236 and 248, all of which employed Bristol Blenheims and provided long-range patrols respectively from Manston in Kent, over the narrows of the English Channel, St Eval in Cornwall, patrolling the 'western approaches', and Dyce in Aberdeenshire, patrolling the North Sea between Scotland and Norway, a key exit route for the German Kreigsmarine. Blenheims would be in use with all three squadrons until late 1941, in part due to a decision to form two new Coastal Command squadrons so they could be trained up on Beaufighters from scratch while the existing Blenheim-equipped squadrons continued in their maritime role uninterrupted. 252 Squadron formed on 21 November 1940, at Bircham Newton, 'for fighter reconnaissance duties' with 'Twenty Initial Equipment Beaufighter 1 aeroplanes'.[3] Key members of staff were called up – including the new CO, Squadron Leader Robert Gordon Yaxley (of whom much more later). The new personnel were then moved to Chivenor in North Devon, where, on 15 December, the squadron received its first aircraft – two Bristol Blenheims. Only on Boxing Day 1940, did the squadron receive a single Beaufighter – the first for Coastal Command.

Over the next few weeks, two more Beaufighters arrived along with several Blenheims, and days were spent either on training flights or grounded with bad weather in a generally cloudy and wet Devon winter. With so few planes and so many eager but frustrated pilots, a problem the new squadron ran into was high levels of unserviceability, which the squadron concluded, 'can only be expected during a period such as this, as the majority of pilots have previously only flown slow twin-engined aircraft such as the Anson, and this experience has led to some amount of minor damage.'[4] By the end of February, with a rare few days of clear skies, 252 had only Blenheims serviceable. Only in March did Beaufighters start to arrive in any numbers – yet when they arrived, they lacked essential equipment: there were no wireless radio sets, dinghies, or Browning machine guns. So while Yaxley was confident the crews were ready for operations, the aircraft weren't. The full complement of twenty aircraft had arrived by the end of March (all still minus the essentials), although this was quickly reduced by one when a new Beau suffered a hydraulic failure, and was written off after a forced landing.[5]

In Bristol and the contracted factory sites elsewhere, the problem of rate of manufacture of the Beaufighter was finally being resolved. While all early aircraft were built at Filton – with the 100th aircraft delivered on 7 December 1940 – on 20 February 1941, the first Beaufighter at Weston-super-Mare had its maiden flight, followed very quickly by the first Fairey-built Beau, on 7 March. The 200th aircraft built at Filton rolled off the production lines two months later. What this meant was that Coastal Command finally started to get significant numbers through in the second half of 1941. While the Beaufighter squadrons moved painfully slowly towards operational deployment, the disastrous losses at sea continued. The eagerness of Coastal Command to get its hands on the Beau was understandable, but as Chief of the RAF Charles Portal was keen to stress, 'on no account should it be supposed that the use of the Beaufighter will enable us to defeat the German attacks on our shipping. In my opinion, shore-based fighters will never offer protection against the kind of attacks we must now expect.'[6]

Portal had a point. German U-boats and aircraft had vast oceans and seas to choose their point of attack. A range of weaponry and technology would be required, not to mention breakthroughs with Ultra intelligence, to properly destroy the German threats to Allied convoys. Competitive fighter performance became immaterial when hundreds of miles from land – loiter time and range were paramount. What the Beaufighter could provide was a cushion of air superiority in the North Sea and Western Approaches, where it was more than a match for the Luftwaffe's maritime raiders like the Focke-Wulf Condors. However, a Beaufighter's effective operational radius was about 600 miles – from a south-western airfield at St Eval or Portreath, this meant Beaus could get as far as the northern Spanish coast, so the Bay of Biscay was within range, while on the northern bases of Dyce and Sumburgh, the Norwegian Sea as north as Trondheim was in range, and just short of Iceland to the west. The reality was Blenheims, with similar range, were adequate in this role, because the Luftwaffe didn't need to compete for this air space. There were much easier pickings out of range of either type – like the areas off Portugal and central Norway. Unlike the nightfighters, the Beaufighter's superior performance wasn't really missed in early 1941. This would change later in the war.

As a result, when 252 Squadron became operational, there was an element of anti-climax. The squadron moved to Aldergrove in Northern Ireland to begin their job as 'convoy stooges', a nickname for long, usually uneventful convoy patrols, in this case over the northern zone of the Western Approaches. The first patrols were carried out on 5 April, with no enemy encounters of any description for eleven days. On 16 April, the Irishman Bill Riley shot down a Focke-Wulf Condor,[7] the first Beaufighter victory for Coastal Command. It would be the only cuckoo of spring for 252. The same afternoon, a flight on patrol made the error of flying too close to the Norwegian coast and encountered a flight of Bf110s from *Zerstörergeschwader* (ZG) 76. The first Coastal Command Beaufighter to be lost was damaged in the encounter and forced to ditch, the crew later being picked up and packed off to a prisoner-of-war-camp. The Bf110 represented the Beaufighter's direct Luftwaffe counterpart, with slightly better speed and manoeuvrability, but while well-armed, not quite to the same extent as the Beaufighter. As an aside, it is surprising is how little these rival aircraft met in daylight – total Luftwaffe Bf110 claims for the Beaufighter amount to thirteen for the whole war,[8] some which can't be matched to Beaufighter losses.

The Beaufighter patrols continued without incident until 25 April when the squadron received orders to send a detachment of fifteen aircraft to Malta. No. 272 Squadron, just setting up as a Beaufighter squadron in Sumburgh in the Shetland islands, got a similar message, and while some aircraft were left behind in the UK, both squadrons from this point would be heavily involved in the Mediterranean for the rest of the war, and for the purposes of this narrative, that story is picked up later. The remnants of 252 at Aldergrove would eventually form the basis of a new Coastal Command squadron, 143 Squadron.

This left four squadrons of Bristol Blenheims – 235, 236, 248 and 254 – performing the endless drudgery of maritime patrol and convoy escort. Outside of their escort cover area, large numbers of ships continued to be sunk, with the U-boats causing most of the damage, despite the increasing success by Royal Navy corvettes. Germany's massive attack on the Soviet Union and Churchill's promise of supplies added a whole new and highly exposed convoy route to Murmansk in northern Russia, space well within range of German raiders, and beyond Coastal Command.

From the summer of 1941, 248 Squadron finally started receiving its first Beaufighters, spending most of summer and autumn completing the conversion. The squadron was led by Squadron Leader David Cartridge, a 22-year-old Englishman who would become one of Coastal Command's few Beaufighter aces.[9] Based at Bircham Newton in Norfolk, 248 got to patrol the Dutch and French coasts, and as a result, they were soon drawn into taking on more offensive operations, as patrols increasingly encountered targets of opportunity like E-boats, merchant ships and flak ships. Almost as a relief from the tedium of the regular day job of endless escort patrols, a new anti-shipping role was being carved out for the Beaufighter.

On 16 December, a flight set out on what 248 Squadron records listed as a 'strike' mission.[10] They targeted Dutch merchant vessels, including one large 5,000-ton freighter and in all about a dozen much smaller vessels of about 300-500 tons apiece, including flak ships. After one of the Beaus turned back with mechanical problems, the other three Beaufighters blasted away at the various ships, expending all cannon and machine-gun ammunition before they returned home, all landing safely despite the heavy flak they encountered. What damage was caused was unclear, the squadron's log commenting: 'Operation thought to have caused much confusion amongst enemy vessels and shore batteries. Several ships were definitely damaged.' A few days later, a similar mission was undertaken, in which a huge cargo liner of 8,000 tons, along with several other smaller vessels, 'were well beaten up'. The big freighter was later found stationary and listing heavily to port.[11] Such attacks of course raised the question of the Beaus carrying more destructive weaponry like bombs and torpedoes.

In the last days of December 1941, Coastal Command's Beaufighters would be involved for the first time in an ambitious combined forces operation. This was Operation Archery, a first mission for Combined Operations under its new 'Advisor', Lord Louis Mountbatten. The plan targeted Maloy and Vaagso island in southern Norway, with 570 commandos landing, supported by one cruiser and four destroyers, with overhead bombing attacks by nineteen Bristol Blenheims and ten Handley Page Hampdens. Providing fighter cover were four Beaufighters from 248 Squadron, and three from 236 Squadron, all flying from Sumburgh airfield in the Shetlands. With their range and armament, they were by far the best aircraft available, but this was a big ask – they would face much faster shore-based aircraft like the Messerschmitt Bf109, which had proved more than a handful for the Beaufighter very recently in North Africa.

However, the Beaus rose to the occasion. They engaged formations of Heinkel He111 bombers and escorting Bf109 fighters and shot down four Heinkels,[12] including the first kill for David Cartridge. One of the 236 Squadron Beaus was shot down, probably by He111 defensive fire. The real evidence of Beaufighter success was that the Luftwaffe had scarcely any bearing on the events on the ground or at sea – a total reversal of the 1940 Norwegian campaign where Luftwaffe domination smashed Allied attempts to build a bridgehead. The landing by commandos and exiled Norwegians still encountered stiffer than expected opposition, including a detachment of elite mountain troops on leave in the town, yet they prevailed, inflicting over 120 German fatalities, with eighty taken prisoner (and back to the UK), for just seventeen killed and fifty-three wounded. They also destroyed their main target in Maloy, a fish-oil processing plant, used for producing high explosives, also wrecking coastal guns and other targets. After an opening bombardment to support the landings, two of the Navy's destroyers, *Onslow* and *Oribi*, ran amok among a coastal convoy. Nine vessels totalling over 15,000 gross registered tonnage were sunk during the raid,[13] and important Enigma code books and tables were taken after boarding an armed trawler.

For 248 Squadron, the success of Operation Archery was followed by a return to patrolling over the Dutch coast and attacking small vessels and even a large tanker. However, in the first week of the New Year, Bf109s intervened three times, although the Beaufighters eluded the attackers. The bulk of the month was less exciting, with a series of convoy escort patrols. No. 235 Squadron, still relatively new to the Beaufighter, had the unappetising task of patrolling the Norwegian Sea in the snow, wind and rain of mid-winter, suffering several losses through accidents. On 9 February, the weather over Sumburgh reported 10/10 cloud at 1,500 feet, deteriorating to 500 feet with sleet and snow in the afternoon. This undoubtedly contributed to two losses on a single day – one Beau failing to return, the other crashing in the low cloud and mist, killing the crew.[14]

Two days later, the Beaufighters would be largely sidelined during the Channel Dash, the passage of two of Germany's remaining battleships, *Scharnhorst* and *Gneisenau*, and the heavy cruiser *Prinz Eugen*, through the narrows of the English Channel. The plan was to make this daring attempt to relocate them from Brest, where they had become hemmed in and subject to repeated RAF bombing attacks, to Kiel in the North Sea, from where they could resume attacks on the northern-bound convoys. The failure to stop the German warships caused an outcry. *The Times* roared, 'Nothing more mortifying to the pride of our sea power has happened since the seventeenth century.'[15]

Coastal Command had dropped the ball by being incredibly slow to respond, taking fourteen hours following their departure from Brest to identify the warships in the Channel. This failure was set in motion when a pair of unreliable Hudsons failed to complete their patrol,[16] causing a gaping hole in reconnaissance coverage at the vital moment, an inexcusable lapse in planning. This meant subsequent attacks were hurried and hindered by the weather, and any co-ordination between fighters, bombers and torpedo bombers was lost – again vital, as a swarm of Luftwaffe Bf109s and Fw190s provided a formidable umbrella of fighter cover. As a result, Coastal Command's three Beaufort squadrons failed to achieve a single hit – nor did Bomber Command's Wellingtons, Stirlings and Manchesters. Worse still was in store for the Fleet Air Arm Swordfish, of which an entire flight of six was gunned down in a heroic yet doomed torpedo attack – a posthumous Victoria Cross was awarded to Lieutenant Commander Eugene Esmonde.[17] Feeling the heat for such a comprehensive failure, Coastal Command chief Sir Philip Joubert complained about a shortage of modern aircraft – Mosquitos and Beaufighters. Yet he had three newly equipped Beaufighter squadrons who were given little part to play in proceedings. No. 248 Squadron was situated ideally to meet the German battleships on their exit from the Channel, yet they spent the two days of the Dash flying fifteen solo patrol sorties, mostly attacking trawlers and other targets of opportunity on the Dutch coast. Just two Beaus were roped into a shadowing recce on 12 February. On the final patrol of 13 February, as the wintry dusk fell, Flight Lieutenant Rose's Beaufighter inadvertently 'flew inside a destroyer's screen at sea level to within 100 yards of the *Scharnhorst* and her escort of seven destroyers.'[18] Sensing discretion to be the better part of valour, Rose extricated his aircraft and headed home. The German warships made it to Kiel, although after all the aircraft attacks failed, both *Scharnhorst* and *Gneisenau* ran into mines, helping ensure the latter never set sail again.

The Beaufighters could have played a role, whether as fighter escort, reconnaissance, or flak suppression, which might have made a difference. However, there was something more fundamentally wrong – Coastal Command's anti-shipping capabilities were dismal, especially compared to the Luftwaffe. It wasn't just the attacks on capital ships – up to March 1943, Coastal Command had sunk just 107 vessels in over three years, at a cost of 648 aircraft.[19] And here, the Bristol Aeroplane Company were already onto something, realising ultimately that the Beaufighter and not its own Beaufort torpedo bomber was the answer. In December 1941, the Air Ministry had contacted the Bristol Aeroplane Company with a proposal to build a more powerful Hercules-engined version of the Beaufort. The Taurus engine had had troublesome reliability from the beginning, but even when they were working, it was clear that the Beaufort was badly under-powered, and the reality was that it hadn't lived up to expectations, suffering heavy losses and sinking few enemy vessels. When Bristol received the request, Leslie Frise made a counter-offer to the Ministry: they would instead build a torpedo-carrying Beaufighter, which was built as a prototype, tested and handed over to the Torpedo development unit on 8 May (sadly it crashed, killing the pilot, after engine failure).[20]

The 'Torbeau' would take some time coming, but in the meantime, anti-shipping strike tactics would be transformed by Beaufort pilots in the Mediterranean, a story which we'll take up in a later chapter. Coastal Command Beaufighters continued in the vital role that it was originally built for – the long-range maritime fighter. Winter brought very few contacts with any Luftwaffe raiders, but spring would see more encounters. On 2 May, a patrol off Norway ran into Bf109s, and were chased for over twenty miles, one of the Beaus taking some damage.

On 17 May, Beaufighters flying out of Sumburgh had spotted a Hipper-class cruiser (actually *Prinz Eugen*) and four destroyers heading into the Norwegian Sea. For the first time in home waters, Beaufighters were employed to escort Beaufort torpedo bombers to attack the flotilla. The action was hopelessly confused, with 86 Squadron's Beauforts and four 236 Squadron Beaufighters flying from Wick failing to link up with 42 Squadron's Beauforts and three 248 Squadron Beaus, flying out of Leuchars. No. 86 Squadron's fifteen Beauforts ran into a mass of eighteen to twenty Bf109s near Feieston Lighthouse off the coast of southern Norway and fought a running battle of twenty minutes in which five Beauforts and one Beaufighter were shot down, its crew being seen in a dinghy. Five Bf109s were claimed shot down, probably with some optimistic overclaiming. No. 42 Squadron's Beauforts and escort did find the *Prinz Eugen*, but ran into heavy flak and enemy fighters, with three more shot down. The squadron records claimed two torpedo hits on the *Prinz Eugen*, although this seems unlikely as very little damage was done. However, 248's Beaufighters distinguished themselves. Wing Commander John Pike carried out a blistering strafe on the leading destroyer: 'Ship was raked from stern to bridge and numerous hits registered.'[22] The French pilot Max Guedj wheeled around for three strafing passes. His less willing navigator, Charles Conder, ruefully reflected, 'I began to realise that my pilot was dedicated to winning World War Two on his own…'[23]

Pike's Beaufighter returned to base peppered with ack-ack damage – with a holed starboard wing, and damaged port engine and propeller, but he and Guedj had shown what brave, aggressive and skilled pilots could do. They also rehearsed a role the Beaufighter would fit perfectly – the anti-shipping strike aircraft. However, it would be in the Mediterranean that this role would be properly shaped. For now, the Beaufighter's Coastal Command role would continue to perplex its boss, Philippe Joubert, who started to toy with gimmicks, such as despatching two Beaus on an attention-seeking flag-hauling low level 'beat up' down the Champs Elysee on 17 June.[24] However, the changing war situation would soon throw Coastal Command's Beaus into one of the least known yet strategically important air battles of the war.

Chapter 5

Rogue Warriors in the Sky

Ground attack operations, North Africa 1941–42

May 1941, Crete

British and Commonwealth forces reeled from crushing blow after crushing blow in the Mediterranean. Hitler had tired of Mussolini's various debacles in late 1940 and early 1941 and decided to intervene. Rommel's Afrika Korps had arrived in the desert and inflicted a series of defeats on the Eighth Army in Libya, forcing them into a lengthy retreat back to Egypt. Malta had suffered a massive Luftwaffe air assault from January 1941, which had comprehensively demonstrated that the Med was not even safe for an aircraft carrier, as the heavily damaged HMS *Illustrious*, victor of Taranto, limped away to Alexandria, not to return.

It got worse. Churchill and his generals had made an honourable but ill-fated decision to help Britain's last remaining ally in Europe, Greece. Greece had been under attack from Italy since December, but Italian failure and the British intervention had led Hitler to order Operation Marita – the massed German invasion of Greece. As a result, an expeditionary force of 62,000 troops, mainly British, Australian and New Zealanders, had scarcely arrived before it was forced into a series of retreats against overwhelming Italian and German forces, and a general evacuation was ordered on 21 April, with 50,000 troops lifted under heavy Axis air attack, mainly to be disembarked at Crete, which loomed next in Hitler's sights.

The rapid change in the war in the Mediterranean had caught the RAF (and Fleet Air Arm) off guard. During the successful Operation Compass and early battles around the Med in late 1940, Gladiators, Fulmars, Swordfish,

Blenheims and even Hurricanes had seen off the Regia Aeronautica and famously mauled the Italian navy. However, these aircraft would struggle against newly arrived Messerschmitt Bf109s, Bf110s and Junkers Ju88s. With the hopeless overstretch caused by the Greek campaign, RAF heads realised they needed much stronger air forces in the Mediterranean, and from April set about sending more aircraft into the region.

With a crucial need for maritime air cover, it was clear there was a role for Beaufighters. And so, having only just got its hands on a proper modern aircraft to replace its Blenheims and Ansons, the ever-put-upon Coastal Command was forced to give them up, as both its new Beaufighter squadrons were despatched to the Med, just weeks after receiving them, to join the hard-stretched 201 Group in the maritime fighter role. As we've seen, the first handful of Coastal Command Beaufighters had arrived in December 1940 at the new 252 Squadron at Bercham Newton, and was followed by 272 Squadron in April 1941. The order for the assignment to the Mediterranean arrived first for 252 Squadron on 25 April 1941, with the RAF wholly overstretched with its commitments in North Africa and Greece.[1]

The first wave of Beaufighters comprised of fifteen aircraft from 252 Squadron, flying via Gibraltar and Luqa airfield in Malta. Two didn't make it to Gibraltar, including one which turned back with mechanical issues, and one which got lost and force-landed in Casablanca. They had originally had a very specific mission – to provide cover for a fast merchant ship, SS *Parracomb*, which was carrying twenty-one boxed Hurricanes from Gibraltar to Malta.[2] After that, they would provide convoy cover for the planned Tiger Convoy in early May. As things transpired, they would find plenty more to do, and would link up closely with 272 Squadron, who arrived in Egypt on 28 May. On arrival in Gibraltar, 252 were given the task of leading several squadrons of Hurricanes in the risky flight across the Med to Malta and then on to Egypt. Single-seat fighters operating at absolute maximum range over the sea with slipper tanks didn't have the luxury of an extra navigator, and a navigational error could be fatal. Malta was intended merely as a service halt, but invariably aircraft got stuck there – sometimes for a few days, sometimes permanently as bombed wrecks. Sure enough, on arrival in Malta, the Beaus soon became embroiled in action, with 252 Squadron's

Bill Riley sharing in shooting down an Italian Savoia SM81 transport.[3] The irrepressible Riley would also be shot down and slightly injured by a Hurricane in an unfortunate instance of friendly fire. Four of the priceless Beaufighters were also destroyed in air raids.[4] However, the main action in the Med was further east, following the German airborne invasion of Crete which began on 20 May.

On 23 May, two of 252's Beaufighters, flown by Squadron Leader Robert Yaxley and Flight Lieutenant Fraser, took off from Malta to escort Hurricanes on to Egypt, just as the battle of Crete had reached its turning point. In the early evening, they took off again to attack the crucial Maleme airfield, which had just fallen and was filling up with Luftwaffe Junkers Ju52s, which were rapidly disgorging paratroopers. A flight of RAF Martin Marylands had previously attacked the base, but Yaxley and Fraser's strafing destroyed four of the trimotors.[5] These were the first of many of the Luftwaffe's transport fleet to fall victim to Beaufighters. Hours later, the withdrawal of the last Hurricanes from the island underlined that air supremacy was firmly with the Luftwaffe, who inflicted heavy losses on Blenheim and Maryland squadrons who dared try to raid the island thereafter.

By the time the next flight of three Beaufighters, led by 272 Squadron's CO Andrew Fletcher, had arrived in Abu Seuir in Egypt, the evacuation of Crete had been underway for four days. The two 272 Beaus were accompanied by the 252 Squadron Beaufighter of the recovered Bill Riley. Again, too little and far too late: the Royal Navy had already taken heavy losses – three cruisers and five destroyers had been sunk by Luftwaffe attack, along with 2,000 men lost[5] – and learned a brutal lesson in what happens at sea when air supremacy is ceded to the enemy. Over the next couple of days, individual Beaus flew accompanied by flights of Hurricanes to provide defensive cover to the ships involved in the evacuation. As before, the 252 aircraft, and in particular Bill Riley, seemed to get most of the action, as Riley managed to collide (without much damage) with a Heinkel He111, and accompanying Hurricanes nipped in to shoot it down.[6] Later in the evening, 252's Fraser shared in destroying a Junkers Ju88, although on his return to base he got lost and ended up with a forced landing, without injury. The next day, 31 May, the last of the Cretan evacuation, the Beaus flew eight sorties and encountered a single Junkers Ju88,[7] which suffered some damage before escaping. At least the final evacuation vessels had been able to reach Egypt without loss.

After such a hefty defeat, it was fortunate that Hitler lifted his foot off the British jugular, as Fliegerkorps X and other units were withdrawn from the Mediterranean in preparation for Operation Barbarossa's launch on 22 June. It was a desperately needed breathing space for the British, although by no means the end to the hazards in the Med – as the battleship *Barham* and aircraft carrier *Ark Royal* would soon become victims of U-boats – but it allowed a comeback of sorts.

The reverberations following Crete were far-reaching, with both army and navy chiefs lambasting the RAF, who'd evidently failed to stop either the airborne invasion or the Luftwaffe onslaught on the evacuation. The newly appointed Arthur Tedder had much to contemplate. The Mediterranean theatre was a hard-fought battle for naval supremacy as well as a fluctuating desert battle front and crucially involved lengthy supply lines over sea and land. It would become something of a tactical test bed for the Royal Air Force. Against the Italians in the desert, the RAF's scant and often outdated aircraft targeted airfields and aircraft and attempted to stymie enemy advances by strafing infantry columns and lengthening enemy supply lines. The original desert air chief, Raymond Collishaw, had identified that softer, vulnerable supply vehicles and depots lay well to the rear of the front line,[8] and deduced that hitting them might be more productive than targeting enemy armour. As a result, Collishaw's paltry four squadrons of Hurricanes and Blenheims had been thrown at the long supply trail supporting the advancing Afrika Korps, using their small-calibre machine guns and small bombs to make themselves a nuisance. However, at the heart of the debacle of Crete, Tedder soon rounded on the problem – a total lack of mutual understanding, leading to recriminations between army, air force and navy.[9]

Things didn't get immediately better, as on 14 June, the British Eighth Army had launched a major offensive, Operation Battleaxe, to try and reverse a series of defeats at the hands of the Afrika Korps. It was unsuccessful, with half of the British tanks wrecked in the first attack. The air battle was also lost, with a chastening beating on the final day of the battle which saw ten

RAF and SAAF fighters lost (including nine Hurricanes) against just one Luftwaffe loss (a Stuka).[10] Beaufighters weren't called upon, as they were required for maritime escort duties, and weren't under Collishaw's direct command. There was an interesting attempt to redress their absence with 113 Squadron using converted Blenheim IV fighter-bombers, with packs of four machine guns and carrying a 20mm cannon in the glazed nose[11] for strafing enemy troops.

In July, Tedder decided to replace Collishaw as field commander for 204 Wing (what would be rechristened the Desert Air Force). The new man would prove an inspired choice – the New Zealander, Arthur 'Mary' Coningham – and the pair would soon revolutionise battlefield air support with their advocacy of 'combined' operations, aided with his own inspired staff choices – notably Basil Embry, who would come to redefine the RAF's tactical bombing strategy later in the war. Perhaps surprisingly, Coningham didn't look to the Luftwaffe, masters of blitzkrieg, for an example, but to his own experiences towards the end of the First World War, when fighters and fighter bombers worked closely in conjunction with tanks and infantry to finally sweep the Germans aside, ensuring their retreat was 'expensive and chaotic'.[11]

It was also clear that a good, properly armed fighter bomber, with the range to carry out extensive sweeps over enemy territory, would be useful. And it turned out the recently arrived heavy maritime fighter, with its four fixed 20mm Hispano cannon and six Browning machine guns, could solve a lot of problems. Even while it lacked a bomb bay or elementary bomb racks at this stage, the Beaufighter would get a chance to prove itself as a superb aerial weapons platform.

While not called upon in the failing Battleaxe, there had been a 'window of opportunity' to try the Beau on different types of offensive operation. The Luftwaffe, so crushingly dominant over Crete just days earlier, had very quickly disappeared from the skies over the eastern Med as squadrons were withdrawn for Hitler's nefarious plans in the east. The standing convoy patrols, while necessary, offered little opportunity for air action. Tedder himself would take the view that 'most of them [his tactical bomber squadrons] had suffered from the long series of defensive patrols over shipping… had inevitably reduced their offensive efficiency'.[12] And so, the Beaufighters were parcelled up into smaller units and despatched to different parts of the Med, the perfect way to restore offensive efficiency.

To the east, a small and largely forgotten war was being fought successfully to retain British dominance in the Levant, with the toppling of a pro-Axis regime in Iraq which would be followed by the defeat of Vichy forces in Syria and Lebanon. In hindsight, the German efforts here were curiously half-hearted. The Kirkuk oil fields of Iraq and the pipeline through Lebanon to Tripoli (the less well-known Lebanese, not Libyan port) might have been transformational to the German war effort. Whatever, a flight of four 272 and 252 Beaufighters flew on to Lidda in Palestine, to carry out a raid on oil storage tanks in Beirut. The idea was for the Beaufighters to strafe the oil tanks, in the hope of piercing the tank walls and igniting the contents with 20mm shells. The squadron records do not speculate what might happen to the low-flying Beaus if one of the tanks erupted in a fiery explosion, but it notes, with a hint of disappointment, 'The CO and F/Lt Moni went in first and attacked a tank, hitting it with no effect, as it was apparently too thick for the ammunition.'[13] An accompanying Martin Maryland then missed with its bombs. A disappointing first raid, but perhaps just as well, as the British and Free French would defeat the Vichy forces within weeks, capturing Lebanon's oil infrastructure intact.

If attacking large oil tanks was not the Beaufighter's forte, attacking Axis airfields would be different. Sicily's coastal air bases were in range of light and medium bombers based on Malta – and Beaufighters. Italian air force bombers, like the Savoia-Marchetti S.79 and CANT Z1007, were a danger to supply convoys in and out of Malta. As a result, Fletcher received orders to take a flight of aircraft to Malta, where he linked up with 252 Squadron aircraft, including Squadron Leader Robert Gordon Yaxley, who had already conducted the Beau's first strafing mission in Crete.

Somerset-born Yaxley was relatively old at twenty-nine, and had trained at Cranwell, earning his commission in the Royal Air Force in 1934. However, his first posting was actually with the RAF's Armoured Car Corps in Mandatory Palestine, where in April 1936, communal tensions had escalated from a general strike into the fully-blown Arab Revolt.

Yaxley earned the Military Cross, 'for gallant and distinguished services in connection with the emergency operations.' This was a brutal counter-insurgency war in which armoured cars were used to restore order, often forcefully, following a violent rebellion which had strong popular support from much of Palestine's Arab population. Good preparation for what lay ahead, because what Beaufighters would be doing was also brutal. Yaxley's first actual posting to fly aircraft would not be until December 1940, entirely missing the Battle of Britain, to join the new Coastal Command squadron, 252 – as a squadron leader. This would prove another inspired choice, but it also underlines where Coastal Command sat in terms of RAF priorities – an ex-armoured car commander wasn't the obvious choice for a maritime fighter squadron. Surely not a coincidence, but one of Yaxley's most aggressive pilots was another veteran of the Arab Revolt, Maurice Bartlett (although with the army).

Over a week in late July, the small Beaufighter force mounted a highly successful series of strafing attacks on airfields at Borizzo and Marsala in Sicily and Elmas in Sardinia in the last week of July. The Beaufighters' cannon and machine guns destroyed an estimated forty-nine aircraft and damaged forty-two others,[14] mainly Italian Savoia-Marchetti bombers and CANT seaplanes. Both Fletcher and Yaxley would receive DFCs for their leadership in this campaign. Yaxley's DFC citation made clear the wider tactical and strategic importance of the raids:

> 'These successes achieved undoubtedly contributed largely to the fact that the convoys were able to proceed without loss; only one ship was damaged, but it succeeded in reaching port.'[15]

The Beaufighters returned to Edku on 2 August, where for the next three months they resumed convoy patrols, which were largely uneventful, except for the loss of one Beau and its crew missing, probably due to a mechanical failure. Partly thanks to the Beaufighter raids, the Regia Aeronautica was much less of a problem, and Allied convoys were able to move around relatively unmolested. Meanwhile, the problem of deploying shipping in conditions of enemy air superiority was handed to the Italians. Malta's

Wellingtons, Blenheims and Albacores, and particularly its submarines, enjoyed a great run of success in the later months of 1941.

In November, Fletcher returned to Britain with the end of his tour, and Yaxley took charge of 272 Squadron, just in time for Auckinleck's great offensive, Operation Crusader. This time, Beaufighters were to be fully involved, and the squadron moved up to the newly cleared air strip LG10. Offensive operations began on 15 November and continued relentlessly over the next two months.

The first mission saw Yaxley leading an attack on an Italian truck convoy, in which several trucks were run off the road or turned over. Next day saw Kiwi Derek Hammond lead a low-level flight of three who wrought carnage, firstly at Tmimi airfield where:

> 'Two Ju87s and mobile W/T truck disappeared in a cloud of dust and gunfire', then they found a lengthy troop convoy near the Via Balbia highway [Mussolini's great Libyan coastal highway]. In their strafing runs, thirty Axis trucks were destroyed or damaged, this despite Hammond striking a telegraph pole. This would have finished most other aircraft, but the Beau managed to return to base, with thirty inches of his starboard wing sheared off, trailing lengths of telegraph wire and insulation materials'.[16]

The next few weeks saw 272's Beaus in daily action, leaving a mounting trail of mayhem and destruction among Axis supply convoys and airfields. On 18 November, the first day of Crusader, and despite being held up by a rainstorm, Yaxley led a flight of six Beaus, arriving at Tmimi to catch five Junkers Ju52s having just taken off. All were quickly destroyed along with a circling Henschel Hs126 reconnaissance plane. They then strafed and destroyed several Savoias, before the Beaus flew on to another aerodrome, where they shot up a detachment of Italian soldiers, finally catching and despatching a Fieseler Storch. In just six days of operations, forty-six Axis aircraft were destroyed, along with dozens of supply and troop-carrying trucks.[17]

Remarkably, no aircraft were lost in this incredibly intensive period of operations, despite the plentiful anti-aircraft and small arms fire, and the physical hazards. To achieve surprise and to avoid interception, the Beaus flew to their targets at barely twenty feet above the dunes, until the final approach when they climbed quickly and shallow dived in from 200 feet. There were no doubts about the Beaufighter's toughness, as several aircraft returned looking like a colander, sometimes on one engine, or with hydraulics shot away and having to pancake without a working undercarriage. Given the difficulties getting any new aircraft to Egypt from Britain, near-wrecked aircraft were now being repaired with remarkable improvisation and efficiency by the new maintenance units set up under Tedder and his maintenance chief, Air Vice-Marshal Grahame Dawson. The efforts in maintaining serviceability of front-line aircraft would prove a key advantage in the months ahead over the Axis air forces. Even Derek Hammond's wing-truncated aircraft made it back for further ops. The ground crew at LG10 basically sawed off an equivalent part of the port wing, making the aircraft flyable enough to make the short distance to Edku's maintenance unit, where full repairs were possible.[18] Still, despite such excellent ground crew support, even they struggled with the unexpected high winds and rain at Edku airfield on 15 December, which flooded the runway, blowing down fifty tents and offices, and destroying vital equipment. Such a crisis called for special measures, and an extra rum ration was issued.[19]

The squadron's run of luck would run out – ground attack was very hazardous, and on 23 November, Norman Lee's Beau was shot down by anti-aircraft fire while attacking Barce airfield, 272 Squadron's first combat loss. Both crew survived but had a long walk home across the desert. Two days later, on a raid on the distant Italian airfield at Agedabia in Libya, Maurice Bartlett made the 400-mile return trip to base minus three feet of wing, having hit a telegraph pole while strafing.[20] The ever-aggressive Bartlett would return to base four times with a badly damaged Beaufighter in less than a month.

On 6 December, the first Beau was lost to a German fighter – the Messerschmitt Bf109F of JG27 gruppe commander Gustav Rodel. Beaus were no match in a turning dogfight, being much more ponderous, and the Bf109F's top speed advantage of 50 miles per hour meant even diving away was no guarantee of escape. On 23 December, another Luftwaffe ace,

Gerhard Homuth, took out two Beaufighters, killing both crews.[21] The following day, Bf109s and Beaus clashed again – this time, Belgian Beau pilot Charles Roman shot down one of the Bf109s, capping a successful mission in which he and his wingman shot up fifteen Axis trucks. Generally, the Beaufighter maintained a remarkably low loss rate to Bf109s, many of which were now the superb new Bf109F, which otherwise were running amok and regularly inflicted one-sided losses on the Desert Air Force's other types. This was underlined on 10 December, when a flight of six Douglas A-20 Bostons from the SAAF's 24 Squadron attempted an unescorted raid on retreating columns. They were ambushed by Bf109s: five were shot down, the lone survivor crash-landing near one of the forward air strips, LG76. With bitter humour, SAAF members came to refer to the massacre as the 'Boston tea party'.[22]

In early December, Beaus were roped into another type of operation – carrying out 'armed rovers', where they focussed on intercepting and destroying German air transport planes. November had been a dire month for the Axis convoys crossing the Mediterranean, with fourteen of twenty-two freighters sunk by Malta-based submarines and bombers, and the loss of sixty-two per cent of Rommel's fuel supplies.[23] The Luftwaffe attempted to make up for the shortfall in supplies with regular flights of transporters, usually Junkers Ju52s, from bases in Sicily to North Africa. As we've seen, the Ju52's first encounter with Beaufighters was disastrous with seven quickly destroyed as they flew into Tmimi airfield. In the week of 11 December, there were several interceptions in which Beaufighters reported destroying one Junkers Ju52 and damaging fourteen others.[24] These were the early skirmishes for more critical air supply operations twelve months later where Beaus would play a full part.

The Beau's main work continued to be the relentless 'beating up' of Germans and Italians in retreat – day after day, after day. The squadron record for two days in mid-December reflects this:

> 16 December: Sortie against Chemines-Agedabia road. Attacks at 12.25 10 miles south of Chemines. Approximately 50 lorries moving north were attacked and hit – lorries chiefly carrying troops. A convoy

> of about 20 trucks moving west of road towards Charqura was seen and attacked. The aircraft returned safely. The second sortie on the same job consisted of one aircraft as the two others were unserviceable. P/O Watters (pilot) and Sgt Gill (observer) attacked at 1405 hours, 45 miles north of Agedabia towards Benghazi. Six vehicles were attacked and damaged, others scattered. Approximately 20 vehicles seen southbound and five northbound. The aircraft returned safely. 17 December: Five Beaufighters took off on operations ... Aircraft flown by W/Cdr Yaxley, P/O Hammond and P/O Orr straffed [sic] Torqe-Benghazi Road. Numerous vehicles were destroyed and damaged and many casualties were inflicted on enemy personnel... F/Lt Bartlett and P/O Crawford went straffing on the South Barce Road. Many lorries and tankers were damaged and destroyed. Personnel were wounded and killed and it was seen that the enemy was retreating.[25]

Unfortunately, 'Heck' Crawford was hit by anti-aircraft fire, and he had to make a forced landing. The dashing Bartlett landed nearby to attempt a rescue – at the same moment a German armoured car patrol turned up. Bartlett's Beau once again took a pounding as he hurriedly took off again under heavy fire, leaving 'Heck' Crawford and his navigator Keith Taylor to be captured.[26] Crawford later managed to make his escape and made it back to 272 Squadron to an uproarious reception on New Year's Eve. Taylor remained 'in the bag'.

The Beaufighter's successes in November and December accompanied hard-fought but significant advances by Commonwealth forces as Operation Crusader played out. The siege at Tobruk was lifted, while Rommel, denuded of armour and starved of supplies, had little choice but to retreat to a new defensive line west of Tobruk at Agedabia. The advancing Commonwealth troops found plenty of evidence of the Beaufighters' work – 458 destroyed enemy aircraft were counted, dotted around newly captured airfields.[27] The Beaus were by no means wholly responsible, as they were joined in airfield attacks by a new special raiding force: 'L Detachment', Special Air Service, working with the Long-Range Desert Group.

This kind of destruction on their rear echelons simply hadn't happened to the Germans in their winning campaigns earlier in the war. The Allies had found the weak spot in the Axis war machine, and had just the right aircraft to poke at it in the Beaufighter. It wasn't just the Beau – the Desert Air Force would also very effectively repurpose their single-engined fighters, notably new cannon-armed Hurricanes and US-built P-40 Tomahawks with their heavy 0.5-inch machine guns, in a similar fighter-bomber role. However, it was the Beaus that led the way – achieving greater destruction for fewer casualties. A recognition of both the efficacy of the Beau, but also the superb commitment of the crews to highly dangerous tasks, was the plethora of awards the pilots of 272 Squadron would receive in the New Year. Distinguished flying crosses would be awarded to three pilots – 'Punch' Campbell, Derek Hammond and the redoubtable Bartlett. A Distinguished Flying Medal was awarded to George Forrest. And Yaxley, scarcely two months after his DFC, would be awarded the Distinguished Service Order. Yaxley's citation lists the considerable accomplishments of the squadron and its leader:

> 'Since the operations in the Western Desert commenced this officer has led his squadron with conspicuous success. Enemy airdromes far west of the battle area as Benghazi, have been attacked daily and other serious damage has been inflicted on the enemy. On the opening day of the operations a number of Junkers 52 aircraft carrying troops were encountered and seven of them were shot down. In addition to a daily toll of enemy aircraft destroyed, heavy casualties have been inflicted on ground crews, while lines of communication have been harassed and petrol tankers set on fire. Altogether, within a space of six days operations, no fewer than forty-six of the enemy's aircraft were destroyed. Much of the brilliant success achieved can be attributed to the courageous leadership and determination displayed by Wing Commander Yaxley. Throughout he has set a magnificent example.'[28]

Sadly, Bartlett never got to receive his medal as, after all of his escapes and near misses, he died following a banal accident on New Year's Day in

1942. He died when his tent caught fire, possibly caused by an unstubbed cigarette.[29]

Operation Crusader was not a knock-out blow – the Allied advance ground to a halt due to their own lengthening and exposed supply lines, and in January the Afrika Korps and Italian allies started to hit back, forcing the Allies back to the Gazala line. Key to this was the 19 December arrival of four freighters into Benghazi with 11,000 tons of supplies, easing the supply problems for Rommel. It had been escorted by no fewer than four Italian battleships and twenty-five other warships. The same trick was repeated on 3 January, this time with over 25,000 tonnes of supplies.[30] This absolute maximum naval effort coincided with the arrival of the first units of over 400 aircraft of Luftflotte 2, mainly from the Eastern Front, with the task to eliminate Malta to ensure Rommel's victory in 1942. Yet Crusader had achieved something major – it had greatly raised the price of victory for Hitler in North Africa and forced him to double-down on a two-front war which Germany was increasingly ill-equipped to fight. In doing so, the Allies now faced a much greater challenge and as early 1942 would prove, the British Eighth Army was not yet a winning force. Nonetheless, there was little doubt that a game-changer in Operation Crusader had been the RAF's close support ground attacks, and this had been led by Yaxley's Beaufighters.

Chapter 6

Mediterranean Night Terror

Nightfighters in Malta 1942

Malta, 25 January 1942

Fifteen Hurricanes from Malta's 126, 185 and 249 Squadrons flew out to provide top cover over convoy ships departing Malta's Grand Harbour to head east to Alexandria. The Hurricanes soon encountered a Luftwaffe formation of Junkers Ju88s and Bf109s. A swirling battle with the escorts took place, in which eight of the Hurricanes were shot down, with just one of the Bf109s damaged. The only piece of good fortune was that seven of the Hurri pilots survived. The Me109Fs were freshly arrived from the Eastern Front as the spearhead of Kesselring's renewed Luftwaffe effort to destroy Malta as the base for attacking Axis convoys to North Africa. Jagdgeschwader 53's new Bf109Fs easily outclassed the Hurricanes, with wing leader Major Gunther von Maltzahn claiming victories fifty-four and fifty-five.[1] Two days later, the Hurricanes of the night-fighting 1435 Flight were caught by Bf109s as they took off at dusk, with Scotsman Alex Mackie shot down and killed. Despite the poor weather in January, the Luftwaffe dropped over 1,800 tons of bombs on the island,[2] targeting the airfields and the docks, and had lost just three bombers all month long. The cost had been ten Hurricanes shot down, but the failure to stop the bombers meant another forty had been destroyed on the ground. Just twenty-eight Hurricanes remained airworthy by the start of February, but they had already ceased to provide effective defence whether night or day.[3]

How had it come to this? Britain's fighter planes, including nightfighters, had obviously been desperately needed in Britain in 1940 and early 1941.

Fighter chief Sholto Douglas was not ready to let them go to other 'sideshow' theatres like Malta. Even Barbarossa and the Luftwaffe's massive redeployment to the east made little difference – in fact it encouraged the RAF and Douglas to throw his Spitfires into the 'endless offensive' to attempt to tie down Luftwaffe fighters in the west. This not only squandered good pilots and aircraft, but also meant Douglas kept Fighter Command's best aircraft in England. Fortunately, some Beaufighters were prised away from Douglas. As we've seen, the Crete crisis had led to Coastal Command's Beaus being redirected to the Med as maritime escorts, but it also meant that Egypt's vital imperial assets came into range of Luftwaffe bombers. Nightfighters would be provided, but not in besieged Malta.

On 25 September, 89 Squadron was established at Colerne, Wiltshire, to prepare for the nocturnal air defence of the Suez Canal Zone and the Nile Delta, including Alexandria, home of the Mediterranean Fleet. Over the next month or so, the squadron received its new Beaufighter IFs, all equipped with AI Mark IV radar. In November, the Beaus were boxed up and shipped to Egypt, arriving assembled at their new base Abu Seuir, just west of the Suez Canal. The first test flights in their new desert environment took place on 18 December. An early errand for each pilot was a flight to Heliopolis airport (now Cairo International Airport) to get new paintwork.[4] The simple all-matt black finish was replaced with sand and brown desert camouflage on upper surfaces of the aircraft, although several sandstorms[5] meant the new paintwork got a sand blasting. It did provide a perfect opportunity to test out the Beaufighter's new Vokes filters – layers of gauze inside enlarged engine air intakes, to stop sand getting into the engine.

The squadron got plenty of time to settle in with practice flights and interceptions, with very little in the way of actual enemy activity to worry about. There were still risks – one Beaufighter crashed through fuel starvation, while another was shot at by friendly anti-aircraft fire. There were a couple of scrambles after radar picked up reconnaissance aircraft during January,[6] but no interceptions until March.

Of course, the greatest need for the nightfighters was somewhere else: Malta. After a torrid start to 1941, during which Stukas blitzed the Grand Harbour and much of Valetta, the Luftwaffe had vanished in June

– Barbarossa trumped everything. The Regia Aeronautica had continued the battle, but without anything like the intensity and effectiveness of the Luftwaffe. They had also switched to small night raids. The consequences of taking the foot off the jugular were disastrous for the Axis supply lines – during the second half of 1941, Royal Navy submarines and shore-based torpedo bombers sent Axis shipping losses soaring. With the loss of supplies, Rommel's advances in the spring and summer were ultimately reversed. The British Eighth Army recovered much of the lost ground in Cyrenaica and inflicted a bloody if inconclusive blow to the Afrika Korps and their Italian allies with Operation Crusader in December, as we've seen, with considerable help from 272 Squadron's Beaufighters in their close support role. And in response to the Axis night incursions, the new AOC Malta, Air Vice-Marshal Hugh Pughe Lloyd, formed the Malta Night Fighting unit, just as the Luftwaffe were disappearing to the east.

The new MNFU squadron leader, a Battle of Britain veteran, Colin Powell-Sheddan, set about utilising what equipment there was. Malta was fortunate by the close of the year to have four fully operational RDF stations – this included the masts at Dingli Cliffs, the very first radar masts installed outside the United Kingdom in 1939. Three smaller GCI stations had been established by 1942,[7] with another completed on Malta's sister island Gozo in February 1942. The radar infrastructure required by the Beaufighters was in place for their arrival. However, for the second half of 1941, Powell-Sheddan had to make do with the only fighters on the island – Hurricanes, which meant using Cat's Eye tactics. Initially with eight Hurricanes, the MNFU had some successes, with a big night on 11/12 August when they shot down three Italian Fiat BR20s. Two of these fell to the guns of David Barnwell,[8] just 19-years-old and the youngest son of the great Bristol designer. The unit would score several more victories over the remainder of the year, when the unit was redesignated 1435 Flight. So far so good – intercepting under-armed Italian CANT Z1007s and Fiat BR20s was achievable with the Hurricanes. Unfortunately, on 14 October, the flight was scrambled to intercept a morning raid, in which Barnwell, after clinching his fifth victory, was shot down and killed by a Macchi C202. Marjorie Barnwell, widowed before the war when Bristol's great designer Frank had his air accident, had lost the last of her three sons, all killed in service with the RAF.

In December 1941, the Luftwaffe returned. With winter on the Eastern Front largely grounding the Luftwaffe bomber fleet, there was an opportunity to move units back into the Mediterranean. Luftflotte 2, including *Fliegerkorps II,* was despatched to Sicily. By March, this amounted to 425 aircraft, including 199 Junkers Ju88s and 137 of the latest Bf109Fs,[9] all with one objective – to crush Malta as a base for operations, ahead of the invasion code-named Operation Herakles. Heading this onslaught was 'Smiling' Albert Kesselring, the man who commanded the Winter Blitz, and whose genial countenance sat uneasily with his brutal enthusiasm for destroying cities.

What had become clear was that the Hurricanes were no longer up to the job: by day thoroughly outclassed by Bf109Fs, by night they struggled to catch the latest marks of Junkers Ju88s. The 1435 Flight's successes entirely dried up, and its new commander, Innes Westmacott, gave up trying to intercept bombers over Malta and set about night intruder raids to their Sicilian airfields, the flight scoring two victories in January. The message had got to Cairo, where Beaufighters were already being readied in early January. A coruscating report by Tedder's envoy, Group Captain Basil Embry, ultimately forced the Air Ministry in London to agree to the air ferrying into Malta of Spitfires.[10] This highly risky series of operations, involving Spitfires taking off aircraft carrier decks in the western Mediterranean, would ultimately, and brilliantly, win back daylight air superiority over the island in the early summer. By then, with less fanfare, the Beaufighters were doing the job at night too.

Both the first Spitfires and the first AI-equipped Beaufighters arrived on Malta on the same day, 7 March, when a flight of four flew from Heliopolis to Takali airfield. Things in Malta were as bad as ever, with overall fighter numbers dipping to twenty, so any new arrival was desperately welcome. The crater-marked Takali fortunately wasn't on the Luftwaffe target list that day, and all four Beaufighters, led by New Zealander Flight Lieutenant Gil Hayton, arrived safely and unnoticed at the cratered and wreck-strewn airfield – described by a Spitfire newcomer, Johnny Plagis, as 'a land of burned out Wimpeys [Wellingtons] and bowsers'.[11]

The priceless new nightfighters needed to be safe-guarded and maintained, and a call went out for any mechanics with experience on Beaus – six were found and immediately drafted into work at Takali (there had been maritime patrol Beaufighters on Malta for a few months, as covered elsewhere). The Beaus made their mark on the very first night, when Welshman Reginald 'Dusty' Miller intercepted and destroyed a Luftwaffe nightfighter, a Junkers Ju88C. Miller also claimed a damaged Heinkel He111 in a fruitful first flight out of Malta.[12]

Over the next few weeks, the Luftwaffe ratcheted up their operations as their numbers swelled, with 6,727 tons of bombs dropped in April alone. The tiny force of Beaufighters was kept busy, and in just over three months, inflicted a steady toll on both German and Italian bombers. Just a few days after their arrival Gilly Hayton claimed a damaged Junkers Ju88 bomber on the twelfth and damaged an Italian Fiat BR20 on 19 March, one of a small raiding formation of six BR20s attacking the airfields. In fact, Axis records show both aircraft were lost.[13] On 1 April, Pilot Officer Oakes and radar operator Sergeant Walsh got amongst twelve Junkers Ju88 raiders, destroying at least one, and damaging two more. In combat with the third of the Ju88s, Oakes' Beau was hit in the engine by defensive fire, and Oakes wrote off his aircraft in the forced landing. It would be some time before he got a replacement aircraft. Incredibly, this was the only write-off in a period of three months in which the four crews shot down nineteen aircraft, which included two Luftwaffe nightfighters as well as seven Luftwaffe and ten Regia bombers. Three of the four pilots, Gil Hayton, Dusty Miller and Edward Daniel, became aces, with Edward Daniel shooting down three bombers on the night of 16 May. Unlike Hayton, Daniel probably overclaimed, as it appears two of his victims got home.[14]

By the end of May 1942, the remarkable efforts of this tiny Beaufighter force alongside the success of the Spitfires meant Kesselring's grand air fleet had been reduced to just eighty-three airworthy aircraft, and there was a break from the savage onslaught of spring. Back in Egypt, the remainder of 89 Squadron had managed to score its first victories. The first fell to a man who would become the highest scoring nightfighter ace in the Mediterranean, an archetypal broad, burly Canadian ex-lumberjack by the name of Robert Fumerton, who predictably acquired the nickname of 'Moose'. Despite his size, he proved a particularly skilful fighter pilot with a deft touch. Prior to joining 89 Squadron, he'd fought in the latter stages of the Blitz with 406 Squadron, the new Canadian nightfighter outfit, for whom he scored their first kill on 1 September 1941.[15] On the night of 2/3 March 1942, he also grabbed the first victory for 89 Squadron, in a dramatic action for which he earned the Distinguished Flying Cross, as described in a narrative as part of his citation.

> 'After a very skilful pursuit in the moonlight, Flying Officer Fumerton closed in to 100 yards and opened fire scoring hits. Thereupon the enemy aircraft opened accurate return fire which wounded the pilot in the right leg and put the starboard motor and the reflector sight out of action. In spite of this, Flying Officer Fumerton pressed home a second attack aiming by tracer effect and set the enemy aircraft on fire. His own port motor cut out also and he was obliged to drop away. He was preparing for a landing in the [Nile] delta when one motor picked up again, the other still being out of action. During the course of the next hour, Flying Officer Fumerton was able by skilful flying and intelligent use of wireless and of signal light to make a homing at another aerodrome and a safe landing with wheels up, the undercarriage mechanism having also been put out of action. The enemy aircraft was afterwards forced to land in the sea, the crew being captured.'[16]

In the grand tradition of buses, having waited months for the first victory, there was a second on the same night, when Squadron Leader Derek Pain also destroyed a Heinkel. Both Fumerton and Pain had been patrolling above the naval port at Alexandria, and it was here that Fumerton would strike again on 7 April, bringing down two more bombers. The arrival of new aircraft from 46 Squadron proved timely as trade picked up over Libya and Egypt as critical battles were fought between the Eighth Army and the

Afrika Korps. No. 46 Squadron had been a Hurricane squadron during the Battle of Norway, but had been almost wiped out by the sinking of the HMS *Glorious* by the *Scharnhorst* and *Gneisenau*. It reformed as a Hurricane squadron during the Battle of Britain, and squadron air and ground crew were despatched to the Middle East in 1941 – without any aircraft. It became operational by converting to Beaufighters seconded from 89 Squadron, and became a type of auxiliary unit, switching from nightfighter to daylight roles as circumstances demanded. They scored their first victory on 2 May, and by the end of October the two units had between them scored fifty-one victories over Egypt and Libya.[17]

21 June would see the changing of the guard in Malta, as the magnificent quartet of 1435 Flight returned to Egypt, returning in three planes and leaving a spare behind. It is a remarkable testament to both the aircrew, the aircraft and the RAF ground crews that three aircraft which had been involved in so much air combat, and subject to numerous bombing raids at Takali, were fully serviceable for the 950-mile flight back to Egypt. 1435 Flight were replaced by what was entitled 'C Flight', 89 Squadron. This time, six crews were sent with four Beaus to Malta, including two pilots who would form a 'subs bench', a wise move given the intensity of the air battle they would immediately be involved in. Fumerton, Australian Mervyn Shipard, and Englishmen Henry Edwards and Nevil Reeves, along with their radar operators, were pencilled in for the starting line up, J.M. Ross and H.E. Mitchell as the substitutes. Malta's AOC, Hugh Pughe Lloyd, was most impressed by the new pilots, commenting, 'The crews were the most experienced to be found anywhere… Against such a team the Axis raiders in twos and threes throughout the night had very poor chances of survival.'[18]

The backdrop of C Flight's arrival was alarming. Tobruk had fallen on 21 June, crowning a devastating run of defeats in North Africa with the Eighth Army in full retreat back to the fortified El Alamein line. Despite the Luftwaffe's increasing losses, 10,000 tons of bombs had been dropped on Malta since the start of the year. Allied supply convoys to Malta were being mauled, and without fuel, ammunition and basic food supplies, all the Spitfires and Beaufighters in the world meant nothing. So things were as bleak as ever in Malta.

The newly arrived C Flight immediately found plenty of trade. Luftwaffe reinforcements for Kesselring's depleted units had arrived in Sicily, as had new Regia Aeronautica aircraft, with the improved CANT Z1007bis largely replacing the outdated Fiat BR20s. With Cairo in his sights, Rommel had made the fateful decision to indefinitely postpone Operation Herakles – trusting in the renewed aerial onslaught on Malta to protect supply lines. It was the pivotal moment in the theatre and meant a return to raids by day and night, by both the Luftwaffe and the Regia.

Despite all the bombing, Malta still had an intact radar defence system, although Italian radio misdirections and Luftwaffe attempts to jam the fairly antiquated AI Mark IV radar had recently been ramped up.[19] All this made the achievements of C Flight all the more remarkable. On each night, two or three nightfighters were on stand-by, and the moment raiders were picked up on radar, these would be scrambled. Within a day of arriving, Henry Edwards had opened the scoring, claiming a probable Junkers Ju88, which turned out to have crashed in the sea. The next night, Fumerton and Mitchell were scrambled twice, bringing down two CANTs and a Ju87.[20] With remarkable speed, all six crews registered scores, amassing sixteen victories in just two weeks of operations. None of the four Beaufighters were damaged in this time. Enemy activity slowed over the next couple of weeks, although later in July, the Aussie Merv Shipard got too close to his victims on two occasions, bringing home a damaged aircraft on each occasion. Shipard, who eventually would tie with Fumerton as the highest scoring Mediterranean ace, also crash-landed a third aircraft following an undercarriage failure. On all three occasions the aircraft would be repaired in Malta and put back into operations.

The efficiency with which this small unit operated is astounding – the flight logs show in the four-week period between 28 June to 25 July, the flight flew seventy-five sorties, averaging one destroyed bomber for every 3.95 sorties.[21] To put that into perspective, on the Luftwaffe's second most successful night of the war, the Leipzig raid of January 1944, seventy-eight bombers were shot down with over 700 nightfighter sorties, or nine sorties per bomber destroyed (the figure is even higher if one factors in aircraft shot down by anti-aircraft fire).[22] This efficiency was crucial. The failure of Operation Vigorous and loss of the tanker *Kentucky* in June meant aviation fuel was scarce. The Beaufighters flew few standing patrols (usually by individual aircraft), and generally waited on standby to be scrambled, to minimise unnecessary flight time. Replacing an aircraft meant flying one in from Egypt, where there was already a backlog of aircrew waiting for aircraft to be shipped from England around the Cape.

July was a much better month for the RAF on Malta and for British fortunes in general. Keith Park's arrival had heralded much more aggressive 'forward interception' tactics for his Spitfires in daylight. The combination of this and night-time losses persuaded Kesselring once again to halt his bombing offensive. Rommel's run of victories had also come to an end at the first Battle of El Alamein. The worst was nearly over. Another arrival in July was 89 Squadron's CO, George Stainforth, who came across with three more Beaufighters. He flew several night ops himself, but the only trade the aviation legend enjoyed was on a guest flight in a 249 Squadron Spitfire. Stainforth's flight ran into a Luftwaffe bomber formation, and he actually claimed a kill,[23] a special moment for one of the original pilots of Supermarine's original S6 seaplane, the design inspiration for the Spitfire.

August saw minimal action for the nightfighters, with the key battle elsewhere, as operations on Malta shifted to the protection of the Pedestal convoy, which, despite heavy losses, breached Malta's siege. The valiant SS *Ohio*'s arrival with thousands of tons of aviation fuel meant the Beaufighters could afford a more expansive strategy. Through September 89 Squadron's attention turned to intruder raids on Sicilian bases, accumulating eight victories over the next few weeks. They would also be drafted in to provide extra escort cover for a new anti-shipping wing. Meanwhile, 'C' Flight were relieved and returned to Egypt, having shot down twenty-six bombers without loss,[24] despite Shipard's various run-ins. Of the six original pilots, three were now aces – Fumerton had added nine to raise his score to thirteen,

Reeves had six and Edwards five. Merv Shipard was one shy of acedom, but he elected to stay on the island.[25]

Unfortunately, September saw 89 Squadron finally suffer its first fatalities of the war. On 25 September, the newly arrived Flight Lieutenant John Waddingham suffered an engine failure, and on returning to base, was fired on by friendly anti-aircraft guns. The aircraft crash-landed, and Waddingham died soon after, although his radar operator survived. He was the only fatality for Malta's Beaufighter nightfighter units throughout the siege. In a cruel twist, the following day, 89 Squadron's totemic CO, George Stainforth, and his radar operator were both killed following an engine failure on a routine patrol in Egypt. A genuine RAF legend, Stainforth is memorialised today with the RAF's annual award for its most effective stations.

Joining Shipard was a new cast of pilots, including the new CO, Squadron Leader Paul Evans, and two future aces, Australian Charles Crombie and Englishman Maurice Pring. The new contingent arrived, but found trade was scarce until 11 October, when the Luftwaffe came back in force with one last week of heavy raids. Shipard and his radar operator Doug Oxby had an all-nighter, flying four patrols through the night, and shooting down two bombers on the first and last of these missions. The Aussie's report on the first was blunt – and not quite accurate. 'One He111 probably destroyed. Rear gunner caught a packet.'[26] It turned out to be a Ju88 and had crashed in the sea, with all the crew escaping but wounded.

12 October was another big day, with five waves of bombing raids in daylight, and Spitfires claiming twenty-seven victories (Axis losses were actually seventeen). Shipard shot down another Luftwaffe bomber, while Maurice Pring ambushed a CANT Z1007 as it tried to land at Castelvetrano airfield in Sicily. Other crews logged reports that their AI radar was being jammed – such Luftwaffe countermeasures almost certainly kept losses to nightfighters lower in October, although this was small consolation given their heavy losses to the Spitfires by day.[27]

With the opening artillery barrage of El Alamein on 23 October, any notion that Malta was still under siege came to an end. Malta would become exclusively the base for offensive operations. The various detachments of

89 Squadron had done a brilliant job, playing a key role in defeating the Luftwaffe and its Regia Aeronautica allies. This was despite being so few and with such resource constraints. Between their arrival in March and the Axis throwing in the towel in mid-October, the unit had shot down fifty-nine aircraft for one pilot killed,[28] a victim of friendly fire. With never more than seven aircraft at its disposal, and a remarkably low rate of attrition, the Beaufighters made night raids expensive, and proof of their success was that the RAF was able to build up both a defensive fighter force and, as we'll see, a highly effective anti-shipping force from the ruins of March 1942.

Chapter 7

Night Defender and Night Intruder

Home Defence and Bomber Command 1941–43

Lübeck, 28 March 1942

Lübeck is one of a series of historic port towns in northern Germany, built through Hanseatic trade, evidenced by a charming historic legacy of medieval buildings. The new Bomber Command Chief, Arthur 'Bomber' Harris, also noticed something else – many of Lübeck's historic buildings were wooden. It had some strategic industry, such as shipyards, but Harris chose it purposefully because he knew his bombers could set the town on fire.[1] He and his men had learned much from the Coventry raid. 234 bombers were despatched, many of them 'tired old cows', as German propaganda had derisively christened the docile-looking and previously ineffective Wellingtons and Hampdens. They were accompanied by a few of the newer, bigger types, including the Short Stirling, the Handley Page Halifax and the troubled Avro Manchester, and were guided most of the way to Lübeck by the new Gee directional radio beam. They dropped a combination of 4,000-pound blockbusters and incendiary bombs on the town centre, starting a major conflagration of a type not seen on German soil – 320 civilians were killed, and over 8,000 buildings were destroyed or damaged, including Lübeck Cathedral.[2] It was by some way the most destructive raid of the war so far. While RAF losses rose above five per cent with twelve bombers shot down, Harris was satisfied. Goebbels and Hitler, who had gloated over the destruction of Guernica, Warsaw, London and Coventry, were horrified to see such carnage and destruction on the

Germans for a change. They were determined to exact retribution and Hitler called in his Luftwaffe bomber chiefs.[3]

The bombing of Lübeck transformed the night bombing war, marking the crossover point where the RAF's night attacks, which had been found to be strikingly ineffective the previous year, became a much more deadly proposition than the Luftwaffe's raids – but it also provoked a much stronger response from the Luftwaffe's nightfighters. At the same time, Hitler insisted on restarting the blitzing of British cities in direct response. As we shall see, the Bristol Beaufighter continued to convincingly answer the nightfighter question in the battle against Luftwaffe bombers, but there would soon be a new question: was there a nightfighter which could help protect the RAF's own bombers?

In the meantime, the Beaufighter had cemented its position as the mainstay nightfighter for Home Defence, although for the second half of 1941, they had much less work on. The last of the great Luftwaffe blitz raids took place on May, following which many UK-facing bomber units were transferred east for Barbarossa. The remaining western bomber force, reformed under the aegis of Luftflotte 3, dropped to just 203 bombers. Meanwhile, the RAF had increased the number of AI-equipped Beaufighter squadrons, with twelve by the end of 1941. Five of these employed the newer, slightly faster Rolls-Royce Merlin-powered Mark IIF. Despite their rapid downsizing, Luftwaffe bombing hadn't halted entirely. Raids were much smaller, with the main focus on aerial mining around port approaches and sea routes.

In addition to there being fewer, the Luftwaffe was getting wise to the Beaufighter's radar. The Germans, who had been working on their own Lichtenstein AI system, had correctly inferred that a problem with the Beaufighter's AI Mark IV radar was that it basically couldn't detect aircraft flying at low altitudes. The Mark IV radar essentially sent out waves from its dipole antennae in all directions – up to a distance of about five miles (about 26,000 feet). However, radar pulses bounce off the ground – and therefore can mask radar pulses from aircraft which are more distant than the nightfighter's altitude.[4] GCI stations also suffered gaps at lower altitude.[5] As a result, Luftwaffe mine-laying bombers flew at a much lower altitude as they approached the English coast. They were still being picked up by ground-based radar, and so Beaufighters could be vectored in on incoming aircraft, with a chance of getting close enough to pick up a radar contact.

No. 604 Squadron's Jeremy Howard-Williams described the new tactics required: '...They seldom fly at more than 1,000 feet and more often less than 500 feet. This means that, to get any range at all, the fighter has to fly about 5,000 feet and hope to establish contact by flying nearly over the top of its target. From this kind of hawklike, hovering position the fighter then has to descend cautiously in graduated steps, keeping the range always less than its own height or else the target blip is swallowed up in the ground returns. This of course is a complete reversal of our preferred procedure whereby we approach from below shrouded in the dark background of the earth or the sea; using the 'Hilo' system it is the fighter who is liable to be silhouetted against the sky for the enemy gunners to shoot at.'[6]

The ultimate solution needed was an upgraded AI radar system with much shorter wavelengths (centimetric not metric) and a directed 'conic' transmission system which could be used at lower altitude – something the boffins were working on. Thanks to the invention of the cavity magnetron in late 1940, the new centimetric AI would become operational, in the form of AI Mark VII and Mark VIII radar systems, in early 1942. These had no need for external dipole antennae – as the antennae were much smaller and embedded in a concave dish, with the whole structure faired over by the thimble-shaped nose (the 'bull-nose' housing the Mark X radar was limited to the Mosquito).[7] Many of the new Bristol Beaufighter VIFs coming on stream in early 1942 would find their looks distorted by the new nasal prosthetics as well as the new angled dihedral tailplanes.

The second half of 1941 had seen a steady trickle of nightfighter victories, and these were largely achieved by Beaufighters, with thirty-four of the forty-one victories scored.[8] New squadrons had begun operations, and by early 1942, there were nine Beaufighter aces, topped by John 'Cat's Eyes' Cunningham. The Boulton Paul Defiant scored its last victory on 11 October and was phased out as a nightfighter in 1942. Cat's Eye nightfighters had had their day and should have been phased out – except for an unforgivable continuation of the hare-brained Turbinlite.

RAF Fighter Command Beaufighter aces

John Cunningham	604	16
Jon 'Bob' Braham	29	14*
John Topham	219	10*
Alan Hodgkinson	219	9*
Rory Chisholm	604	7*
Edward Crew	604	6
Thomas Pike	219	6
Keith Geddes	604	5
Graham Budd	604	5

*Includes a single Blenheim victory in each case.

Turbinlite was the brainchild of Australian inventor Sidney Cotton, first proposed in September 1940, working with an RAF officer, William Helmore. At that time, exploring other solutions was understandable, given the ineffectiveness of AI fighters in responding to the first Blitz raids. However, there the logic ended, as to work, Turbinlite relied on the Havoc's AI being successful in finding the enemy, which was then illuminated with a powerful searchlight, yet having found the enemy, the Havoc had no weaponry and was reliant on accompanying 'Cat's Eye' Hurricanes to shoot it down. In practice, such cumbersome attack plans were not difficult for enemy bomber crew to spot and then evade. Fortunately, the Beaufighter was passed over for involvement, and instead US-built Douglas Havocs were used.[9]

The project continued well into 1942, consuming significant time and resources. In the end, nearly 100 Havocs were converted for use, along with five Hurricane squadrons which were assigned to provide accompanying interceptors. The Havocs could have been better used elsewhere, but the Hurricanes and their pilots were desperately needed, most notably in South-east Asia, where just two squadrons of the hopeless Brewster Buffalo faced the looming threat to Malaya and Burma from Japan. As it was, Turbinlite operations were responsible for the destruction of a single bomber in a full year of operations. The single tangible benefit was that the Hurricane squadrons involved – 1, 3, 32, 151 and 253 – gained further experience with night operations, and would be used as the first night intruders on the Continent. The cynic might suggest that Sholto Douglas was simply finding ways to keep all his squadrons despite the declining threat of invasion. Whatever, it was a shocking waste of resources when they might have helped prevent one or other of the humiliating disasters of early 1942. The Turbinlite project was finally axed following a scathing report by none other than John Cunningham.[10]

The RAF's Lübeck raid meant the Beaufighters would get to face a new 'blitz' from April 1942. Hitler had directed his Air Chiefs, 'that the air war against England be given a more aggressive stamp. Accordingly, when targets are being selected, preference is to be given to those where attacks are likely to have the greatest possible effect on civilian life. Besides raids on ports and industry, terror attacks of a retaliatory nature are to be carried out on towns other than London'.[11] A Foreign Ministry official, Gustav Brun von Stumm, let the cat out of the bag, stating, 'We shall go out and bomb every building in Britain marked with three stars in the Baedeker Guide [a German tourist guide],' in doing so, giving the new campaign its name.[12]

For Hitler, the gloves were off – any town, regardless of military value, was fair game. Particularly the picturesque ones with nice churches. But if Hitler thought he was getting a repeat of the Blitz, he was badly mistaken. The pressures on the Luftwaffe were as heavy as ever, with the spring offensives on the Eastern Front, and the battles in North Africa and Malta making increasing demands too. Luftflotte 3 was left with too few aircraft, despite a whip round and gutting the maritime bomber force.[13] The result was the Baedeker raids would consist of woefully small numbers of aircraft, never exceeding a hundred, and in planning the raids, only cities or towns with ports or which lay relatively close to the coast were selected for bombing, to minimise the time spent flying over land and therefore the chances of nightfighter interception. The targets chosen – Exeter, Bath, Norwich, Cowes, Canterbury – were and are lovely cities to visit with immense historical architecture, but strategically unimportant. In some cases, reaching the targets meant bombers flying elaborate dog-leg and fish-hook routes, meaning many bombers simply didn't find the target.[14] Pretty much everything that had clicked so monstrously well at Coventry and during the Blitz was absent, leading to a wholly futile campaign. This was the deterrent effect of the Beaufighter.

As a result, the first two raids were carried out on Exeter over the nights of 23/24 and 24/25 April, with forty-six bombers the first night and sixty on the second when eighty civilians were killed. The Regency city of Bath followed, then Norwich. A return to Exeter saw the cathedral hit and 164 civilian fatalities.[15] The RAF's nightfighters were certainly wrong-footed by the strategy, and the initial raid on Exeter saw just a single bomber shot down, with none in the more destructive raid the following day. Even John Cunningham, who managed to vector in on a Dornier, came away from the contact empty-handed. The Beaufighter was also facing another problem – Dornier had produced a faster bomber.

In late 1941, the first operational Dornier Do217s arrived with Luftflotte 3, and while outwardly similar to the Do17, it was actually a heavily redesigned aircraft, powered by the superb new BMW 801, altogether boasting 3,400 horsepower. While the German aircraft manufacturers struggled to produce the quantities of bombers required to meet the burgeoning needs of their multi-front war, they would take a big step ahead with development of the BMW 801, which delivered 400 more horsepower than the contemporary Bristol Hercules. It powered the superb new Focke-Wulf Fw190A fighter, which provided a brutal shock to the RAF's Spitfire pilots in the autumn of 1941. The Do217 also marked a leap forward in performance, with a top speed of 320 mph at altitude, and an increased bomb load of up to three tonnes.[16] According to Taffy Bowen's formula, this new bomber was too quick for the Beaufighter, even the Merlin-engined IIF version. In other respects, the Do217 wasn't great, with the same cramped crew arrangement and light defensive armament of its predecessor, and it was simply too small for a proper strategic role. It also proved to be a lousy nightfighter.

This performance advantage wasn't always apparent, as when in the small hours of 8 July, four Beaufighters of Canadian 406 Squadron were vectored towards a formation of twenty-five Do217s heading towards Middlesbrough, destroying five in short order.[17] However, the Do217 prefigured other newer and faster Luftwaffe bombers like the Messerschmitt Me410 *Schnellbomber*, ultimately leading to the Beaufighter being supplanted by the much faster de Havilland Mosquito, the first of which arrived with 157 Squadron in May 1942.

While the Luftwaffe losses on the Baedeker raids were relatively low compared with the Blitz, with forty losses on the fourteen raids,[18] the loss rate still bit deeply into Luftflotte 3's limited reserves. Newly trained crews suffered particularly heavy losses. At least two crews lost had recently trained for anti-shipping strikes, a vital and wholly under-resourced tactical role. The raids had no bearing on the Allied war effort, despite the damage and great distress in the target cities. Yet even in assessing the carnage as some kind of grim score, with 1,650 fatalities from all fourteen raids,[19] was roughly the same as the death toll in a single night of the Blitz on London on 11/12 May.

In June, raids continued, but there was a return to more strategic targeting – the eastern port of Hull was struck, along with a three-day campaign attacking the industrial city of Birmingham. Bombers followed a route up the Severn estuary into the heart of the West Midlands, which offered up more opportunities for interceptions – sixteen bombers were lost. Other raids were carried on through the summer, sometimes with as few as twenty aircraft involved, and the more strategically important the target, the more the losses to Beaufighters stacked up, along with the first victories for the Mosquito. By August, the Kampfgeschwader 2 wing reported just twenty crews remaining, having lost sixty-five through the course of the spring and summer.[20] This added to a similar scale of losses over Malta and in the Med, and the continuing attrition on the Eastern Front. Even with Milch galvanising the bomber manufacturers, the Luftwaffe's tactical bomber strength was ebbing away.

Other bombing tactics were tried, such as extreme high-altitude bombers (using the specially built Junkers Ju86P), which scarcely justified the term 'nuisance', although this led to accelerated high-altitude engine development. Another tactic was to employ 'Jabos' – Focke-Wulf Fw190 fighter-bombers, each carrying a 500-kilo bomb. This had been done without much success in the latter stages of the Battle of Britain, but the highly capable Fw190 initially proved very difficult even for daytime defenders to intercept. From

October 1942, these nuisance raids caused casualties and some disruption. When employed at night, the Fw190 had little difficulty outpacing the Beaufighter, and the writing was on the wall. Until early 1943, Mosquitos had been drafted into replace Defiants and Havocs in the Home Defence squadrons but would start replacing Beaufighters. Even the Beaufighter's great exponent, John Cunningham, who had spent most of 1942 resting from combat in an instructor role, was reassigned to command 85 Squadron, who had just replaced their Havocs with Mosquitos.

By the end of 1943, Mosquitos had replaced Beaufighters in all but five squadrons – 604 being one of the last, giving up its Beaus for the new Mosquito Mk XIIs in March 1944. Just two Beaufighter squadrons, 406 and 68 Squadrons, would be involved in the final big Luftwaffe bombing campaign – Operation Steinbock, which took place over January to May 1944. This campaign saw the rout of the Luftwaffe's bombing force, with 227 bombers lost on operations,[21] the majority shot down by Mosquitos, just seven falling to Beaufighters. An even stronger testament to the nightfighter defence was that twelve of the twenty-six raids managed to drop less than two tons of bombs on target cities,[22] and five missed entirely, while attacks on London were abandoned in favour of more peripheral coastal locations like Falmouth and Weymouth.

However, the Beaufighter nightfighter story in England would have one further, glorious chapter – as a night intruder. Just as the Luftwaffe bombing raids had shrunk continuously following the Blitz, the RAF's bombing campaign had done the reverse. Bouncing back from the embarrassment of the Butte report, Bomber Command was galvanised by the arrival of Arthur 'Bomber' Harris and bigger and better bombers, in the form of the Stirling, the Halifax and the supremely effective Avro Lancaster. Following the successful Lübeck raid, Harris launched ever more ambitious raids on an ever-widening range of German cities, including the very first 1,000-bomber raid on Cologne on 30/31 May 1942. The development of target-marking Pathfinder squadrons had ensured more accurate and concentrated bombing, with much more damage and injury inflicted. Bomber Command was becoming an ever more effective strategic weapon.

The problem was the Luftwaffe was inflicting an ever-bigger toll on the bombers – while forty-one lost over Cologne (a 3.9% loss rate) was deemed acceptable given the huge number of sorties, a similar size raid over Bremen saw bomber losses reach fifty.[23] The inadequacy of the RAF's bombing campaign in 1941 has tended to mask the fact that the Luftwaffe's nightfighter force had also been finding its feet, being entirely reliant on a system of ground-based Wurzburg radar and searchlights until the arrival of Germany's own AI radar with Nachtjagdgeschwader 1 in June 1941. Between October 1940 and early July 1941, RAF bombers flew 18,291 night sorties over much of western Germany, with several as far as Berlin, and lost just 2.1 per cent of the aircraft despatched.[24] While the Luftwaffe was blitzing London for the final time in early May, the RAF struck Hamburg on three successive nights, losing just eleven bombers. However, as the RAF also found to its cost, the arrival of AI and improving ground Freya and Himmelbett radar stations and nightfighter control led to much better results for the Luftwaffe. Lichtenstein AI, which necessitated the nose-mounted 'cat's whiskers' aerial structures which characterised Luftwaffe nightfighters, became operationally ready in June 1941 – however, it took a long time to supply sets across the whole nightfighter force. Those that reached the squadrons did prove effective – NJG1's Ludwig Becker shot down six bombers in his Lichtenstein-equipped Dornier Do215 over the course of the summer of 1941.[25] However, with or without AI, Luftwaffe nightfighters began to inflict more serious casualties, with a race emerging to be top ace between Helmut Lent, Werner Streiss and Paul Gildner, all of whom shot down twenty RAF bombers in 1941. Between July and November 1941, the RAF loss rate soared to 3.5 per cent.[26]

The heavier losses led to the RAF sending night intruders to the Continent to take on and disrupt Luftwaffe nightfighters. As we've seen, the Luftwaffe had done the same in the spring, with very little success. However, the RAF at this stage didn't use the obvious choice of aircraft, the Beaufighter, which in addition to all its other attributes, also had the range to do the job. The RAF didn't want to risk AI radar falling into enemy hands and exposing the truth about its carrot-munching nightfighter aces.

Instead, the task was allotted to several under-employed Hurricane squadrons – including those achieving next to zero with the Turbinlite project. Some of the squadrons had new cannon-armed Hurricane IIcs and used newly developed drop-tanks to provide extra range to reach the Continent. The mission was twofold – to intercept nightfighters, or seek out targets of opportunity, which usually meant they gravitated towards front-line bomber airfields. They achieved a measure of success too, although at a cost. Very early into operations on 12 December, the outstanding Cat's Eye ace Richard Stevens was killed on a raid on a Luftwaffe airfield in the Netherlands.

On 1 June, 3 Squadron's Peter Gawith, a New Zealander, managed to shoot down a leading Luftwaffe nightfighter ace, Helmut Woltersdorf. No. 1 Squadron's Czech pilot Karel Kuttelwascher proved particularly adept, running up the extraordinary total of fifteen victories, although all were shot down over French or Dutch airfields, and all appear to be bomber types – Heinkel He111s (including three in one night on 3 May), Junkers Ju88s and Dornier Do217s.[27] While these were certainly damaging losses to the bomber force, the Hurris only rarely intercepted nightfighters.

Later in the year, 23 Squadron's new Mosquitos were deployed in intruder raids, including their new recruit, Kuttelwascher. The squadron used 'Mark II specials' – meaning their AI Mark IV radar had been removed as it was next to useless for identifying Luftwaffe fighters hiding in a stream of RAF bombers. No. 23 Squadron's raids returned nine victories, and as with the Hurricanes, most were achieved near airfields. Examination of the records[28] show that while one of these victories would later be confirmed as a Bf110 nightfighter, the others were a motley variety of other types, including two inoffensive trainers, a biplane Bucker Bu-133 and a Klemm KL-35, a 105-horsepower monoplane with fixed undercarriage which was misidentified as a Stuka. Despite the heroic efforts of intruder crews, the results were all a bit random. Kuttelwascher's successes also encapsulated the problem with intruder missions. Without AI, the chances of identifying and then intercepting nightfighters attacking the bomber stream were vanishingly small; while hanging around airfields at least produced a return, but did little to actually disrupt the Luftwaffe's nightfighter effort. So, while

Harris continued to pursue his area bombing strategy with ever greater intensity, the loss rate continued to rise, reaching 4.5 per cent in the last four months of 1942. Leading the charge for the Luftwaffe was Helmut Lent, who received his Knight's Cross with Oak Leaves, and ended the year with fifty-six victories.

What was needed was technology to target actual nightfighters. AI radar had taken a big step forward with the development of the cavity magnetron and the resultant centimetric AI radar, which was being fitted to the Beaufighter VIFs and Mosquito XIIs now equipping nightfighter squadrons. The cavity magnetron was such a closely guarded secret that it was felt it could not be risked in operations over Europe – but the old Mark IV could be. This became doubly significant when radar boffins discovered the fortuitous coincidence that the old Mark IV antennas were able to pick up Luftwaffe Lichtenstein signals due to the same wave lengths being used. To identify a nightfighter, the radar operator would have two display boxes – the radar's own transmitter box and a box tuned to the Lichtenstein – the Seratte box. This displayed the direction to the German aircraft, but not the range. By following the Lichtenstein contact before switching back to pick up the same pulse on the Mark IV radar, the nightfighter could be intercepted in the safe knowledge it was an enemy aircraft, not a friendly bomber.[29]

'Operation Seratte' was assigned to 141 Squadron, a nightfighter squadron that had changed from Defiants to Beaufighters a year earlier. This was a bit of a hard luck outfit, one of the original Boulton Paul Defiant squadrons that fought in the great daylight battles of summer 1940. On 19 July, 141 suffered the single worst mauling suffered by a squadron in the Battle, with seven Defiants shot down in a clash with Bf109s,[30] and ten crew members were killed. Dowding quickly shifted them out of the line and into night defence, where their Defiants were traded for Beaufighters towards the end of 1941. Even this didn't improve things, and the last straw came with the decision to move the squadron leader, one of the flight lieutenants and the adjutant. The new man to lead 141 was someone we've met before: Jon 'Bob' Braham, whose promotion made him the youngest wing commander in the RAF. Braham had already achieved plenty of success with 29 Squadron, having amassed twelve victories, and trailed only John

Cunningham among Beaufighter aces. On his arrival, Braham found all his energies were focussed on raising rock-bottom squadron morale, and after racking up his first victory for the squadron on 31 January, he took them out of the line to Predannack in Cornwall, with the very different job of supporting Coastal Command.

In April 1943, the squadron returned east to Wittering and started training for the Seratte mission. Some of the training involved night dogfighting, with 'pairs of Beaufighters chasing each other around the dark heavens',[31] as after all, the Luftwaffe had their own AI and might be the ones intercepting them. The fortuitous capture of an intact Junkers Ju-88 nightfighter which confirmed the Lichtenstein radio frequency was also very helpful. Bomber Command's war was about to enter its most successful period, with the battles over the Ruhr and Hamburg, and Braham's Beaufighter squadron would play a small but significant part – although to Braham's frustration, the opportunity to quickly scale up the Seratte effort with more squadrons was rejected. The first operation, providing 'bomber support' for a raid on Oberhausen, was carried out by six of 141's Beaufighters on 14 June. Braham and his radar operator 'Sticks' Gregory would encounter a Luftwaffe nightfighter first time out, as Braham later wrote:

> 'Then there was excitement in Stick's voice, as he called, "Bob, I've got another signal, turn gently port." As I manoeuvred the Beau I counted three other aircraft on fire in the air [probably bombers] within my range of vision… "Bob, I think this one is behind us. The signal is strong." "Have you anything on the AI yet?" "No, but keep turning." It was an eerie feeling, knowing that we were playing a deadly game of hide and seek with an unseen foe. "Bob, I've AI contact 2,000 yards behind. Hard as possible port." "Are you sure it isn't one of our bombers?" "Yes. It isn't. The Serrate and AI signals match up. Keep turning, he's only about 1,000 yards and 20 degrees on your port and a little above. Now ease the turn a little and watch it. You're closing fast, you should see him in a second. He's only 600 yards and still well over to port." "I've got him. I've got him," I yelled excitedly. In the moonlight I caught a glimpse of an aircraft on my

> port beam. At that moment he straightened out, heading south at 10,000 feet. An Me110. Perhaps he had lost me on his AI. At 400 yards range I opened fire, gradually easing the deflection so that as I rolled in astern of him the dot of my electric gunsight was centred on his fuselage. Explosions appeared all over the Me. Burning brightly he dived steeply towards the earth.'[32]

Braham's description underlines the intuitive trust, communication and understanding needed between the two Beaufighter crew members in achieving an intruder interception and turning it into a kill. Such great partnerships were rare – it was much more difficult than defensive nightfighting, where the third man at GCI took on much of the load. Later in June, Braham and Gregory discovered the dangers of the mission when they found themselves under attack by two Junkers Ju88s – they were hit, with one of their engines set alight, but managed to dive into some cloud and escape. In fact, the Beaufighter's resilience to damage was tested to the full on these trips with aircraft often returning home riddled with bullet and shrapnel holes. Despite running the gauntlet of enemy nightfighters, anti-aircraft fire and the friendly fire of bombers, the squadron's losses were just three aircraft over the course of four months of operations, just one claimed by German nightfighters. Intruder work was stressful. Braham recognised the burn-out in his radar operator, Sticks Gregory, and insisted he accept a ground detail for some rest and recuperation – replacing him with another trusted r/o partner, 'Jacko' Jacobs. He also discovered one of his pilots was regularly turning back due to what seemed to be recurrent problems with his radar sets (in fairness, they did regularly fail) – when he sent the same aircraft and sets out with another crew, all worked well. The original radar operator confessed he had made the problems up because he couldn't face the missions. He was reassigned elsewhere.[33]

However, the results achieved by 141 Squadron entirely vindicated the AI-equipped intruder concept. In the four months up to Braham's enforced sabbatical, the squadron shot down sixteen Luftwaffe nightfighters, a very healthy ratio of 5.3 victories for every loss. All but two of these were by three pilots – Braham (six victories), Howard Kelsey (four) and Harold White (four). On 17/18 August, the squadron had its biggest night, accompanying the first wave of bombers on the raid on the V1 factory at Peenemunde in northern Germany. Braham encountered Bf110s of Nachtjagdgeschwader 1 (NJG1) and after destroying one, was attacked by a second, which he managed to turn inside and raked with his cannon and machine guns at very close range, nearly colliding with the flaming Messerschmitt.

While Braham was unaware at the time, research has shown that both Bf110s were piloted by aces – Feldwebels Georg Kraft (with fifteen victories) who was killed and Heinz Vinke (on twenty-eight victories at the time), who baled out and survived. Braham saw Vinke dangling in his parachute and briefly considered firing but Sticks dissuaded him. Vinke would score twenty-five more victories before being killed in action in March 1944. The Peenemunde raid was a spectacular success for Bomber Command and is believed to have set back V1 production for months. It would also be the most successful single night's operations for 141, with four Luftwaffe nightfighters shot down and another damaged. Remarkably, Braham probably shot down and killed two more leading Luftwaffe aces on 27/28 September, he appears to have shot down Hans-Dieter Frank, at the time the Luftwaffe's third leading nightfighter ace with fifty-five victories. Frank was flying one of a handful of pre-production Heinkel He219 A-0s in operation – a purpose-built nightfighter with an alleged top speed of 420 mph, faster even than the Mosquito. It shouldn't even have been a contest. The damaged He219 subsequently collided with another Luftwaffe nightfighter, and both crews were killed. Frank actually used the new aircraft's innovative new ejector seat – one of the first instances anywhere of an ejector seat being used – but failed to unplug his radio-cable, which strangled him. The following night Braham shot down a Bf110 flown by August Geiger, a fifty-three victory ace (number five on their list). Geiger and his radar operator baled out over the flooded Zuider Zee area of the Netherlands, and both drowned.[34] This would be Braham's last operation in a Beaufighter, as like Gregory, he was showing clear signs of combat fatigue, and he was rested.

On 11 November, 141 Squadron were incorporated into Bomber Command's new 100 Group for 'bomber support' operations, which included night intruder operations alongside all manner of radar and radio communications detection, jamming and spoofing. Mosquitos replaced the Beaufighters, not just for their speed but also their superior range – vital with Bomber Harris' planning on deeper penetration raids into the Reich. Perhaps because of the switch to Mosquitos, and despite the appointment of an experienced nightfighter pilot as its CO, Rory Chisholm (who had served alongside John Cunningham in 604 Squadron), the group took some time to start replicating the success of Braham's 141 Squadron. This was also due to the Luftwaffe getting wind of Seratte and adjusting the wavelengths on their aircraft's radio sets. However, the other aspect was numbers – just two new squadrons were brought into the group in time for Harris's Battle of Berlin, which meant deeper penetration raids at extreme range for the intruders, and they would turn out to be too few to make a critical difference.

But there was also something special missing – the loss of Braham's leadership and example, in harmony with the trusted and proven Beaufighter. The replacement Mosquito NFIIs were relatively well-used aircraft grudgingly given up by Fighter Command squadrons and simply didn't perform well, with several losses due to unreliability. A more ambitious approach, implemented earlier and with a larger number of squadrons, might have avoided the crushing losses of Harris's Berlin campaign. Nothing better illustrates that than the Nuremburg raid on 30/31 March, when a raid deep into Germany was unaccountably allowed to proceed in a clear moonlit night sky where bomber contrails were visible for miles around. Ninety-six RAF bombers were shot down as the Luftwaffe nightfighters had their deadliest night of the war. 100 Group despatched just nineteen sorties on this night and claimed just one Luftwaffe nightfighter shot down.[35] Nuremburg was a severe wake-up call for night intruder strategy, which would be much more effective following the addition of three new squadrons in May 1944. These were properly equipped with the latest Mosquito marks and fully up-to-date centimetric radar. 'Mosquito panik' was finally unleashed.

An analysis of the numbers shows that despite ever bigger and often successful raids, the Bomber Command loss rate was down during its 'Beaufighter summer' – starting at 4.3% loss rate in the spring and down to 3.5% in the autumn.[36] This excludes the July/August raids on Hamburg where 'Window' greatly reduced losses. However, the Beaufighters of 141 would achieve the best success rate of all the night intruder squadrons throughout the war, with a victory achieved in every eleven sorties. Even beyond that, there was a nasty shock for the Luftwaffe. For all their big scores and hefty decorations, not even the Luftwaffe's top aces could deal with Beaufighters flown with the express intention of taking them out. There may not have been 'Beaufighter panik' – but the Beau started what the Mosquito would eventually pick up and continue until the end of the war: the physical and psychological disintegration of the Luftwaffe nightfighter force.

100 Group intruder missions[37]		**Intruder sorties**	**Vics**	**Losses**	**Vic rate**	**Loss rate**
141	(pre-group)	179	16	3	8.94%	1.68%
141	Nov-43	1214	70	11	5.77%	0.91%
85	May-44	864	71	7	8.22%	0.81%
157	May-44	1122	37	5	3.30%	0.45%
169	Dec-43	1247	25	13	2.00%	1.04%
23	Jul-44	1067	3	8	0.28%	0.75%
239	Dec-43	1394	51	9	3.66%	0.65%

Chapter 8

Il Flagello Di Dio

Mediterranean shipping strikes 1942–43

14 April 1942, South-east of Malta

The front had been steady on the Gazala line in Libya for nearly three months. Ultra intelligence had picked up an Axis convoy consisting of four transports and five destroyers sailing south from Naples, and a strike force of nine Bristol Beaufort torpedo bombers of 22 and 39 Squadrons set off to intercept from Bu Amud airfield in Egypt. It was led by Flight Lieutenant John Lander and escorted by four 272 Squadron Beaufighters, under the command of Irish Beaufighter ace Bill Riley. The small force included every airworthy Beaufort torpedo bomber in North Africa, but within minutes, one hit mechanical problems and turned back. Loaded down with their torpedoes and flying at under 100 feet, the Beauforts were flying at their limit of range, and flying on to Malta. Initially, they missed the convoy at the estimated interception point, about seventy miles south-east of Malta, and had to circle around again. The Beaufighters had found themselves zigzagging to stay with the tortoise-like Beauforts,[1] whose underpowered Taurus engines struggled in Mediterranean conditions. Riley spotted some Bf110s at altitude and the Beaus were drawn into an air battle, with Riley shooting down one (actually a Dornier Do17Z) and badly damaging another. Short of fuel, the Beaus peeled away to head home.[2]

Eight unescorted Beauforts pressed on, and finally found the convoy and mounted their attack, at which point they were set upon by about fifteen Bf109s. Three of the Beauforts were quickly shot down, two shot down just short of Malta, and two crash-landed at Luqa. The Beauforts had launched just five torpedoes and none hit home. As a result, thousands of tons of supplies reached Rommel's forces, and just over a month later, Rommel unleashed his devastating offensive against the Gazala line.

The failed Beaufort raid provoked an enquiry and encapsulated a whole heap of problems facing the RAF when it came to attacking enemy ships. Torpedo bomber crews had the worst survival rate of any airmen in the Royal Air Force. An RAF survey in November 1942 estimated that a torpedo bomber crewman faced excruciating odds of six to one (17.5 per cent)[3] of surviving a single operational tour. Even heavy bomber crews faced better odds. Not only that, but RAF torpedo bombers weren't destroying that many ships, even by comparison to the Fleet Air Arm's seemingly antiquated biplanes. The reason was that Axis shipping by and large tended to sail near the coast and within range of land-based Luftwaffe or Regia Aeronautica fighters – this was the case in the North Sea, the Baltic, Bay of Biscay, and the whole length of the Mediterranean Sea. Unlike British merchantmen, they were very rarely to be found on the open ocean, out of fighter range, where they could be picked off more easily.

Torpedo bombers, which had to fly slowly in a straight line at low level in order to discharge their weapon successfully, were incredibly vulnerable to being bounced by fighters, and even in the absence of enemy fighters, were also very vulnerable to anti-aircraft fire. Even if the torpedo was released on target, the aircraft had usually been sighted and the ship could take evasive action, and even then, the torpedo had to work properly – detonating pistols might not go off, or the torpedo might be too low in the water and skim under the target. The great successes for torpedo bombers – like Taranto, Pearl Harbour, the *Bismarck* and Force Z – all saw torpedo bombers getting to work almost entirely unmolested by fighters, and in the first two cases, their targets were at anchor. Allied air superiority wasn't likely to happen any time soon in the Med – they needed to find a better way of protecting torpedo bombers in hostile skies. And the price for not doing this would be a properly supplied and replenished Afrika Korps.

In Cairo, a young torpedo bomber pilot, chafing against a dreary desk office job at RAF's 201 Group HQ, tormented by the heat, dust and unappealing local food,[4] finally got his wish and a posting to 39 Squadron, one of what remained of two Beaufort 'squadrons' in Egypt. Patrick Gibbs was a Welshman – the son of international rugby player Reggie Gibbs. He had joined the RAF in 1936, but spent two years flying Swordfish off the decks of carriers with the Fleet Air Arm, and had become an instructor in aerial torpedoing at Gosport. From here, he had the rare experience of surviving a full tour as a torpedo bomber pilot with Coastal Command, flying Beauforts attacking North Sea convoys, although with little success. He would attribute his survival to a training accident, which meant he missed several high-casualty raids while recovering from injuries. Unfortunately for Gibbs, when he arrived at 39 Squadron, they had next to no aircraft left after 14 April. It took some time, but new planes would eventually arrive, and Gibbs would bring an analytical approach into rebuilding the squadron and developing much more effective tactics in time, crucially, for the lead-up to El Alamein. And the key to the Beaufort torpedo bomber's success was in the use of its Bristol stablemate, the Beaufighter.

Following the successes of 272 Squadron's Bristol Beaufighters in Operation Crusader at the end of 1941, a squadron and a half of Beaufighters would be in much demand all over the Mediterranean – the problem was there were far too few, and just the task of maintaining airworthy numbers continued to be difficult with the harsh desert climate. This was the case with most aircraft types, with Cairo rapidly filling with RAF air crew with no aircraft, nicknamed the 'wastage pool'.[5] The Luftwaffe onslaught on Malta had renewed with heavier bombing than ever, which cut the more direct way of getting aircraft to the Desert Air Force in Egypt. It meant sending aircraft by freight instead – and while new Beaufighters did arrive in late December 1941, as we've seen these were AI-fitted aircraft for essential nightfighter defences. There was much talk of what would be arriving, and 1942 would eventually see the arrival of hundreds of US-built aircraft (mainly Martin Marylands and Baltimores and Curtiss Kittyhawks), Spitfires and more Beaufighters, and finally major USAAF units, including the latest models like the B24 Liberator and P38 Lightning. In other words, jam tomorrow. In the meantime, the British faced some of their worst crises of the war.

Nos. 272 and 252 Squadron's Beaufighters carried on in their old and new roles – as long-range maritime fighters moonlighting as close-support fighter bombers. However, with the battle front in Libya quietening down, the focus reverted to flying maritime patrols, providing air cover for the convoys which formed a lifeline to Malta. However, if these patrols in mid-1941 tended to be quiet, they would provide great challenges in 1942. Thanks to the advances of Operation Crusader, 252 Squadron would operate from Tmimi airfield, recently used by the Luftwaffe, and the cleared LG10 airfield in nearby Girwala in Libya. As before, small units would be assigned from time to time to Malta. 272's recently decorated commander, Robert Yaxley, ended his tour and was replaced by a light bomber pilot, John Hoggarth, who took over on 1 February. The first couple of months of the New Year saw some days with patrols looking out for enemy convoy activity; on other days, pairs or flights of Beaufighters went out looking for targets of opportunity on the main Axis supply routes, shooting up trucks, bowsers, motor bikes and troops as they found them. Unfortunately, there was a run of casualties in the first week of Hoggarth's command, starting with 'Heck' Crawford, who was shot down and killed on 6 February.[6] Crawford's navigator John Patterson managed to survive and evade capture, much as Crawford had once done, turning up at LG10 three weeks later, bearing sad news. The new CO, Hoggarth, was in one of two Beaus which got shot down on 9 February in a fruitless attack on shipping at the port of Sirte.[7] The crews of both aircraft became prisoners of war.

The remainder of February and March was conducted on convoy escort duties, with two major convoys sighted on 9 March – 252's Beaufighters missed the rendezvous, while 39 Squadron's Beaufort force found and attacked (without escort) the force of warships and cargo vessels, but faulty Duplex firing pistols prevented any damage. This failure of co-ordination by the fighters and torpedo bombers was a problem which would come to a head on 14 April. Two days later, 252 were guarding an Allied convoy, and intercepted some attacking German Heinkels. They claimed six shot down, although Luftwaffe records showed just one aircraft lost, but did no damage to the convoy, although a destroyer was later sunk by a U-boat.

The Beaufort calamity of 14 April had led to an inquiry and some difficult questions, but the crux was that the Beauforts shouldn't have attacked unless the Beaufighters took them all the way to the target. A big problem which

Patrick Gibbs would identify was the performance of the Beaufort Mark Is, with their Taurus engines. For whatever reason, whether it was drag from the big and ugly Vokes filter fittings or sand getting into the engines, they were too slow, particularly compared to Mark IIs which were powered by US Twin Wasp engines, several of which had recently arrived. It had meant Riley's fuel-starved Beaufighters had had to break away before the Beauforts had found the convoy.

Yet there was another fundamental that had to change. Eight Beauforts to attack a large convoy which included Italian warships was woefully inadequate, and it's also questionable that just four Beaus tackling dozens of Bf109s, Bf110s and Ju88s was a wise proposition, for all the aircraft's magnificent attributes. Egypt's Beauforts and Beaufighters were hopelessly overstretched. Despite this, a few days after the raid, 22 Squadron's remaining Beauforts flew out of Edku, bound for Ceylon, to fulfil their original assignment following the bruising Japanese attack on Admiral Somerville's Eastern Fleet.

With increased enemy build-up around Gazala, the Beaus were called back to do what they did so well during Operation Crusader: attacking the enemy rear echelons. The 1 May saw a flight of 272 Beaus carry out an offensive sweep on the Benghazi-Agedabia road and found a convoy. They shot up seven tankers and twenty-one lorries, while in addition Riley forced a Ju52 into a crash-landing.[8] A few days later, 252 would have more success against the Luftwaffe air transport fleet, as covered elsewhere. This good news would be the last for some time.

On 26 May, Rommel launched his great offensive against the Gazala line, and for the next five weeks, his Axis forces inflicted defeat after defeat against a technically larger Commonwealth army which had been unwisely split up into 'penny packet' units. The totemic Tobruk, which had defied Rommel for months in the spirited defence of 1941, this time crumbled and fell in a matter of days. By the end of June, over 60,000 Eighth Army soldiers had been taken prisoner, and the British had been pushed back over 350 miles to a defensive line near the small coastal village of El Alamein, well to the east of the Egyptian border. They say worse things happen at sea – and there was even some truth in this.

The situation in Malta was becoming ever more parlous, and in an attempt to get vital food, fuel and munitions to the besieged island, the British attempted two simultaneous convoys from opposite ends of the Mediterranean – Convoy MW11, codenamed Operation Vigorous, sailing from Alexandria, and Convoy MW4, Operation Harpoon, which sailed from Gibraltar. The Italians, probably acting on information gleaned from carelessly unencrypted signals from their US attache, Bonner Fellers, put their navy to sea, headed by the mighty battleships *Littorio* and *Vittorio Veneto*, to intercept and destroy either or both of the two convoys. Both Beauforts and Beaufighters would be fully involved, but this time separately.

A great air battle developed in 'Bomb Alley', where Convoy MW11 was in easy range of attack from Luftwaffe and Italian aircraft based in Crete and Axis-occupied Libya, with the Beaufighters of 252 and 272 Squadrons thrown into action as escorts, trying to break up an unrelenting series of attacks by torpedo-carrying Savoia S79s and Junkers Ju88s as well as Ju87 Stuka dive bombers. The Luftwaffe and Regia sank several ships, but it proved a harrowing experience for 272 Squadron in particular, the 272 Squadron records bleakly recording:

> 'Two of the blackest days in the squadron's history. Twenty-six sorties protecting a naval force of approximately fifty ships including eleven MV [merchant vessels] for Malta. Seven aircraft were lost …'[9]

The Beaus had been too few – they could maintain no more than six in the air at once, and there were major gaps in cover on the two critical days in the 'alley'. The ageing cruiser HMS *Coventry* had on-board radar and provided fighter direction for the Beaufighters, but the absence of an aircraft carrier with a full radar plotting room was keenly felt. As the 272 records noted:

> 'The Fighter Direction system was incapable of dealing with more than two aircraft at a time; sections of six were fired on by blind barrage and often vectored on to each other.'[10]

At least two Beaufighters were shot down by friendly anti-aircraft fire. The other problem was that the convoy passed within range of the Luftwaffe's Bf109 fighter groups at Derna in Libya. In the late afternoon of 14 June, six patrolling Beaufighters and a Lockheed Hudson reconnaissance plane were set upon by sixteen Bf109s of Jagdgeschwaders 27 and 53, the escort for a group of Ju87s. The Beaus fought a heroic battle over the next hour, with two of them shot down along with the Hudson and one of the Bf109s. A third Beau, flown by Belgian Flight Sergeant Tedesco, was shot down on the way back to base – struck by friendly anti-aircraft just as he squared up behind a Ju88.[11]

The following day, just two 272 Beaufighters were available to escort 39 Squadron's Beaufort attack. Patrick Gibbs led his Beauforts into action, with a heroic torpedo attack on the Italian battleships, in which three of his twelve aircraft were shot down. While all the torpedoes missed, the Italian battle fleet turned around and headed back north. A further Beaufort attack using aircraft newly arrived from England (and en route to Ceylon) saw the Italian cruiser *Trento* crippled, later to be sunk, while battleship *Littorio* also suffered minor damage. The escorting Beaufighters were both lost tackling Bf109s, who also claimed the three Beauforts lost. By the evening of 15 June, 272 squadron could put up just a single Beaufighter for escort duties.[12]

Yet for all the sacrifices, and with a seemingly clear run left to reach Malta, Rear Admiral Philip Vian reluctantly made the decision to turn the convoy around, with ammunition and fuel running dangerously low among the escorting destroyers. Both the aborted Vigorous and Harpoon suffered heavy losses – one cruiser, five destroyers and three merchant ships, while just two merchant ships from Harpoon made it through to Malta. This alleviated the growing food shortages but the lack of aviation fuel would become a major problem in coming weeks. The failure of the convoys reflected the events in North Africa. An awful lot of bravery and sacrifice, but the British were losing and needed to rethink. In the case of the Beaufighter, this superb aircraft wasn't being used effectively in its original role as a maritime fighter.

One fortuitous consequence of Operation Vigorous was that Patrick Gibbs crashed his damaged Beaufort on Luqa in Malta. It quickly became obvious to him that he should have been flying out of Malta in the first place, rather than from bases hundreds of miles away in Egypt. As a result, Gibbs lobbied Malta's AOC, Hugh Pughe Lloyd, to get 39 Squadron's Beauforts moved to the island, which lay in the way of any Axis convoy or fleet sailing from Italy to Libya. As he would reflect, what was the point of holding Malta if not as a base for offensive operations? Malta been the base for successful Fleet Air Arm and RAF operations in late 1941, using Blenheims, Swordfish and Albacores. Along with Royal Navy submarines, all had contributed to significant losses for the Italian merchant fleet, aided greatly by facing few Italian fighters. However, the resumption of Luftwaffe bombing in early 1942 and destruction of many torpedo bombers meant Axis shipping losses tumbled.

As it happened, Gibbs had chosen the perfect moment to ask the question. Malta was being used as a transit point for supplying other theatres of the war, and there was a squadron of recently arrived Beauforts at Luqa – 217 Squadron, en route to Ceylon (these had taken part in Vigorous, as a 'one-off'), and Beaufighters from Coastal Command's 235 and 248 Squadrons, which were earmarked for future convoy support from Malta. Having acted on Gibbs' proposal to bring 39 Squadron to Malta, the AOC North Africa then went further and instructed 217 Squadron to stay too.[13] Gibbs' Malta squadron had become a wing. They were based at Luqa, and helpfully shared it with 69 Squadron, the Photo Reconnaissance Unit led by the brilliant Adrian Warburton, with its unusual mix of Spitfires and Marylands, with 69 taking on the role of preliminary recces for convoys before Gibbs' wing attacked.

Their first missions were very much done in the conventional way, with Beaufighters flying at height as top cover and uninvolved in the actual attack. Often, they didn't have much to do other than watch as no Axis fighters turned up, while the Beauforts bore the brunt of the anti-aircraft fire – in the first mission two Beauforts were shot down and five damaged, including Gibbs' plane, whose elevator flaps jammed. It was clear the Beaufighters could be doing more, and the very first manifestation of 'flak suppression' was for Beau observers to drop empty beer bottles on to the vessels below.[14] This was in the hope their shape and the whistling sound would lead AA gunners to think they were being bombed by the Beaufighters, and turn their guns away from the torpedo bombers. On 24 July, a whole flight of three Beauforts was lost to anti-aircraft fire, while the Beaus watched from above and dropped beer bottles, failing abjectly to draw any fire. There were extenuating circumstances. The flight was recently arrived from 86 Squadron in the UK, still sported North Atlantic camouflage with black underside,[15] and had actually climbed up to 300 feet for the attack,[16] exposing themselves against the sky to the flak gunners in the convoy. Leaving this aside, it was clear to Gibbs that a more active role for the Beaus was required on these missions – perhaps dropping real bombs?

Just prior to the mission, there had been a major change in command in Malta. Keith Park had arrived on 14 July to take over the AOC role, earning a rebuke from the about-to-be-relieved Lloyd for landing in a flying boat during an air raid. The two leaders exchanged terse words before going their separate ways, and the dynamic force that was Keith Park took charge. Park would take the time to visit and interview all his squadron commanders, sent the tour-expired and combat-fatigued home, and brought in new, aggressive and highly effective forward interception tactics for his Spitfire squadrons. These inflicted painful losses on the Luftwaffe's bombers and broke up raids before they ever reached the island, forcing his old Battle of Britain adversary Kesselring to abandon his July bombing offensive after just five days. Park was also intent on revitalising Malta's role as an offensive base against Axis supply routes, and paid a visit to see Squadron Leader Gibbs, shortly after the debacle of 24 July. Gibbs recalled: 'After listening to my explanation of that disaster, he [Park] was not only willing to try the effect of bombing on the next sortie, but went a step further and agreed to my suggestion that the Beaufighters should adopt a more offensive role and cover us during the attack by firing on the escort with their four cannons.'[17]

From this conversation, the strike wing was born, and the Beaufighter would be its spearhead. And for good measure, Patrick Gibbs ended the conversation a wing commander, commanding a Beaufighter squadron as well as his Beauforts.

On 28 July, intelligence reported a convoy consisting of one merchantman, escorted by two destroyers, heading south in the Ionian Sea, giving Gibbs' new tactics their first go. The raid comprised of three waves of aircraft

– Beaufighters first, then bomb-carrying Beauforts, and finally torpedo-carrying Beauforts, who flew towards the expected interception point near Cephalonia. On sighting the convoy, Gibbs fired off two Very flares, which the Beaufighters, led by 235's Squadron Leader Ross Shore, took as a signal to climb into position to make their diving strafing run on the escorts. They were followed by the bomb-carrying Beauforts. Gibbs' wave-skimming Beauforts split into two sections, flying around each flank of the convoy, looking to position themselves to attack the freighter's two broadsides. 'It looked as if our two sections might be able to close like the jaws of a nutcracker, without being detected.'[18] At that moment, pandemonium broke loose, as the Beaus opened fire, the anti-aircraft guns on all three vessels erupted and the freighter turned sharply, just as Gibbs' Beauforts were releasing their torpedoes. Adding to the chaos, one of the dive-bombing Beauforts streaked in front of Gibbs, releasing its bomb load slightly short. The Beaus were then involved in keeping several Macchi C202 fighters at bay. One torpedo struck the freighter, causing serious damage, and later recce photos showed it lashed between two destroyers and heading back to port. Several thousand tons of munitions and supplies had been denied to Rommel. Two Beauforts were missing, including one of Gibbs' most experienced pilots, Ted Strever, who had been seen in a dinghy floating towards the Greek coast.[19]

The raid and the new tactics had been reasonably successful – the target was crippled, although Beaufort losses hadn't been avoided and the importance of well-timed choreography was underlined when the bomb-dropping Beauforts almost wrecked the torpedo-bomber attacks. In the event the tactics were regarded as a great success – but this might partly be due to an astonishing event the following day. Gibbs recalled sleeping uneasily at the loss of Strever, a pilot he held in the highest regard. The following day, Ted Strever and his three crew members turned up at Luqa, with the most incredible story.[20] They had been picked up by the Italians in Greece, given a lavish wine-fuelled dinner, then flown back to Italy where they boarded a lightly manned Italian flying boat bound for Taranto and a POW camp. When their guard was indisposed with flight sickness, Strever and company mounted a hijack, eventually cajoling the pilot to head for Malta, where they somehow avoided interceptions by both Bf109s and Spitfires. The story caused a sensation throughout Malta, an adrenaline shot after so many grim months of bombing and hunger. And it meant there was no question about continuing with the new tactics.

However, there would be an interval before the next strike missions, as despite Strever's antics, the shadow over besieged Malta of increasing shortages in food, fuel and ammunition was ever darkening. Adult Maltese civilians were surviving on just a few hundred calories daily.[21] Livestock was being slaughtered to supplement the population's diet and to free up pastural land for crops. Fuel shortages meant Park had to be very careful about mounting another mission on the scale of 28 July, as it used up so much scarce aviation fuel.

Following the partial failure of the Operation Vigorous and Harpoon convoys, the Royal Navy was planning another massive effort to break the siege – Operation Pedestal. This time, there was an acknowledgement that the eastern Mediterranean and 'Bomb Alley' had become too hazardous, so the plan was for a single large, heavily armed convoy to come from Britain, through the Straits of Gibraltar. The convoy of fourteen merchant vessels, including the vital oil tanker *Ohio*, would be guarded by two battleships, three aircraft carriers, seven cruisers and thirty-two destroyers and set out on 8 August although the older aircraft carrier *Eagle* was lost early in the mission to U-Boat attack. No. 248 Squadron's Beaufighters on Malta were joined by six more Beaufighters from 252 Squadron.[22] These were allotted a major part in the operation, being tasked with strafing attacks on Sardinian and Sicilian air bases, providing escort for Beauforts in the event of an Italian fleet intervention, but they would also take over from the Fleet Air Arm's carrier-borne fighters in providing air cover for the convoy from Skerki Bank, near the Sicilian Narrows. This was a pre-determined point where the big battleships and aircraft carriers would turn back, as the navy deemed the risks to its capital ships from air attack were too great this far into the Mediterranean.[23]

Their first action was a strafing sweep of airfields in southern Sardinia, led by 248 CO Wing Commander John Pike. Heavy AA limited damage at Elmas airfield to one Savoia S79 destroyed and six S79s (and four Luftwaffe aircraft) damaged. However, they surprised the defences at Decimomannu and destroyed four SM79s and damaged nine more, getting away with no losses as Fiat G50s tried to give chase.[24] Thanks to Pike's raid, about twenty Italian torpedo bombers were taken out of the attack on Pedestal. The Beaus also reported a flotilla of Italian cruisers and destroyers heading south – this would have ramifications later. The disruptive effect of the raid continued the following night, when G50 pilots at Elmas attacked returning Ju88s, thinking they were Beaufighters, shooting one down.

The Pedestal convoy proceeded until at about 6.35pm on 12 August when the new aircraft carrier *Indomitable* was hit.[25] The carrier wasn't seriously damaged, but its flight deck was rendered useless, also rendering its fighter squadrons inoperable – all its aircraft aloft at that moment would have to land on the remaining carrier *Victorious*, crowding its deck, and meaning several aircraft had to be pushed over the side. As a result, the big units of the fleet and some of their escorts turned around at 6.55pm, about twenty minutes earlier than planned and short of Skerki Bank,[26] and three hundred miles from Malta. Up to that point, the Fleet Air Arm's motley collection of Grumman Wildcats, Fairey Fulmars and Hawker Sea Hurricanes had done a superb job. Over two days they had broken up wave after wave of attacking Italian and German dive bombers and torpedo bombers, claiming thirty-nine shot down.[27] Only one freighter had been seriously damaged, the *Demoucile*, and it was still ploughing on for Malta. This was in large part thanks to excellent fighter direction control on board the fleet carriers, which meant aircraft could scramble from the carrier decks and vector in on incoming enemy aircraft.

The effect of the *Indomitable* hit and capital ship withdrawal, to use a cricketing analogy, was like the loss of a high-scoring batsman in the final overs of the day in a Test match. Suddenly, the nightwatchman gets brought in and opportunities open up for the bowling, precipitating a batting collapse. Which is pretty much the story of Pedestal from the evening of 12 August. All Fleet Air Arm aircraft still in the air were forced to break off from patrolling in order to land on *Victorious* which was heading away in the opposite direction – the final Fairey Fulmar landed at 8.15pm.[28] In the original plan, the turn-around would have allowed patrols until dusk, and 'close of play' for the Axis bomber force. Instead, there was a window of daylight for the Luftwaffe and Regia bombers to cause havoc.

While the main carrier-borne radar fighter direction was heading west, there was cruiser-borne radar – for another hour. At 7.56pm, the Italian submarine *Axum*, captained by Captain Renato Ferrini, unleashed an incredible salvo of torpedoes which struck two cruisers, the *Nigeria* and the *Cairo,* and the convoy's vital oil tanker, the *Ohio.*[29] The cruisers were the only two remaining ships equipped with fighter direction radar, and they were rendered inoperable, *Nigeria* limping back to Gibraltar, while the older *Cairo* was abandoned and scuttled.

And so, with the withdrawal of the carriers, the only air cover for this critical phase would be Malta's Beaufighters, who would have no radar fighter direction. Six of 248's Beaufighters had taken off to carry out a patrol above the convoy at 6pm. Squadron records show they found the convoy but attracted heavy anti-aircraft fire from Royal Navy vessels. They saw no enemy aircraft, so they turned for home fifteen minutes early.[30] In this case, it was not the time for an early bath, as there was no relief patrol ready to take over until darkness fell. The remaining Beaufighters on Malta were otherwise engaged. Fifteen Beaufighters were on standby to form a strike mission with Gibbs' Beauforts, expecting the call to attack the Italian flotilla seen previously. Another flight of Beaufighters, four aircraft in all, had been despatched on an airfield strafing mission, hoping to catch Italian bombers returning from convoy attacks at dusk. The flight leader turned back with engine problems, but the other three strafed, destroying or damaging six aircraft.[31] Two justifiable tactical choices, but both assignments meant they were absent when needed over the fleet.

At 8.35, with dusk falling over the Mediterranean, thirty-seven Luftwaffe bombers duly arrived, and unhindered by fighters they made hay, sinking two freighters and badly damaging two more, both of which would be finished off later. Throughout the night, Italian and German submarines and E-boat motor torpedo boats picked off more of the now scattered freighters, and several were left badly damaged and sailing at a greatly reduced speed. When dawn broke, just seven freighters remained, some damaged and falling behind, and spread out over a wide area, with destroyers split into groups trying to shepherd each through the last desperate miles to Malta. At least the convoy was now in range of Malta's radar stations, and there was radar direction from HMS *Charybdis*, which had been recalled to the convoy. Malta's Spitfires could now take a part in proceedings, alongside the Beaufighters. The strike-assigned Beaufighters also joined the air battle as Gibbs' planned strike mission was not required. The British submarine *Unbroken* had torpedoed and crippled two Italian cruisers,[32] causing the Italian fleet to turn back. Five freighters finally made it through to Malta's Grand Harbour, including the huge US tanker *Ohio*, lashed between two destroyers and sporting a crashed Junkers Ju87 on its foredeck, which limped in two days later. After the disasters of the previous evening and night, it was enough to save Malta. Operation Pedestal was one of the few major battles where the Beaufighter disappointed, but the arrival of the *Ohio*'s 11,500 tons of aviation fuel meant Gibbs' Beaufighters and Beauforts would get their chance for redemption, with major consequences for Rommel and the Axis war effort.

On 20 August, the various Beaufighters and crews at Luqa airfield from 235 and 248 Coastal Command squadrons were officially formed into 227 Squadron.[33] Their commander was Wing Commander Donald Ross Shore, another veteran of the pre-war RAF armoured car regiment. That day, ten Beaufighters led by Shore would form up for their belated second strike mission, along with twelve Beauforts led by Patrick Gibbs. Ultra intelligence had alerted them of an Italian convoy leaving Messina, consisting of a 7,750-ton tanker, *Pozarica*, as well as two destroyers, two torpedo boats and a smaller German merchant ship. This strike was a bit of a setback – the Beauforts' torpedoes missed and two Beauforts and two Beaufighters were shot down, with one man killed and ten crew taken prisoner.[34]

However, the raking damage from the Beaus' cannon on the Italian destroyer *Camicia Nera* wrecked her superstructure and caused many casualties, causing her to limp back to base. The sheer savagery of the Beau's strafing attacks had earned it a nickname with Italian sailors: 'il flagello di Dio' (the scourge of God). The wing tried again the following day, with nine Beauforts, four bomb-carrying Beaufighters and nine escort Beaus. This time there was no mistake as three Beauforts planted their torpedoes in the hull of the *Pozarica*.[35] The badly damaged tanker had to be run aground, denying the Afrika Korps and Luftwaffe thousands of tons of fuel as they prepared to go on to the offensive. Beaufighters also shot up another destroyer, *Aviere*, and shot down five Luftwaffe and Regia Aeronautica escort planes. Over the next week, the wing carried out three more convoy attacks, including successive missions where the freighters *Dielpi* and *San Andrea* were destroyed. *San Andrea* went down with 4,000 tons of fuel, intended to replace a comparable amount on *Pozarica.*[36]

These successes of Gibbs' wing had an exquisitely quantifiable effect on the war in Egypt. Rommel mounted his last great offensive at Alam Halfa, which ran up for the first time against Montgomery and his reinforced and revitalised Eighth Army. Subsequently, deciphered messages show that Rommel was expecting to receive 6,000 tons of fuel and about 2,500 tons of munitions from Italian convoys. Thanks to the Beauforts, just 1,500 tons of fuel arrived,[37] so Rommel's offensive started with strict rationing of fuel for his armoured vehicles. To make matters worse, the lengthy lines of communication, which for Rommel stretched hundreds of miles from Benghazi and Tobruk to Alamein, were being hammered by the Desert Air Force. This included strafing attacks by the Beaufighters of 272 Squadron, who on 31 August attacked a marching column on the Sidi Barrani-Mersa Muttrah road, causing an estimated fifty casualties.[38] They also shot down two Junkers Ju52s. The result was that Rommel halted his offensive on 2 September, citing Allied air attacks and lack of fuel in his report to Berlin.[39] Alam Halfa was a very significant failure – it was arguably the precise moment that the war turned irrevocably against the Germans. There was another significant consequence – it also forced the Germans to ramp up air supply operations. Gibbs' Beaufighter-Beaufort strikes in the last week of August played a very obvious part in this.

The wing continued its attacks over the rest of September, further weakening the Axis forces in the run-up to the Allies' own great offensive. Beaufighters with underwing bomb racks had replaced the Beauforts in the dive-bombing role, while Gibbs, increasingly stressed and unwell in the hot, dusty Maltese summer, had stepped back from leading the raids, with Donald 'Hank' Sharman and Ken Grant stepping up.[40] At the start of September, Park notified Gibbs of his award of the Distinguished Service Order, and on the same day, an Air Ministry order arrived to send him home. On 6 September, Gibbs planned one last mission as word arrived of a new convoy – much to his chagrin, he was ordered to stand down, so Hank Sharman led the mission. The wing faced heavy flak and a swarm of Macchi and Ju88 fighters. Two Beauforts, including Hank Sharman, fell to flak, with most others damaged and two Beaufighters were shot down in the dogfight that developed above the small convoy. The Beauforts hit the main target, the freighter *Manara,* and disabled her – once again stopping the supplies reaching Rommel. Among the escorting Beaufighters, drawn from 89 Nightfighter Squadron, ace Nevil Reeves shot down a Ju88 for his sixth victory.[41]

Ten days later, the wing tried another tactic. Intelligence had revealed *Carbonia*, a small Italian freighter (1,237 tons), had left Tunis without an escort, heading east to Tripoli. This time, the Beauforts and their torpedoes were left at home, and 227 Squadron's Beaufighters took on the job alone, each armed with two 500-pound bombs on wing racks. Led by Squadron Leader Wigmore, the Canadian Dallas Schmidt hit the vessel with a bomb, which he followed up with five strafing passes. The flaming *Carbonia* was abandoned and sank.[42]

By 22 October and the eve of Montgomery's great offensive at El Alamein, the Italian merchant marine, entrusted with keeping the Afrika Korps and their Italian allies supplied, had been decimated. The previous three months had seen only half of their ships getting through to the North African ports, with the destruction wrought by Gibbs' wing augmented with sinkings by the Maltese submarine flotilla as well as Wellington bombers adapted to carry torpedoes for night attacks, nicknamed 'Fishingtons'. US B-24 Liberators weighed in too. So with the front erupting with Allied and Commonwealth attacks, Rommel was informed that his Panzerarmee had just a few days of fuel and spare parts. Two convoys, TT and J, were despatched to Tobruk, Rommel's easternmost port, and while still over 400 miles away, the closest to the Alamein front. This time, a wing of Egypt-based 47 Squadron's Beauforts, bomb-carrying Bristol Bisleys (a more powerful version of the Blenheim) and escorting Beaufighters from 252 Squadron made the attack. They hadn't used Gibbs' strike tactics before and it showed, with all but two Beauforts attacking the wrong ship (they had orders to attack oil tankers first), two aircraft colliding with each other, and another colliding with a ship's mast. Fortunately, the Beaus were able to keep a swarm of Ju88s and Macchis at bay, while the ice-cool Canadian Ralph Manning hit the turning 5,000-ton tanker *Proserpina*. The torpedo was observed to bump along the side of the tanker before it exploded, and the tanker quickly sank.[43] The destroyer escort *Calatafimi* was also damaged by a Beaufighter strafing attack. The other large vessel in Convoy TT, *Tergestea*, carrying thousands of tons of ammunition and fuel, was attacked that night by Fishingtons – when struck it erupted in a huge explosion, killing all eighty on board. The two smaller tankers in Convoy J would also be hit by this souped up 'tired old cow'. One was destroyed and the other damaged and forced to turn back.

With the battle of El Alamein raging, the Allies had tightened the screw on the Axis shipborne supply lines across the Mediterranean. The Beaufighter, working with Gibbs' strike wing tactics alongside its stablemate, the Beaufort, had helped render the Axis' maritime supply routes untenable – a remarkable achievement given the tragic disarray of 14 April. Supplies to Rommel across the Med were reduced to what could be carried on Luftwaffe transport aircraft and on small and speedier vessels. This wasn't enough, and on 29 October, Ultra Intelligence was picking up urgent signals about Rommel's dire fuel situation,[44] and shortly afterwards, Rommel's forces faced comprehensive defeat and were in full-scale retreat. As we shall see this was a lesson unlearned by Hitler and his generals. They should have baled out of North Africa at this point – but they ignored the mastery of the RAF and Allies over their vital supply routes and doubled down once again.

Chapter 9

Aussie Battler

New Guinea and Timor operations with RAAF

Darwin, Australia - 19 February 1942

Four days after the shocking surrender in Singapore of 85,000 troops, including two whole Australian brigades, 242 Japanese aircraft mounted an attack on Darwin, the port town and capital of the Northern Territory. Darwin had some heavy anti-aircraft artillery, but crews were untrained and many shells didn't detonate. There was no radar, and the RAAF defences consisted of Commonwealth Wirraway trainers and some Hudson and Beaufort light bombers, no match for the Zeroes escorting the Japanese bombers. Some more modern USAAF P-40s had stopped over in Darwin, but these were overwhelmed. The result was Darwin port was hammered, with six freighters sunk, including the ammunition-packed MV *Neptuna* which erupted in a huge explosion. Dozens of aircraft were destroyed in Darwin's two airfields, and there was also damage to civilian areas, with casualties amounting to about 250 dead. Hundreds of Darwin's residents fled the city. The whole population was shocked as the Japanese tsunami threatened to engulf Australia, and with the cream of its troops fighting in North Africa, it seemed no one could stop them. The Americans had been badly bruised by Pearl Harbor and were in full retreat in the Philippines, and far less the British Empire, humiliated in Singapore and with Churchill trying to cling on to Australian units to help deal with crises on several fronts.

Fortunately, Beaufighters were on their way. The Royal Australian Air Force had been very quick to realise the potential of the 'Beaufort Fighter', with the Australian Air Board placing an order with Bristol as early as May

1939.[1] Unfortunately, war intervened in Europe and the RAF's immediate wartime priorities trumped the still theoretical Japanese threat. While this delayed things, Bristol was able to commit to delivering fifty-four Beaufighters to Australia by March 1942,[2] just weeks after Darwin and the Fall of Singapore.

On 9 March, RAAF Long-range Fighter Squadron 30 was established at Richmond in New South Wales with the objective of equipping with Beaufighters. Over the next few weeks, the squadron grew rapidly in terms of air and ground crew, including a new CO, Wing Commander Brian 'Blackjack' Walker, and his navigator, John Mason. The Beaus were on their way but would take longer – they had been dismantled and were in crates aboard various ships working their way around the globe. On arrival, they arrived at Air Board depots where mechanics, who had never seen the plane, set about assembling them, under the watchful eye of a single Bristol factory representative.[3] The first airworthy Beaufighter 1C reached 30 Squadron in Richmond on 15 June, with the full complement arriving within the next month. In preparation, the squadron's new air crews had been practising in a dual-control Beaufort, with the RAF's dapper and experienced Squadron Leader 'Handlebars' Ellis leading training on the precious new aircraft. With most pilots' experience limited to aircraft like Avro Ansons and Airspeed Oxfords, the Beaufighter's immense power came as quite a shock. As one of the new squadron, Jim Wilson, remarked, 'I'm not telling any lies, when I say that I saw a number of shaking and white-faced pilots after their first flight in a Beaufighter.'[4]

In August, a second squadron, Number 31, was set up near Wagga Wagga in Outback New South Wales – their wait for aircraft was much shorter, with the first Beaufighter arriving with the squadron just nine days later.[5] There was a need for haste. While the carnage at Darwin hadn't been repeated, despite further air raids, the war was getting much closer to Australia.

On 23 January, the Japanese Army had landed at Rabaul on the island of New Britain, their first step to an invasion of New Guinea and capture of its southern-facing capital Port Moresby, which had been identified as the key base for neutralising Australia as a base for offensive operations (in fact an actual invasion of Australia had been ruled out by Japanese commanders).

In March, they landed unopposed on the northern coast at Lae and Samalaua. At this stage nobody expected the Japanese to try to cross the distinctly uncongenial mass of jungles and mountains at the heart of eastern New Guinea. Indeed, the Japanese thought the same. However, in May, the Imperial Japanese Navy's attempt to reach Port Moresby was blocked by the US fleet at the Battle of the Coral Sea – one of the first glimmers of success for the Allies after six months of disasters.

And so, on 11 June, the Japanese embarked instead on a land invasion of New Guinea, with the aim of driving out the Australians and taking Port Moresby. Having got used to sweeping everyone aside in the Philippines, Indonesia, Malaya, even Burma, with breathtaking speed and ruthlessness, the Japanese had inadvertently found the perfect place to get bogged down. They would be stuck in New Guinea for three more years and over 200,000 would die in the godforsaken place, mainly victims of a range of hideous tropical diseases. But that's jumping ahead, as they still had to be stopped, and this task would largely fall to the armed forces of a bruised, chastened and anxious Australia, most of them home defence militias and reservists, the derisively nicknamed 'chocolate soldiers.' And some brand new Beaufighters.

In July, Japanese midget submarines attempted a daring attack on shipping entering Sydney, once again stirring alarm in the Australian population. Fortunately, a US Catalina spotted them and 30 Squadron would take off on its first meaningful combat mission, although they wouldn't find anything. On 6 August, the squadron was issued a warning to prepare to move to an unspecified destination.[6] Where to became obvious when all squadron staff were issued with active service kit for the tropics, and eleven aircrew were dispatched on a northbound train with seventy tents. An advance flight of three aircraft flew into Milne Bay on 6 September, and the following day were pressed into their first mission, providing flak suppression for an attack on the Japanese cruiser *Tenryu* and destroyer *Arashi* – an early use of strike wing tactics developed in Malta, with Beauforts from 100 Squadron following with torpedoes. Unfortunately, one of the Beaus slid off the runway and hit a Hudson, but the other two carried out their strafing run, and the Beauforts were able to mount their torpedo attacks, but no hits were recorded.[7]

The squadron's ultimate destination was an area of cleared jungle named Ward's Strip, a few miles outside Port Moresby. The Beaufighters flew in on 12 September, initially landing at the wrong place, Waigani airfield, before reaching Ward's Strip in the early evening. With all the ground crew and those seventy tents following in the steamer SS *Taroona,* which arrived two days later, the Beaufighter aircrews faced an uncomfortable night sleeping under the stars with prodigious numbers of bloodthirsty mosquitos. The arrival of the tents, ground crew and a semblance of organisation hardly made it good. One of the aircrew glibly summarised their insalubrious new circumstances: 'At the end of the day and buggering about in the dark, I flopped on my allotted ground space, caked in mud, and stinking like a sewer.'[8] Tropical idyll, this was not.

The Beaufighters had arrived at a dangerous moment. The Japanese had already done the difficult bit – they had trekked across the jagged peaks and through the tangled jungle of the Owen Stanley range and they were positioning their artillery in the foothills in sight of Port Moresby and the Coral Sea. Japanese journalist Seizo Okado described the celebrations among the Japanese troops: 'The sea! It's the sea of Port Moresby! Wild with joy, the soldiers who were stained all over with mud and blood, threw themselves into each other's arms and wept.'[9]

On 16 September, the Japanese commander Tomitoro Horii, camped near Ioribaiwa and just twenty-five miles from Moresby, had written his final order for the attack on Moresby, but received orders to dig in and rest his exhausted men and wait for supplies to arrive before initiating the final victorious push.[10] Horii wrote that the Australians were 'in a state of utter confusion, to a great degree have lost the will to fight'. On the face of it, everything was going to form – the Japanese had pushed the 'Chockos' back (albeit with heavy losses) and Port Moresby and the final Allied foothold on New Guinea were now set to fall, exactly as had happened everywhere else. Yet chinks of weakness were already appearing in the Japanese war machine. The Coral Sea battle had been followed by the shock defeat at Midway, while in early August, the Japanese had tried a small flanking landing on the eastern tip of New Guinea, at Milne Bay. Such was Japanese overconfidence that this was entrusted to too small a force, and despite fighting with suicidal ferocity, they were defeated by Australian forces on 9 September, leaving behind 750 dead and a similar number unaccounted for.[11] It was Japan's first land defeat.

The Japanese logistics of the main thrust towards Moresby depended entirely on a single trail – the undulating and winding 100-mile Kokoda track through the impenetrable jungle and jagged mountains of the Owen Stanley range, with some parts single-file, and in some stretches reaching an altitude of over 7,000 feet. The shock weapon of Malaya – the bicycle – had to be left at home. The Japanese had to march on foot through taxing terrain, accompanied by some horses and mules, and hundreds of conscripted carriers, recruited from Rabaul, Korea and Formosa.[12] In Malaya, plantations and jungle fringes offered potential for both flanking moves and seizing relatively plentiful food supplies. The jungles of the Kokoda trail offered few such fruitful diversions and next to no subsistence. The attackers were exhausted and hungry, suffering from the cocktail of diseases which exacerbated the slightest injury – this despite capturing Allied food dumps at Kokoda and elsewhere on the trail. The Kokada campaign highlighted a key flaw in Japanese army operations – the indifference to the health and well-being of their men, and carelessness in the logistics of supply. The key aim for Australian and US air forces became interdiction: to forbid supplies reaching the stretched Japanese front-line units forced to use a single, narrow track. And this is where the Beaufighter's armament of four 20mm cannon and six machine guns would prove particularly potent.

Prior to the arrival of the Beau, the combined US-Australian air force consisted of RAAF and USAAF P-40s along with US Douglas A-24 Banshees (the army version of the US Navy's very successful dive-bomber, the Douglas Dauntless) in jungle-cleared air bases near Port Moresby. This would be supplemented by light and medium bombers (B-25 Mitchells, B-26 Marauders and Douglas A-20s) based in Townsville in northern Australia. There were also some Beaufort torpedo bombers, Hudsons and even Wirraways providing some reconnaissance and which were occasionally used for ground attack.[13] The initial focus of the aircraft had been to attack Buna, where barges and boats delivered supplies – these were much easier targets for the medium bombers and dive bombers to hit. However, they had to run the gauntlet of strong anti-aircraft fire and Mitsubishi Zeros from the elite Taiman Kukugi air group, whose pilots included several noted Japanese aces, including Saburo Sakai.[14] The US bombers would on occasion suffer heavy losses, and didn't cause a lot of damage. Attempts to strafe the Japanese supply columns on the Kokoda trail were tried – but only the P-40 fighters had adequate armament for this, and there is little evidence this had much effect in stemming the Japanese advance.

Interestingly, the Beaufighter's example as a weapons platform was coincidentally one being learned by the Americans when Beaufighters arrived in Townsville. US aviation manufacturers up to now had been building light and medium bombers using pre-war doctrines, i.e. bombs formed the offensive weaponry, with guns used only for defence, and all featured a glazed nose to assist bomb aiming. In the early summer of 1942, the newly arrived US air chief in Australia, General George Kenney, had discovered that one of his enterprising officers, Paul 'Pappy' Gunn,[15] had converted an A-20 Havoc to carry four 0.50-cal heavy machines in a solid non-glazed nose, the guns taken from wrecked and unserviceable aircraft. Until this point, the A-20 was too short range to reach the northern coast, so was next to useless. Kenney instructed Gunn to convert all of the A-20s, and these would join the Beaus in the next phase of shooting up the Japanese supply lines. It didn't end there, with Gunn also setting about converting the B-25 Mitchell, which eventually included one version with eighteen 0.50-cal machine guns, and another with a 75mm cannon.

On 17 September, twelve Beaus performed 30 Squadron's first strike mission, targeting barges which were landing Japanese troops and supplies at Sananand a and Buna on the northern coast.[16] They left three barges blazing fiercely, amid a great pall of smoke. No aircraft were lost, and US commander Douglas MacArthur, in a rare compliment for an Australian unit, called the raid 'a honey!'[17] That night, the Japanese countered with a bombing raid on Ward's Strip. Such raids on and around Port Moresby were frequent – with about one hundred during the year, but they were usually small and rarely caused much damage. This attack spurred crews to dig slit trenches around the airfield – a wise precaution but one that had its drawbacks. The trenches would quickly fill with rain, and even worse, an assemblage of biting spiders, centipedes and in one case a small crocodile, all delightful surprises for airmen diving for cover during an air raid.

The next day saw the Beaufighters mount their first strafing attacks on the Kokoda trail. A big challenge was the topography – in one incident, Des Moran-Hilford only just cleared a hilltop as he pulled up from an attacking strafing dive.[18] Five days later, the same pilot was attacked by two Zeros over Buna. He successfully evaded by diving to sea level and opening up the throttles, taking advantage of the Beau's top speed being similar to the Zero. This became an established tactic among Beau crews, and this, alongside the aircraft's toughness, meant Beaufighter losses to Japanese fighters were light. The next few days continued with daily missions over Buna and the trail, but 23 September saw the squadron's first loss. One of its most experienced pilots, George Sayer, and his navigator William Mariet were both killed when their Beau was hit near Buna by anti-aircraft fire from what other crews came to regard as 'the hottest gun-pit around' and crashed in a mangrove swamp. Sayer had seen action in several theatres, and had escaped Java in a small lifeboat, surviving a forty-four-day ordeal to reach northern Australia. The Buna raid had been Sayer's first combat mission with 30 Squadron.[19]

The arrival of the Beaufighters was a precursor of a major expansion of Port Moresby as an Allied base, overseen by US South-East Pacific Commander, the controversial Douglas MacArthur. Australian War Correspondent George Johnston wrote, just a couple of weeks after the Beaufighters' arrival: 'The strength of Moresby is staggering — thousands of motor trucks, new roads everywhere and seven magnificent airfields. We could put 100 fighters in the air against a Jap raid. Huge forces of modern bombers [are] now here.'[20]

This rapid build-up must have been soul-destroying for Horii's Japanese force. In addition, the expected supplies hadn't got through, and his depleted force was reduced to a few ounces of rice per day. Perched in sight of Port Moresby and the sea, Horii relayed his latest orders to his men – to advance to the rear.[21] As the Japanese retreat began in late September and early October, the Beaufighters would come into their own, stepping up to a relentless schedule of daily attacks in support of the revitalised Australian advance. Key to this was liaison with the Australian front-line forces, who radioed into RAAF liaison officers when they had located Japanese resistance.

The same jungle canopy which provided cover to troops, particularly from the strafing by lightly armed fighters, would become a deadly killing ground when pulverised by the full weight of a Beaufighter's cannon and machine guns, with trees shredding into deadly flying shards and splinters. Obviously, this was out of sight of the Beaufighters, and these lethal maelstroms had to happen in the very close vicinity of troops and pack animals to have real effect. Actual results attributable to actual attacks were very difficult to confirm – but the regular discovery of piles of Japanese dead on the trail suggests some of the Beaus attacks were highly effective. Okado Seizo described finding large numbers of bodies 'here and there', with 'a nasty, stifling smell, like that of burning old cloth, filled the air, giving us a stifling sense of nausea. It was the smell of dead bodies, rotting human bodies lying in all possible postures... I approached one of the bodies and found that it was a heap of maggots bred in the belly, where the rotting process seemed to set in before any other part of the body.'

The topography and terrain became ever more challenging as the Japanese pulled back, and on 13 October, 30 Squadron lost its second Beaufighter and its crew when they flew into the hillside, failing to pull out in time after strafing.[22] The Owen Stanley mountains around the trail rose dramatically, with Mount Stanley touching 13,000 feet, and had some very steep slopes, meaning it was a lethal environment to navigate, particularly with rapidly forming rain and storm clouds, not infrequent with New Guinea's tropical climate.

No. 30 Squadron's Beaus weren't exclusively attacking the Japanese supply lines. They took part in a couple of major daylight bombing raids on Japanese air bases, acting as long-range escorts to the burgeoning selection of US heavy and medium bombers in attacks on Lae and Buna, with the US and RAAF mustering over one hundred aircraft on 21 and 24 November, including B-17s, B-25s, A-20s, escorted by P-40s as well as the Beaufighters.[23] The Beaus targeted a couple of the Japanese airfields, destroying a number of Zeros on the ground (they were actually Nakajima Ki-43 Oscars as this was an army air force base).

During the course of December alone, 30 Squadron flew 302 hours of operations, firing 155,000 rounds of ammunition.[24] The intensity of operations for the Beaufighter was more than matched by the intensity of the struggle on the ground. Here the Australians battled both their own supply issues and bitterly defended Japanese strong points at Templeton's Crossing, Eora Ridge and Oivi-Gorari. At the overrun Japanese defensive position at Gorari, the diary of a dead Japanese lieutenant simply noted, 'all morning their planes have bombed and strafed us.'[25] If the physical privations and suffering weren't enough, the Australians also had to put up with the machinations and interference of distant, notably self-aggrandising commanders Thomas Blamey and Douglas MacArthur.[26] If the top brass were unloved, there was no doubt where the Beaufighter lay in the affections of the Aussie troops, as the Australian *Sun* newspaper reported:

> 'The story of the tree-topping wave-hopping Beaufighters begins in the rain, mud, slime and malaria of Port Moresby in September. Although inadequately sheltered, tormented by mosquitoes and improperly fed, the Beaufighter boys had their aircraft ready in three days for the first of hundreds of devastating sorties. The amazing firepower of the Beaufighter has probably inflicted more Japanese casualties than any other type of aircraft.
>
> 'It can deliver more than a third of a ton of lead every minute and can concentrate more cannon and machine-gun fire than can a Fortress or a Liberator. The Japs began a very costly acquaintance with the Beaufighter when the AIF was smashing its way towards Buna. The soldiers told the Beaufighter pilots the location of the enemy troops, and the co-operation was so harmonious that although the aircrews never saw the Japanese in the jungle, they killed them in their hundreds. Following through, our Army lads found the areas strafed by the Beaufighters to be littered with enemy dead. Through the festering jungle, over which the aircraft flew low enough to set the tree-tops quivering, the Beaufighters left a long trail of enemy dead, of blasted installations, silent anti-aircraft positions, mangled equipment, and charred equipment.'[27]

The storied history of ground attack is replete with exaggerated estimates of damage actually caused. In this case, it is impossible to precisely assess the Beaus' contribution – the crews could rarely see the targets they were shooting at, borne out by debriefs and mission logs, which are prosaic in the extreme – no numbers, no gore, no indication of apocalyptic destruction. The head of the US 5th Air Force in New Guinea, Ennis Whitehead, noticed this phenomenon, speaking of one Beaufighter raid, 'This is one of the quite frequent occasions on which the pilots have seen no movement or effect of their attack and would probably consider their mission was of no value, whereas in fact it was most successful.'[28] There were plenty of other contributors to Japanese losses, not least the indefatigable Aussie soldiers and untreated disease and injury in the pitiless tropical environment. However, Beaufighters played a very important role – in both the interdiction of supply routes, but also as aerial artillery in terrain where deploying tanks and field guns was difficult to say the least.

By December, the Australian troops had crossed New Guinea and reached the sea, seizing the beachheads at Buna and Gona. The Japanese had left 4,500 troops behind on the trail, all dead. It had been a remarkable achievement, and while churlishly unacknowledged by MacArthur, it did not escape the notice of British General Bill Slim, who wrote: 'It was the Australians who first broke the spell of the invincibility of the Japanese Army.'[29] Slim and his Indian Army colleagues would spend the next year absorbing and implementing the lessons of Milne Bay and Kokoda, which would pay great dividends in 1944. One of the lessons learned was that cutting the supply lines was critical for victory. It was primarily the Beaufighters that did the cutting.

The battle in New Guinea would continue for many more months, and 30 Squadron's operations continued with attacks on Lae and Rabaul, which both continued to be major Japanese bases. Losses to aircraft and aircrew occurred along the way, although the worst loss would be a practice strafing exercise when Bob Harding's lead Beaufighter, carrying two new crew as a 'work shadow', collided with the target ship's mast.[30] The two pilots on board were lost, while the two radar operators somehow escaped.

On 3 March, 30 Squadron were called in for one of their most ambitious raids, which would be filmed by celebrated Australian cameraman Damien Parer, flying on board one of the Beaus. The raid would be recognised as the last of five key battles which saved Australia from invasion. A troop convoy had been sighted leaving Rabaul, consisting of eight troop ships, eight escorts and carrying 6,900 troops, heading across the Bismarck Sea to Lae, to stem the Allied advances following victory at Kokoda. The convoy had been attacked by Fortresses on the previous day, and one of the troop ships was destroyed. The raid would see 30 Squadron joined by large elements of the US 5th Air Group, with a multi-layered attack plan which owed much to the shipping strike tactics that had been pioneered by Patrick Gibbs in Malta in the summer of 1942 (described elsewhere).

The attack started with a conventional heavy bomber raid at altitude, with heavy P-38 escort in order to draw off Japanese fighters. Then the Beaufighters would go in at wave height, aiming at 'flak suppression' by targeting anti-aircraft guns, and would be followed immediately by B-25s and A-20s 'skip bombing' (another Pappy Gunn-inspired tactic) with 500-pound bombs. The thirteen Beaufighters deliberately approached low and slow in order to give the appearance of a torpedo attack by Beauforts.[31] This had the desired effect as the Japanese convoy was ordered to turn towards the Beaus in order to minimise the chances of a torpedo strike. Instead, they opened themselves up for strafing the full length of the ship. As 30 Squadron radio operator Harry Suthons recounted:

> 'You've gone around behind the warships, but they're still banging away with their big guns, pom-poms and ack-ack. You can see tracers whipping by. A cargo ship is in the sights. She is camouflaged and has goalpost masts. She looks blurred at first, but then comes into focus. The first thunder of fire [from the cannons] gives you a shock. It jars at your feet, and you see the tracers lashing out ahead of you, and orange lights dance before your eyes [as the bullets strike] on the grey structure of the ship. You keep on following the tracers to the ship, but before you get there "Torchy" eases back the stick and you feel the tearing at your stomach and your knees want to buckle with the terrific strain of the pull-out. You have to hang on to the framework behind the pilot — and the ship becomes a dark mass. Again, you see a lot of sky …'[32]

Suthons' account very much accords with the film taken by Damien Parer – what is evident is that beyond the ship's grey shape and the tracer and bullets streaking towards it, there isn't much detail discernible on deck, with the ship disappearing below the aircraft before any chance of observing the results. Following behind in a skip-bomber, the B-25 co-pilot Garrett Middlebrook had a somewhat more lurid and colourful description of the effects of the strafing attacks on troop ships with decks crowded with troops:

> 'They went in and hit this troop ship. What I saw looked like little sticks, maybe a foot long or something like that, or splinters flying up off the deck of the ship; they'd fly all around ... and twist crazily in the air and fall out in the water. Then I realized what I was watching were human beings. I was watching hundreds of those Japanese just blown off the deck by those machine guns. They just splintered around the air like sticks in a whirlwind and they'd fall in the water.'[33]

The follow-up attacks by Mitchells and A-20s were also successful, while Beaufighters wheeled around attacking again and again until their ammunition was spent. By the end of the day's raids, seven troopships were either sunk or blazing hulks, and US PT boats finished off the last crippled one in the night. Four destroyers were also sunk in a highly successful operation, and an estimated 2,900 troops were killed. The flak suppression clearly worked – just one Mitchell was lost, and one Beaufighter was written off after a 250-pound bomb exploded beneath it. The surviving Japanese destroyers managed to pick up about 2,700 troops who were safely returned to Rabaul.[34]

The next day, volunteers were requested for possibly the Beaufighter's most controversial mission – the machine-gunning of troops on rafts or in the sea, to prevent their reaching Lae. One of 30 Squadron's observers, Alf Nelson, described this: 'Very bloody show. The water in the barges was red with blood. You could see the sea was stained all around.'[35] Mention of this distasteful task is notably omitted in George Turnbull Dick's squadron history. While tactically this can be justified, it underlined the savagery of the war with Japan by early 1943. However, the Bismarck Sea action was a great victory for the Allies and a bitter blow for the Japanese and ended any realistic chance of a renewed push on Moresby and Japanese victory in New Guinea. The Beaufighters had played a huge part through their highly destructive strafing attack which had cleared the way for the US light and medium bombers to conduct bombing runs unimpeded and accurately with minimal losses.

The battle in New Guinea and 30 Squadron's missions continued for several more months, attacking Japanese forces around Lae, as well as further afield on New Guinea. It wasn't entirely one-way traffic – on 22 March, a large Japanese air raid hit Ward's Strip, destroying one of the Beaus and damaging others. Operations continued at Ward's Strip, except when a mission demanded a deployment on a forward airstrip, which were basic in the extreme, as pilot Keith Nicholson found: '…We staged to Dobodura [in western New Guinea] the night before. It was an awful strip, the mud squirted through the holes in the pierced steel planking (PSP) as the aircraft rolled down the runway.'[36]

On 22 July 1943, the squadron moved to Goodenough Island to the north-east of New Guinea, moving again to Kamiri aerodrome on Noemfoor Island following its successful invasion in mid-1944. It was from here that a raid was carried out on 20 September, when Beaufighters targeted Japanese troop-carrying barges at Bomberai Peninsula, the westernmost point of New Guinea. One of the Beaus flown by Flight Lieutenant Moody and Flight Sergeant Aitcherley was shot down by anti-aircraft, with both men surviving and evading the Japanese. Despite Western New Guinea's wholly inhospitable interior, the pair made a valiant effort to try and reach Allied lines which lay much further east. Unfortunately, having trekked about 300 kilometres, and presumably in a state of absolute exhaustion and malnutrition, they were picked up by the Japanese and suffered a tragic and macabre fate. Post-war investigation revealed that after three months of torture, the Japanese unit's CO had fallen ill, and in a disgusting act of savagery had them both executed, before getting his men to wrap their entrails around him as some kind of quack cure.[37] Such were the risks of missions conducted at long range over both difficult terrain and, with increasing regularity, open ocean, and this would particularly face the other RAAF Beaufighter unit, 31 Squadron.

This squadron had remained in Australia, deploying to Coomalie Creek Airfield about forty-five miles to the south of Darwin, under the command of Charles Read.[38] It was initially planned that the Beaus would be deployed in their original intended role – as long-range maritime fighters. However, for the first, most successful period of the squadron's existence, they fought in support one of the most unjustly forgotten campaigns of the Second World War – the battle for Timor. Another long, slim Indonesian island with a mountainous spine, it had long been split by rival European colonial powers the Netherlands and Portugal. It had a more amenable climate than New Guinea, with a distinct dry season, and large areas of deciduous forest, some of which had been cleared for farming. For Australia, its position to the north-west meant it was an increasingly important strategic 'barrier', particularly following the fall of Malaya. As a result, the Australians, in cahoots with the Dutch, occupied the Portuguese half of the island. Despite this, the Dutch and the Australian 'Sparrow Force' were defeated quickly following the Japanese invasion on 19 and 20 February, exactly as had been occurring to Allied armies everywhere else in the region.

However, what was different was that a sizeable force of Dutch and Australians, many with specialist training, would retreat to form a 'commando' unit, in the southern mountainous parts of what had been Portuguese Timor. The force was nurtured, supplied and reinforced from Australia, and would harass the Japanese forces for a whole year, tying down a whole division of at least 12,000 men, and inflicting serious casualties in ambushes and raids. The unit worked with the local population, who would become embroiled in the fighting, and while many Timorese 'criados' and Portuguese settlers joined the Allied guerilla force, innocent civilians suffered heavily as a result.

No. 31 Squadron's role was to provide close support for the commandos, target enemy bases, and assure some level of air superiority and escort for supply operations. Timor lies 450 miles away from Coomalie Creek, and in mid-1942, the Beaufighter was probably the only aircraft in the world with the required ability to project firepower from such a distance. No. 31's first operation was on 19 November, with the Beaufighters strafing several targets on Timor, usually Japanese bases or units, but also 'hostile native concentrations', a grimly vague term for strafing villages whose inhabitants had sided with the Japanese. Obviously in strafing a village, the bullets and cannon shells made no distinction between those actively helping the

Japanese and those innocently going about life in their village. Operations continued on a daily basis, and on 26 November, the biggest raid yet saw six Beaufighters escort ten Lockheed Hudson light bombers in bombing and strafing the villages of Beco and Nova Lusa, starting a number of fires. Beaufighters were also involved in escorting a small Royal Australian Navy flotilla intended to drop off fresh Dutch troops and supplies and help evacuate at risk Portuguese civilians and some of the original Australian commandos, who were finally being relieved. The Beaufighter escort headed off the largest attack of fourteen bombers on 30 November, but the fourth attack by torpedo bombers the next day got through, and two torpedoes struck HMAS *Armidale*, which sank with 100 sailors and soldiers lost.[39] Just one day later – or one day too late – the Beaus carried out a highly successful raid on Timor's main Penfoei Airfield, destroying eighteen aircraft and damaging several more, without loss.[40]

The Allied effort had provoked a huge Japanese reaction – through November and December 1942, the Japanese had poured men into Timor, to take the full strength up to 12,000 (nearly twice the number used in the Battle of Kokoda), and making inroads into the commando-held areas. With the loss of *Armidale* it became clear that to continue the campaign would need serious reinforcements or face destruction. With the US and Australians focussed on New Guinea, there was little appetite for this, and having inflicted disproportionate casualties and diverted Japanese resources away from the New Guinea battlefront, the Allied commando force was withdrawn by early January. The Beaufighter raids continued, not least because Penfoei had become the main Japanese base for launching attacks into mainland Australia, with Darwin struck several more times. Flying Officer Eric 'Basher' Barnett recalled one particularly hairy attack on Penfoei.

> 'Crossing the coast, we climbed up through 10/10th cloud which was down to ground level. At 1200 feet we emerged from the cloud into bright sunshine and almost immediately, Squadron Leader Savage, Flight Lieutenant Madden and myself observed our target through a break in the cloud.

'It was directly in front and below us, so we dived down for a low-level attack, heading northwards across the strip.

'At about 500 feet I decided to test-fire my 20-mm cannons on a large building with a red tile roof … It was located on the western side of some low hills to the west of the airfield. I fired a short burst and watched it hit the roof ... the building immediately disintegrated in three tremendous explosions and flattened everything within a 2-mile radius. It turned out I had hit a munitions factory nobody knew about. I was momentarily stunned and recovered to find myself flying upside down at about 1000 feet, in the explosion both cockpit windows had been blown out and everything movable had been sucked out of the aircraft's cockpit, including my smokes and matches.

'I was bewailing their loss to my navigator just after he had finished a report to HQ and the transmitter was left open and the whole area was informed of my loss.

'A large mushroom cloud of thick black smoke had risen from the site where the building had been and was already up to the base of the clouds. A deep-red-coloured fire was burning in the remains of the building.

'Having checked that my aircraft hadn't been damaged, I dived to attack the airfield, flying about 20 feet off the ground. I fired my cannons and machine guns at two 'Bettys' on the strip outside some pens. One of these aircraft caught fire and is considered to have been destroyed. At the northern end of the strip I turned left and opened fire with cannon and machine guns on two more 'Bettys' parked on the main strip. One of these bombers caught fire, considered destroyed, while the other was damaged. I then fired into some blast pens and damaged a 'Zeke' fighter, following which I attacked a heavy AA position, killing or wounding three personnel. At this point I began a gentle right-hand bank and decided to have a quick look over my shoulder back down the strip, turning back to see where I was going, I instantly applied full power and went into a steep climbing left turn.'[41]

An even more successful Beau raid came on 28 February, when thirteen Japanese aircraft were destroyed on the ground, and one Zero shot down. Unfortunately, on 16 May, the Japanese were prepared for another 31 Squadron attack, with alert and well-positioned anti-aircraft batteries. These shot down two of the Beaus on their strafing run, and damaged a third which was forced to ditch off Timor, with the loss of its crew. The remaining four Beaus all survived a long chase by Japanese fighters which pursued them over 100 miles across the Timor Sea.[42]

Unlike 30 Squadron, the Beaus of 31 Squadron would achieve a number of air-to-air victories – and produced the RAAF's only Beaufighter ace. This was new Squadron Leader Reginald Lloyd 'Butch' Gordon, who shot down two Kawasaki Ki-45 Toryu 'Nick' heavy fighters on 9 October, on his way to scoring five victories. The encounter saw Gordon take some damage from the defensive fire of the first Ki-45 before he shot it down. A second Ki-45 attacked and scored multiple hits on Gordon's Beau. However, the Japanese pilot made the fatal mistake of thinking Gordon was finished, flew past him, and into his sights and was blown away. Gordon had lost his port engine yet still made the return journey of 400 miles of ocean to crash-land at Livingston airfield in the Northern Territory. An examination of his aircraft revealed fifty 'cannon' holes (most likely larger 12.7mm machine-gun rounds) and 220 smaller 7.7mm rounds.[43] It demonstrated perfectly the toughness and resilience of the Beau – it also underlined that the 'Nick's' offensive armament was inadequate for a heavy fighter. Among the other aircraft Gordon shot down was a Nakajima A6M2 Rufe – a floatplane fighter conversion from a Mitsubishi Zero – one of three shot down by 31 Squadron on 21 November.[44] Sadly, Gordon was killed in February when he was testing a Beau with a defective propeller.

The man Gordon replaced as squadron leader, Charles Read, had been promoted to wing commander in June 1943, and in March 1944 he would form the new 77 Wing, finally bringing Australia's two great Beaufighter squadrons together, along with 22 Squadron, a light bomber squadron which had fought alongside 30 Squadron in New Guinea and had later switched to Beaus from Havocs. All of the squadrons had started to receive Australia-built Beaufighters – built under licence by DAP (Department of Aircraft

Above: To capture the power of the Bristol Hercules meant huge propellors (12′6″ in diameter), long undercarriage legs and a cockpit well above the ground. All well-captured in this photograph of an RAAF Beaufighter, possibly at Townsville. (State Library of Victoria)

Below: Mechanics working on a Beaufighter's stripped-down Bristol Hercules engine, revealing its twin rows of cylinder heads. Two Beaufighter VIFs can be seen being given an overhaul or modifications at Southern Aircraft Ltd's Lowfield Heath hangar at Gatwick. (Peter Amos, via Historic Military Press)

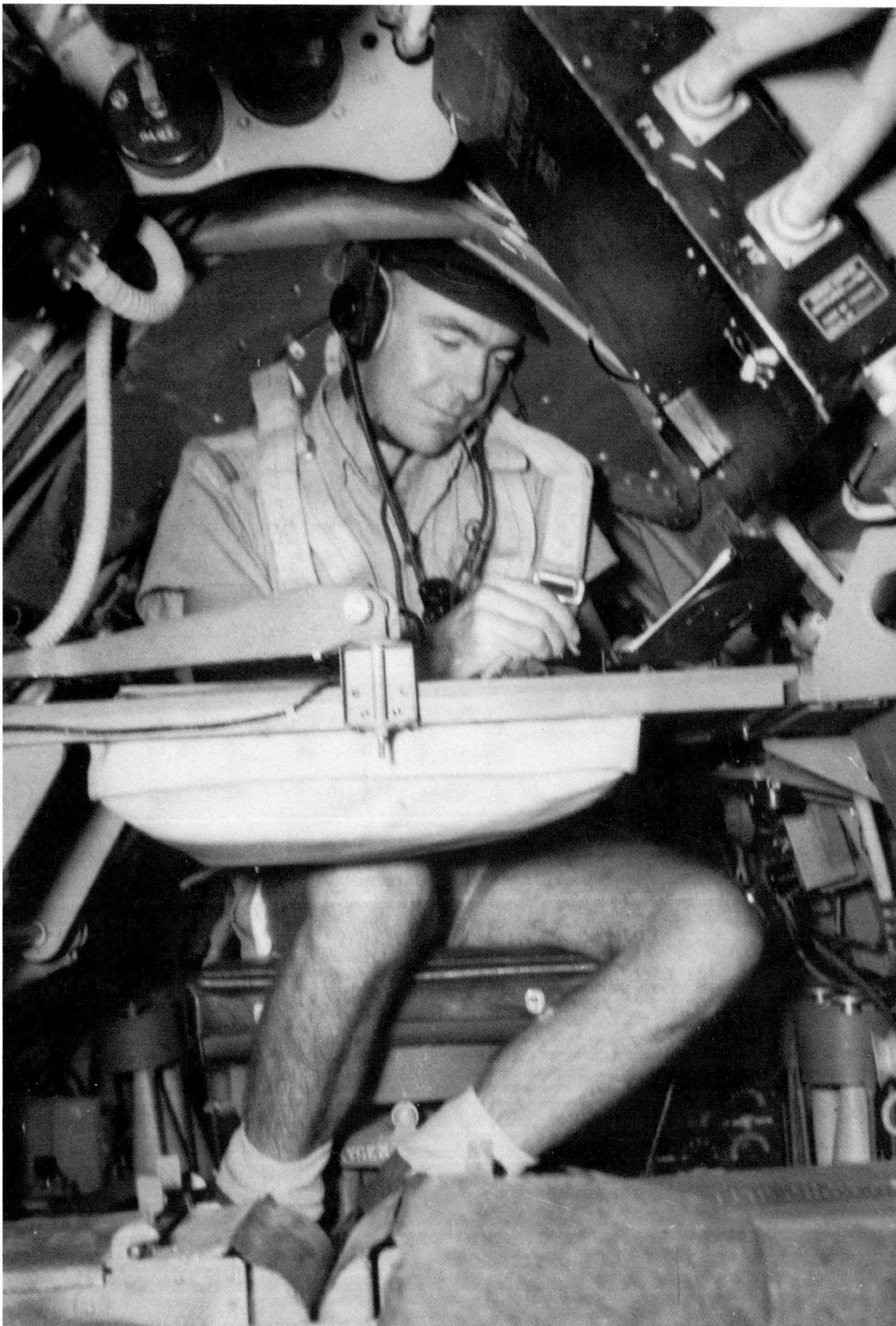

RAAF 31 Squadron's observer and navigator John Neville Marr at work in flight in the tight confines of the rear Beaufighter fuselage. (State Library of Victoria)

The Beaufighter was legendary for its ability to survive collisions with all manner of objects during its low-level attacks. In this case, a strike wing Beaufighter from 455 Squadron has three feet of mast from an armed trawler embedded in its nose, following the attack on Marsdiep Harbour in the Netherlands on 17 November 1944. Posing with the offending item are navigator Lee Turner (left) and the pilot Steve Sykes (right). (Historic Military Press)

Above: The ever-present key to the Beaufighter's success as a combat aircraft were its four Hispano 20-millimetre cannon. Here, as mechanics work on the engines, the armourers of 30 Squadron RAAF at Noemfoor, Dutch New Guinea, are readying 20mm cannon to be fitted on the Beaufighter. (State Library of Victoria)

Below: A patched-up Beaufighter IC of 252 Squadron on a desert airstrip in Libya, possibly Gambut, in 1943. This was one of the two original Coastal Command squadrons reassigned to the Mediterranean, where they began the Beaufighter's glorious career in the theatre. (Historic Military Press)

Above: Personnel of 'B' Flight of 409 Squadron, one of Fighter Command's two Canadian night-fighter units, posing for a formal portrait with one of their Rolls-Royce Merlin-powered Beaufighter IIFs at Acklington, on a snowy day in January 1942. (Public Domain)

Below: A German merchant vessel on the receiving end of cannon and rocket fire from Beaufighters of 455 Squadron RAAF of the Anzac wing, led by Flight Lieutenant R.A. Wills. (State Library of Victoria)

Above: The crew of a 144 Squadron 'Torbeau' stand by the cockpit of their aircraft at Tain, Ross-shire, in North-west Scotland. Note the Mark XII aerial torpedo and the aerial camera port in the nose. (Air Force Museum of New Zealand)

Below: An aerial view of a 489 Squadron (RNZAF) 'Torbeau' of the Anzac strike wing.

Above: Beaufighters of 404 Squadron, Dallachy wing, attacking German shipping on 15 October 1944. The targets were the flakship VP1605 *Mosel* and the Norwegian freighter *Inger Johanne*. Following the attack, *Mosel* blew up and sank. (Historic Military Press)

Below: A 'Torbeau', in this case a 254 Squadron Beaufighter TF.X, one of the North Coates strike wing squadrons. Note the 'thimble nose' designed to house the centimetric AI Mark VII or VIII radar with its cavity magnetron (even though in this case, no radar was carried). (Historic Military Press)

A crash-landed Beaufighter VIC at Langham following an anti-shipping raid on 14 May 1944, flown by Flying Officer Ian Masson and Flight Sergeant Knight. The aircraft is from 455 Squadron, one of the Anzac wing. Note also the small 'Beaverbug' armoured car to the right of the aircraft. (Historic Military Press)

Above: A USAAF Beaufighter VIF of 416 Nightfighter Squadron, nicknamed *Fluff*, at an airfield near Grottaglie, Italy, in late 1943. This aircraft sports the dipoles in the nose and on the wings of the outdated AI Mark IV radar. Other USAAF Beaus sported the thimble nose and Mark VII radar. (NARA)

Below: A classic view of a 30 Squadron Beaufighter passing a mountain peak in the rugged highland interior of Eastern New Guinea. Beaufighters faced hazardous mountain crossings on a regular basis in both New Guinea and Burma. (Australian War Memorial; OG0001)

Air crew leaving the air strip following a mission. Behind them, an RAAF 30 Squadron Beaufighter, its missile launch rails empty. (State Library of Victoria)

Above: RAAF 30 Squadron's Leading Aircraftmen N.R. Hewitt and R. Nicholls lift a rocket into place on a Beaufighter's wing rails. This appears to be a high-explosive version, with rounded tip and sixty-pound charge. (State Library of Victoria)

Below: The aftermath of a Japanese air raid at the 30 RAAF Squadron base at Ward's Strip, near Port Moresby. Beaufighter A19-50 suffered a direct hit and was totally destroyed on 12 April 1943. (Permission granted by Jim Turner, RAAF 30 Squadron Association)

Above: 30 RAAF Squadron CO Brian 'Blackjack' Walker and his navigator John Mason emerge from their wrecked aircraft following a crash landing, after a strafing attack on the Japanese airfield at Lae, on the northern coast of New Guinea on 17 November 1943. Both look remarkably unperturbed given their close shave, while the aircraft, A19-4, would ultimately be repaired and transferred to a training unit. (Photograph Brian Walker, permission granted by Jim Turner, 30 Squadron Association)

Below: A pair of RAAF 30 Squadron Beaufighters swoop in at low level over a cleared encampment in the tropical forests of New Guinea. (Permission granted by Jim Turner, 30 Squadron RAAF Association)

Beaufighter VIC, probably from 27 Squadron, landing at an airfield in the Arakan in Burma. (State Library of Victoria)

A stunning photograph of a South African Air Force squadron Beaufighter TFX of 16 Squadron, firing off a salvo of rocket projectiles at targets in the snow-covered German-occupied town of Žužemberk, Yugoslavia, on 6 March 1945. (Historic Military Press)

An altogether more tranquil scene showing a flight of Beaufighters from an RAAF training unit, 6,000 feet above prime Australian farmland. (State Library of Victoria)

Above: While there are currently no flying Beaufighters to be seen, there are some spectacular examples at air museums around the world. This is a Coastal Command Beaufighter, replete with D-Day stripes, at the RAF Air Museum in Hendon.

Below: Neighbouring the Beaufighter at the RAF Museum is an even rarer bird, a Bristol Beaufort. Note the smaller engines and propellors, shorter undercarriage and much bulkier forward fuselage. The Beaufighter may have started as the 'Beaufort Fighter', but in reality it was transformed.

Production) at Fishermen's Bend in Melbourne from early 1944. The DAP Beaufighter was specially numbered 'Mark 21' and was fitted out to carry a torpedo. A total of 364 were built, of which about half reached squadrons before the end of the war.[45]

The war in late 1944 had shifted decisively towards Allied victory and had moved away from New Guinea and Timor. The Beaus would switch to bases in the western part of the Indonesian archipelago, such as at Noemfoor, Morotai and Tarakan, continuing in various dangerous roles, from strafing, to anti-shipping strikes, to maritime escort over Leyte and the Celebes Sea, and providing close support for Operation Oboe, the Australian and free Dutch amphibious landings on Borneo. No. 93 Squadron carried out its first operational mission on 26 July 1945, with two Beaufighters mounting a rocket attack on a Japanese residential compound at Situ, just outside Jakarta. With opportunities for meaningful combat missions rapidly receding, 93 Squadron carried out its most notable mission on 7 August – an attack on what it believed to be a Japanese oil tanker. The sunk ship turned out to be *Mia Moana* – the personal yacht of the Rajah of Sarawak![46] Missions in Indonesia continued past the end of the war, with a Beaufighter damaged by flak as late as 28 August, with 'show of strength' flights in September over areas where Japanese soldiers had still to lay down arms in the spiralling turmoil of post-war Indonesia. Before the end of the year, all the Beaufighter squadrons were back in Australia.

By the end of the war, sixty-five aircrew from 30 Squadron had been killed, seventy-nine from 31 Squadron and ten from 22 Squadron. All told, just fifty-two Beaufighters were lost to enemy action, of which at least eight were shot down by Japanese aircraft and thirty-four by anti-aircraft fire.[47] While not a dogfighter, the Beaufighter's top speed was surprisingly competitive with the key Japanese fighters, the A6M Zero and Nakajima Ki-43 Oscar, and it had the power to dive away, and ability to absorb plentiful damage, meaning it was very difficult for Japanese fighters to shoot down. No. 31 Squadron was credited with twenty enemy aircraft shot down, but none of the other squadrons posted a confirmed kill. It wasn't their job.

The arrival of the Beaufighter in New Guinea and Timor in late 1942, was, to use an over-used expression, a game-changer in the Australian fightback after the humiliation of Singapore and disaster of Darwin. More than any other Allied aircraft, the Beaufighter became beloved of the RAAF – in part due to its transformational role, but it also embodied certain Australian qualities – strong, rugged, bloody-minded and a great mate for the Diggers battling through in the jungles below. The aircraft's sheer destructive power was something the once invincible Japanese didn't expect and couldn't handle. It is no idle boast to claim the war in the South-West Pacific changed dramatically when the Beaufighter arrived.

Chapter 10

The Bloody Flax

Daylight operations, Mediterranean October 1942 to July 1943

Libyan coast near Derna, 12 May 1942

Cairo HQ had been alerted by an irregular forward reconnaissance unit, the famed 'Popski's Private Army', led by Russian emigre Major Vladimir Peniakoff, that the Luftwaffe was flying regular transport flights between Crete and Derna airbase in Libya, using the same route each time.[1] The 12 May would be different, as Beaufighters from 252 Squadron and P-40 Kittyhawk fighters of 250 Squadron were waiting for the next flight. Sure enough, flying into the trap came a formation of thirteen Junkers Ju-52s, escorted by a single Messerschmitt Bf110. Each of the Ju52s was carrying about twenty troops to provide reinforcements in the build-up to Rommel's great offensive later in the month. The escort was very swiftly dealt with by 250 Squadron's John Waddy, one of Australia's leading aces of the war. Waddy claimed a second Bf110 – after the war he was adamant that the German records were wrong and the escort comprised of two Bf110s.[2] The remaining P-40s and Beaufighters set upon the Ju52s, and had a field day, claiming eleven shot down. There was overclaiming, but nonetheless Luftwaffe records show seven were shot down into the sea, two crippled aircraft crash-landed at Derna, and the other four were damaged – 175 troops ended up in the Mediterranean, just forty-seven being rescued. Five Ju52s were claimed by 252's Beaufighters.[3] Despite being shorn of their escort, the Ju52 defensive fire had proved dangerous, and one Beaufighter was hit and dived into the sea.

This wasn't the first encounter Beaufighters or other Allied fighters had with Luftwaffe air convoys. This was the first use of a new tactic of coupling Beaufighters with more manoeuvrable fighters to deal with any escort (what later became known as 'delousing'), and it had proved a spectacular success. This well-orchestrated massacre by the RAF should have sent a sharp message to the Luftwaffe High Command, who were at that precise moment labouring under a delusion that their transport fleet could supply and nourish huge armies when cut off from other means – in fact they were at that moment celebrating the greatest Luftwaffe airlift of the war.

On the Eastern Front, in the wake of the Red Army's winter counter-offensive in front of Moscow, a dangerous salient had emerged in Demyansk, roughly halfway between Moscow and the besieged northern city of Leningrad. Taking advantage of the freezing cold and snow of February 1942, a Soviet pincer movement cut off about 95,000 Germans in Demyansk, completing the manoeuvre by 12 February. Nearby, 3,000 more were cut off in the tiny, pocket of Kholm.[4] Luftwaffe commanders assured Hitler they could fly in a daily total of 300 tonnes of supplies into the pocket, enough to supply and feed the armies trapped in Demyansk. The Luftwaffe were as good as their word, flying in 24,300 tons of supplies, 15,466 replacement troops and evacuating 22,093 wounded, in the three months before the Germans broke the encirclement.[5] They even exceeded the 300 tons per day promise. This was achieved in the dead of winter with temperatures falling to forty degrees below zero, when aircraft were often grounded and unserviceability rocketed.

Unfortunately for the Germans, this success led to unrealistic expectations. In his later treatise, *Lufttransportfuhrer* Fritz Morzik, a capable officer who organised the Demyansk airlift, would reflect bitterly:

> 'It is tragic to have to admit that it might have been better if the Demyansk action had failed plenty in its initial phase. This would have forced German leaders to order the 2nd Army Corps to attempt a breakthrough towards the west ... At the same time, German leaders would have been forced to realise that the personnel and material resources available were inadequate to assure fulfilment by air of the

> entire supply requirements of an Army unit numbering 100,000 men … The potential for success of the air transport forces was viewed with far too much optimism.'[6]

The Demyansk action provided Hitler with the perfect rebuttal to nervous generals requesting permission to retreat. The transport fleet had become the safety net, the saviour when armies were surrounded or supplies cut off. Overlooked in the great deliverance were the huge costs to the Demyansk operation – 265 transport aircraft were lost, and over 300 aircraft and instructors were removed from training units for over three months, compounding a shortage of new pilots which would never be resolved.[7] This is why 12 May, and the efficacy of the RAF's Beaufighters as transport destroyers, should have set off alarm bells in Luftwaffe High Command.

Yet even for Beaufighters, getting to grips with the supply flights took time. One would have expected the massively armed Beaufighter would have no problem simply blowing away a line of Junkers Ju52s, the workhorse which formed the nucleus of the Luftwaffe transport fleet. It was a slow, cumbersome trimotor designed originally as an airliner in the early 1930s – an export version was even fitted with Bristol Pegasus engines. It was capable of just 170 mph, but it was stable and easy to fly, with a payload of two tonnes or up to twenty troops. Yet intercepting the Ju52 wasn't simple, as the Luftwaffe had developed quite effective defensive tactics.

In the Mediterranean, the Ju52s flew from bases in Crete or southern Italy, in large and close formations of anything from three to fifty aircraft, at very low altitude, just about skimming the waves. The low altitude meant they were very unlikely to be picked up by radar and also meant they remained difficult to see from ground or sea until quite close. The discovery by escort fighters that flying just above the sea meant that an exhaust trail was visible from above as a black line meant an adjustment to flying at 165 feet – still very low.[8] This ultra-low flight altitude created two problems for attacking fighters – it meant they couldn't attack unseen from below, so they had to attack from above where they were easily seen against the sky – and thus exposed to targeted defensive fire, sometimes from a whole formation of Ju52 turret gunners. The Ju52 mounted a single heavy 13mm machine gun in a dorsal turret, and a couple of beam-mounted 7.9mm machine guns which its passengers would generally operate. The second problem was that for a fighter making any kind of diving pass, there was little altitude left to pull out of the dive, particularly if the fighter had picked up some damage – and when pulling up, it exposed itself to close-range raking fire from beam gunners. In addition, there was the likely presence of escorting Bf110s, with Bf109s flying out to meet the formation as it neared its North Africa destination. During an actual attack, the Ju52 pilots were drilled to close formation further and descend as low as possible, with gunners immediately opening fire whatever the distance, in an attempt to deter or interfere with the attacking pass.[9]

Hence the early entanglements of 272 Squadron saw mixed results as the Allies got to grips with tackling the formations. As we've seen, the first meeting between Ju52 and Beaufighter was catastrophic – five were shot down in minutes and two more later when 272 Squadron's Beaufighters caught them landing at Tmimi airfield.[10] The Tmimi air battle aside, the first sustained effort made to tackle Luftwaffe transport formations came as Operation Crusader reached its climax in December 1941. Rommel's Afrika Korps were suffering increasing shortages due to shipping losses, so the Germans turned to air transport. As well as 272's Beaus, Martin Marylands of SAAF's 12 and 21 Squadrons were assigned to the interception job – these US-built light bombers were lightly armed by comparison to the Beau, with four wing-mounted 7.7mm machine guns, but were quite fast, topping 300 miles per hour. They were quite successful on 11 December, claiming three Ju52s shot down, although at the cost of two Marylands lost.[11] However, the following day they suffered heavy losses to Luftwaffe fighters and were soon withdrawn from the role. On 12 December, two Beaufighters attacked a small formation of Ju52s, claiming one shot down and others damaged. Unfortunately, both Beaus were hit by defensive fire – Wing Commander Yaxley's observer was struck in both lungs, while the second plane had to crash-land.[12] The same afternoon saw 272's Beaus grapple with more Ju52s, damaging six, but this time avoiding damage to themselves. Luftwaffe records show that four Ju52s were actually lost on this day,[13] so 272's pilots probably underclaimed, but the dangers in such attacks became readily apparent.

This minor series of engagements, along with the new tactics and great success of 12 May, would provide some preparation for what occurred following Monty's great El Alamein offensive which began on 23 October. As we've seen, Beaus working in concert with Beauforts had caused havoc with the Italian navy, which had been unable to get vital freight vessels across the eastern Med to supply Rommel's forces in Egypt, in effect creating a blockade of maritime supply routes. A direct result of the difficulties caused by Gibbs and co. was that the Luftwaffe's air supply had been ratcheted up, bringing fuel and ammunition into Maturba and Tobruk, the westernmost supply bases and closest to Rommel's front line. This had far-reaching effects not only in the Mediterranean.

Under the aegis of Kesselring's Luftflotte 2, two large transport wings were set up in Naples and Sicily, consisting of about 250 aircraft, mainly Junkers Ju52s. Starting in late August, the early air convoys to support Rommel's Alam Halfa offensive were largely uninterrupted by the RAF. They were well-routed to avoid Malta and RAF air bases in Egypt (well to the east following the reverses of May and June), while the focus of the RAF was over the Alamein front and the battle of the convoys. As a result, 11,500 sorties delivered 15,000 tonnes of supplies[14] – an impressive number, until one considers that all that could have been carried by two large merchant ships. A big priority was ferrying in fuel, but a problem was that a Junkers Ju52 on its shuttle run used about half the amount of fuel again as what it could actually deliver. Nor could large artillery or armoured vehicles be carried, although they did manage to fly 41,678 troops into Tunisia.[15] Monty had no such problems, and at El Alamein in late October, his newly equipped and retrained Eighth Army was able to finally deliver a decisive victory over Rommel's Afrika Korps. This led to the rapid retreat west, with Tobruk changing hands once again, which shifted the whole calculus of supply operations, as air and shipping routes fell into fighter range for the RAF and the increasing numbers of USAAF squadrons.

The calculus would be properly smashed a matter of weeks later with Operation Torch, the first major combined operation of the war, which saw the Allies land in the French territories of western North Africa. In one bite, the Germans found the Allies were pushing on the Tunisian border, restricting their length of occupied coastline to roughly 1,000 miles between Tobruk, which the Allies regained on 13 November, and Bone in Algeria. The positive aspect was the Germans now had access to Vichy French ports in Tunisia such as Tunis, Bizerte and Sfax, and requisitioned three-quarters of a million tons of French merchant vessels,[16] much needed as the Italian merchant marine had been so reduced. Westerly routing and protection from air bases in Corsica and Pantelleria meant merchant ships had a better chance of getting through – but still meant targets for the Malta strike wing.

Newly arrived Luftwaffe units made life very uncomfortable for a few weeks for the Allies after Torch, not least the sitting duck Beaufighters of 255 Squadron (covered elsewhere). But crucially it also stripped vital air units away from the Eastern Front – with six fighter and five bomber gruppes moving to the Mediterranean. With the defeat of Alamein, a further 150 Ju52s arrived, and later in November 170 more,[17] many taken from the Eastern Front. In fact, prior to Torch, the Luftwaffe had increased the assemblage of transport aircraft in the theatre from 205 to 673.[18] They were joined by Italian Savoia SM81s and SM82s, also trimotors and of similar modest performance as the Ju52s – 'but these hardly counted', in the disparaging words of Fritz Morzik.[19] Morzik's dismissal of Italian aircraft is both telling and misplaced – the Savoia models were a match for Ju52s (in fact the Luftwaffe had its own 'Savoia staffel') and performed way better as transports than some of the bombers the Luftwaffe later used. There were also the very first operational Messerschmitt Me323s, huge 50-ton six-engined transports that could lift over ten tonnes – and nicknamed 'Gigants', and several of the equally gargantuan Blohm und Voss Bv222 flying boats, again boasting six engines, and challenging the Gigant as the biggest aircraft in the world in 1942. The Luftwaffe in the east was stripped, and with it, Hitler's insurance policy.

The Luftwaffe transport fleet wasn't the only one on the move. On 5 November, sixteen Beaufighters of 272 Squadron took off from Edku, all of them new Mark VICs, and carrying an extra load of seventeen ground crew between them, on its way to its new home at Takali airfield in Malta. Hugh Lloyd, AOC of 201 Group, sent a typically understated message to the departing squadron:

'The scene changes temporarily. You are still 272 Squadron and belong to 201 Group. I regard you as a well-trained squadron with a reputation. Keep it, and good luck to you.'[20]

After over fifteen months of operations from Egypt, the squadron had accrued forty-four aerial victories as well as destroying dozens more aircraft, trucks and tankers on the ground.

The squadron's main purpose in Malta would be to disrupt the now regular Luftwaffe air supply formations, and its first mission was to attack the airbase at El Aquina, near Tunis, one of the several bases now being used to receive and turn around transport aircraft – so recently had the Germans and Italians moved in that there were no anti-aircraft guns in place. Attacking in two waves, the nine Beaus shot up and claimed to have destroyed ten aircraft, including two Junkers Ju290s (four-engined transports), five Ju 52s and what the squadron records reported as a 'large glider (probably 150-seater)'.[21] The glider was actually the first Messerschmitt Me323 to be destroyed. One Beaufighter was hit by small arms fire and had to force-land on a nearby beach, both crew being taken prisoner.

Two days later, 272 Squadron intercepted its first aerial transport convoy, when a patrol of seven Beaus led by Squadron Leader Anthony Watson intercepted six Savoia SM82s, flying at 200 feet, one of them already trailing behind. All six were reported shot down, with one ditched, with an attempt to tow the stricken plane to the nearby island base of Pantelleria, 'several khaki-clad figures were seen struggling in the water'.[22] Italian records showed that one of the six actually managed to stagger on to its destination.

The Malta-based Beaufighters of 227 Squadron, in between anti-shipping missions, were also tasked with intercepting the transports. They too had had something of a change-around: tour-expired pilots had been replaced, and new commander Cedric Masterson took over as the CO; they also received new Mark VIC Beaufighters. The new 'delousing' tactics were also employed, with flights of Beaufighters now often accompanied by Spitfires from one of Malta's three fighter squadrons. On 13 November, they intercepted a much larger formation of about forty-five transporters, claiming six shot down in a running battle, in addition to a Dornier Do24 flying boat shot down earlier. While 227 Squadron's crews identified their victims as Savoia SM82s, in fact they had destroyed five Junkers Ju52s and damaged three others.[23] This formation had been a much tougher nut to crack, with one Beau shot down, while the tough Canadian Dallas Schmidt, having bagged two Ju52s, limped home on one engine having been hit by defensive fire.

Next day, 272 returned to El Aquine airfield, although this time anti-airfield defences had been readied and a heavy barrage met the first section to attack, with Squadron Leader Watson's aircraft set on fire and crash-landing nearby. Watson and his observer escaped and made it back to Allied lines. The second section leader Flight Lieutenant Bale fared even worse, failing to return after leading a second attack, while a third Beaufighter hit electric powerlines, although the damaged Beau still made it home, despite the attentions of a flight of Bf109s. It had proved a costly raid in which losses outweighed the several aircraft seen to be set on fire or damaged. Nonetheless, the squadron received a congratulatory message from the AOC Malta, Keith Park: 'Beaufighters are doing grand work and have opened their batting well.'[24]

No. 272 Squadron also received a new commander, Wing Commander John Buchanan, who flew in on 20 November. The stylishly moustachioed Hampshire man would prove an inspired choice, having racked up immense experience – except it was all on bombers. He had earned a DFC flying Wellingtons in England in July 1940, then moved to the Middle East, where he had flown Wellesleys and Blenheims in obscure air campaigns in Sudan, Eritrea and Iraq.[25] By the time of his arrival at 272 he had flown 230 bombing missions, but if there were questions over his ability to adapt to fighters, he answered them in short order. On his first mission, he shot down an Italian CANT Z506 floatplane, as well as strafing a German flak ship which was left smoking and stationary.

The attacks on the air supply flights continued, and the toll racked up by the Beaufighters continued to rise. On 22 November, 272 Squadron's Ern Coate encountered a huge six-engined Blohm und Voss Bv222. Attacking out of the sun, Coate fired off two prolonged bursts, setting the behemoth alight. It plunged into the sea and blew up, killing all fifty-eight men on board.[26]

A second Bv222 was destroyed just two weeks later by a 227 Squadron Beaufighter. Both the Australian Coate and Buchanan would become aces in the space of a few days before the end of November, although even these sterling efforts would be trumped by 227 Squadron's Dallas Schmidt, who achieved eight victories in a run of just six sorties, including six Ju52s.[27] The Canadian Schmidt was a fearless attacker, meaning his aircraft was always getting hit by defensive fire. He staggered home from scrapes that left him with just one working engine on four occasions and was forced to bale out on another. He also tried out new ways of attacking the transports – attacking one large formation of Ju52s, he flew under the formation at barely fifty feet to avoid the defensive fire and heavy fighter escort. It worked, as he shot down two more of the trimotors, while his wingman Cas de Bounevialle dealt with a Bf110 which latched on to Schmidt's tail after he emerged from the 'tunnel'.[28]

Over November and December, the Luftwaffe lost 128 Junkers Ju52s, including many of their crews, to Beaufighters and other Allied aircraft, with many others damaged, a total that amounted to eleven per cent of all Junkers Ju52s in operation with the Luftwaffe.[29] These losses, perhaps not enormous in the grand scheme of things, would prove highly consequential.

On 19 November, about 2,000 miles to the east, Soviet forces completed Operation Uranus: a pincer movement around the bitterly contested city of Stalingrad, pushing aside ill-equipped Italian and Rumanian forces, and leaving nearly 250,000 troops of the German Sixth Army surrounded. Luftflotte IV, responsible for the southern Soviet area of operations, was notably short on transport aircraft following the aircraft transfers to the Mediterranean. Fatefully, Hitler insisted on a repeat of the Demyansk Air Lift plan, following assurances by Luftwaffe chief Herman Goering, and his deputy, Hans Jeschonnek, that they could deliver the necessary weight of supplies each day.[30] Looking at the Demyansk operation, Goering's minimum target of 300 tons per day seemed achievable – this had actually been done in Demyansk. However, the reality was that there were more than twice as many men to supply, and the real requirement was more like 600 tons per day.[31] And, unlike Demyansk, a large chunk of the Luftwaffe's transport aircraft were elsewhere and being wasted by Beaufighters.

Goering was either recklessly gung-ho or excessively eager to please his boss – either way it was a disastrous decision. A plan was agreed on 23 November, steam-rollering the views of Luftflotte IV's commander, Wolfram von Richtofen, who said it couldn't be done.[32] There was certainly urgency in implementing the plan. The Luftwaffe turned immediately to the emergency option, going to the flying schools, where instructors and aircraft were seconded to the airlift effort. Bombers like the Heinkel He111, Junkers Ju86, Focke-Wulf Fw200 Condor and later the brand-new Heinkel He177 were pulled into the line-up,[33] although only the He111 proved anything like as reliable as the Ju52. The process was rushed by often inexperienced commanders, and vital logistic tasks like preparing airfields and setting up fuelling facilities and repair workshops in the right places were too often skimped on. The state of the airfields within the pocket would also have a huge bearing on things, frequently becoming overcrowded with aircraft with insufficient capacity to unload and disperse supplies. It would take a week to get the first 350 tons into the pocket,[34] and only at the start of December could the Luftwaffe get even 200 aircraft into place. What is very evident is that the Stalingrad airlift fell massively short of that in Demyansk, averaging just 117 tons per day,[35] and this led to the rapid deterioration in the physical health and nutrition of the Sixth Army as temperatures plunged.

The Beaufighter didn't win Stalingrad, but there's an interesting counter-factual here which deserves airing. One of the big problems for the Luftwaffe was that on the fateful day of 19 November, nearly half the Luftwaffe's transport were in the Mediterranean, including over 600 of the workhorse Junkers Ju52s, including, crucially, their experienced crews. Things might have been different had they not been reassigned to the Med. And this is where the Beaufighter had played an important role, by transforming the effectiveness of shipping strikes in the summer of 1942. Hitler and his army commanders either distrusted the Italian Navy, and/or feared the RAF's anti-shipping squadrons, and they chose to move the air transport fleet to keep Rommel properly supplied in the Med.

Astonishingly, no immediate call was made on Luftflotte 2's legion of Junkers Ju52s until Christmas Day, when finally, about half of the fleet were sent east[36] – leaving behind 200 Ju52s and the Me323 Gigants. By this time, the fleet had been significantly reduced by Beaufighters and other Allied aircraft. They should have been moved a month earlier. While the aircraft would have required modifications to deal with the Russian winter, many crews had served in the east earlier in the year. Instead, the Luftwaffe airlift started slowly and with poor November weather. From mid-December, the weather was only going to get worse, meaning unserviceability rocketed and winter fog and snowstorms wrote off whole days of airlift missions. The state of the Sixth Army's soldiers as they entered winter was already diminished and going downhill. The belated transfer of Mediterranean Ju52s came too late, with winter and the loss of key airfields to the Red Army ensuring the air lift was doomed. In the end, the Sixth Army starved, its soldiers suffering and dying in great numbers, with just 90,000 emaciated ghosts surrendering on 31 January 1943.

Ironically, Tunis in December/January was not under immediate threat after the overstretched British First Army had been halted at the Tunisian border. Tunis was still being served by sea, particularly faster merchant vessels which could do the run between Corsica and Tunis entirely in darkness. In January, with far fewer aircraft, the Luftwaffe air supply flights were wound down, and the two Beaufighter squadrons returned to other missions, including shipping strikes alongside the two Beaufort squadrons. The newly arrived US Army Air Force was also making a telling contribution. On 22 January, Algeria-based US B-17 Fortresses mounted a highly successful attack on El Aquina airfield, a key hub where the Luftwaffe transport fleet was gathered, and destroyed twenty-three of the remaining Ju52s.[37]

Within a few months, following the calamity at Stalingrad, Axis forces were facing another in Tunis. Reverses for the Allies in mid-February were followed by victories for Montgomery and the new US commander, General George S. Patton. The war against Rommel's supply vessels had continued, with further successes for Malta's strike wing, and they were joined in the anti-shipping effort by the US 12th Air Force's B-25 Mitchells. The key Axis ports were now in range of US and RAF heavy bombers, so even those ships that slipped through the net into Bizerte and Tunis ports faced bombardment, with many being sunk in port. The two Malta-based Beaufighter squadrons, 227 and 272, continued to be involved in shipping strikes, but their main priority was convoy escort, as the Allies continued to build up forces in North Africa. By April 1943, quarter of a million men were clinging on in Tunis, cut off by Allied dominance of the sea, and as at Stalingrad, entirely dependent on air supply.

The loss of so much shipping meant there was much less call for anti-shipping strikes, and on 21 March, John Buchanan led the last 'full' Malta strike wing attack involving Beauforts and Beaufighters against a convoy of two freighters, a destroyer, two torpedo boats and a submarine, but the mission failed, with several pilots complaining their cannons were jamming, while some torpedoes failed to detonate. Nonetheless the convoy turned back to Messina, while one Bf110 was shot down with several other Luftwaffe aircraft damaged, for the loss of one Beaufort and one Beaufighter.[38] A few weeks later, a Beaufort would achieve the type's last sinking in Mediterranean waters when 39 Squadron's Stan Balkwill struck and finished off the crippled 5,000-tonne tanker *Aquino.*[39]

At the start of April, with Tunis almost entirely cut off from sea supply, the Allies implemented 'Operation Flax', with the aim to eliminate the German air supply flights. Despite the huge losses of the winter, the Luftwaffe had rebuilt a fleet of 430 transport aircraft, comprising Junkers Ju52s, Messerschmitt Me323 Gigants and Savoia SM82s. This time, the Beaufighters were stood down. Since November, the US 12th Air Force had grown massively, and other fighters fitted the role well. The Lockheed P-38 Lightning shared the range and some of the heavy punch of the Beau, while being much faster. Using lessons learned from earlier interceptions, this time the transport flights met massed formations of RAF, USAAF, RAAF and SAAF fighters – Spitfires were tasked with 'delousing' the fighter escorts, while the transport aircraft were tackled by the (slightly) more heavily armed Curtis P-40 Kittyhawks and P-38 Lightnings. So the Beaufighter took a back seat as Ju52s were hacked down – seventy-six were claimed shot down during the 'Palm Sunday massacre' (in fact twenty-four were destroyed, but over thirty were damaged, many crash-landing).[40] On 22 April a large flight of Me323s was intercepted, with sixteen of the six-engined monsters shot down by mainly South African Spitfires and P-40s.[41] Such huge losses forced Goering to stop the daytime flights, with only night flights permitted (covered elsewhere), severely reducing daily supply drop-offs. German and Italian troops fought on until 13 May, surrendering nearly 270,000 troops, and ending any Axis presence in North Africa after nearly three years of battle. There was less carnage and suffering than Stalingrad, but the defeat was just as significant.

The very crux of the victory in North Africa had been air power, and the interdiction of Axis supplies. The final battle was won because the Allies could gather their forces, armour and sustain it, while the Axis powers got cut off, despite the legendary prowess of Rommel, the Afrika Korps and the elite regiments of the Italian army. At every stage following its introduction in late 1941, Beaufighters showed how this was done – starting with strafing trucks, tankers and aircraft, developing strike wing tactics to wreck convoys and finally, attacking and destroying the Luftwaffe transport fleet (with grave consequences elsewhere too). And that was just the story by day.

Chapter 11

Mud, Gubbins and Glory

Nightfighting operations, Torch to Tunis 1942–May 1943

20 November 1942 Maison Blanche, Eastern Algeria

'It was a bright moonlit night and conditions were all in favour of the raiders as the visibility was excellent and there were no AI aircraft available, nor was there a GCI station working at the time. Although it was thought that only a dozen German bombers carried out the raid on the drome, they did considerable damage, scoring hits on hangars and aircraft and starting many fires. It was during this intense period of the raid that the squadron suffered a great loss: Flying Officer Hugh Wyrill, DFC (of "B" Flight) was killed by shrapnel as he going out to his plane to take off. His radio navigator Flight Sergeant "Jock" Williams, DFM who was already waiting in the aircraft, fortunately got away with severe fractures of his right arm and splinter wounds. Three of our Beaufighters, three Flying Fortresses (one with crew) and several Spitfires and Lightnings were completely destroyed by bombs or fire and at least five Beaus and many other aircraft damaged, and fourteen people were killed and others injured.'[1]

Flight Lieutenant Alfred Lammer's diary entry encapsulated the chaotic events at the holding airbase of Maison Blanche in Algeria in late November 1942. Lammer and 255 Squadron's Beaufighters had been dropped into a bit of a hole.

With El Alamein won, the British, American, and Allied forces had moved quickly into their first big, combined operation of the war – Operation Torch, the conquest of Vichy French Morocco and Algeria in western North Africa. Meanwhile, on the eastern side of North Africa, Monty's victorious

Eighth Army was chasing Rommel through Libya. The British First Army had raced to the Tunisian border, bypassing various former Vichy French airfields, starting from west to east, sweeping past airfields which would need to be specially liberated by British parachute brigades and US Rangers. Nobody anticipated the Germans being so aggressive in countering the attack, pulling in fighter and bomber wings amounting to 445 aircraft,[2] substantially denuding their eastern air fleets. The RAF could have been better prepared and it didn't expect to be outnumbered, but this wasn't the first such situation for the Beaufighter.

No. 255 Squadron had been formed during the First World War as a pioneering but ineffective anti-shipping squadron, which was quickly disbanded at the end of the war. The squadron was reformed in late 1940 at Kirten Lindsey as a nightfighter squadron, where it had the misfortune to be equipped with Boulton Paul Defiants, later supplemented by a few Hurricanes, employing Cat's Eye tactics. Success was rare, with just a couple of victories in the first six months of operations, but this changed on the early morning of 9 May 1941, when the squadron achieved six victories against Luftwaffe bombers in a night of raids against Hull, Nottingham and Sheffield.[3] This even earned a letter of congratulations from the Secretary of State for Air, Sir Archibald Sinclair. Soon after, the squadron switched to AI-equipped Beaufighters. These were the Rolls-Royce Merlin-equipped Mark IIF, which were dogged with unreliability and had several accidents, including four due to engine failure. With a relative lull in Luftwaffe operations in the early months of 1942, the squadron would eventually start replacing its Mark II Beaufighters but saw little further action in the defence of Britain.

A new squadron leader joined at this point, Dillon Kelly, who had flown Spitfires in the Battle of Britain, but had switched to nightfighters and the Beaufighter in early 1941. His usual flight partner and the squadron's most senior radar operator was also the squadron's wonderfully droll diarist, Alfred Lammer. Lammer was not a typical radar operator – he was an exiled Austrian aristocrat, Ritter von Lammer, and if your vision of an Austrian aristocrat is the character Georg von Trapp in the hit Hollywood musical *The Sound of Music*, you haven't gone far wrong. The von Trapps were close family friends of young Alfred von Lammer.[4] Both families were bitterly anti-Nazi, and both would find themselves bankrupted following the Anschluss (this financial aspect seems to have escaped Hollywood's screenwriters), with the von Trapps escaping to Switzerland. Von Lammer sought refuge in England, where he joined the RAF as an Austrian refugee, starting out as a gunner in a Boulton Paul Defiant, before dropping the 'von' and being granted British citizenship in late 1941. Ever the renaissance man, Lammer became a leading photographer and design teacher following the war. Perhaps the most successful remaining pilot was Henry Wyrill, who had claimed a victory on 255's big night on 8 May, and also added one of the squadron's few Beaufighter victories in April. As with 89 Squadron, the lack of much previous success in the squadron would not prove a hindrance once they got into action.

In September, the squadron was withdrawn from operations in order to practise and train for Torch with eighteen newly arrived Beaufighter VIFs at Honiley in Warwickshire.[5] The 9 November saw Operation Torch and the multiple landings on the North African coast begin, and three days later, 255 received orders from Fighter Command to proceed immediately to Portreath in Cornwall, a Coastal Command base which was by a small margin the shortest distance from their interim destination en route to North Africa – Gibraltar. They weren't the only Beaufighters to make the trip – 600 Squadron, veterans of the Blitz, would follow. While Spitfires were dissembled and packed into boxes, the Beaufighters got to fly the route, saving the aircrew the discomfort the squadron's ground crews had on board the crowded SS *Majola*,[6] a requisitioned P&O liner which they shared with hundreds of troops. Crucially, they wouldn't arrive in North Africa until two weeks after the aircraft and the crews who flew with them.

The flight to Gibraltar was followed by a briefing on the morning of 16 November on their destination in North Africa – Maison Blanche airfield in Algeria. At the time of the briefing, this was technically in enemy hands, i.e. Vichy French, with a detachment of Royal Marines and US Rangers entrusted with ensuring a friendly reception when the Allied air squadrons did arrive. Fortunately, things went to plan, and not too long after the first aircraft arrived at Maison Blanche. Aside from not being in enemy hands, there wasn't much else to commend the place, which, 'bulged with aircraft of all types and activity bordered on organized chaos. The fighter squadrons had a built-in disadvantage since their ground crews were still in convoy somewhere in the mid-Atlantic. We had limited assistance to each squadron from small groups of about a dozen RAF Servicing Commandos, whose efficiency was a little impaired by the contents of their toolkit which appeared to be confined to a spanner and a screwdriver.'[7]

Seventeen of 255's Beaufighters had arrived at between 1230 and 1330, but without their secret new centimetric AI Mark VIII radar sets – they would come by ship. It saved weight, but the secret of the cavity magnetron couldn't be risked in a forced landing in Portugal or Spain.[8] The radar would arrive over two weeks later, preceded by Pilot Officer Gloster, who had been left behind in Gibraltar on 15 November with engine problems. It wasn't just essential equipment that was absent – the Beaufighter crews had also been made to leave behind camping kits to save weight on their long flights. Instead, crewmen were handed a couple of blankets and given some space on the concrete floor of some huts on the fringes of the airport.[9] And as Alfred Lammer noted, 'To start with, there was no ground crews, nor was there a bowser. There was petrol a plenty, it is true, but it was in four-gallon tins and nowhere near our Beaus! However, a lorry was eventually scrounged to collect petrol tins from one of the numerous dumps on the aerodrome, and the slow process of refuelling from cans was completed just about as darkness descended on us.'[10]

Within a day of arrival, Beaufighters were flying night patrols, a necessity with frequent, but generally small Luftwaffe raids. With their AI radar on a boat somewhere, the Beaufighters had little hope of intercepting intruders. Adding to the sense of chaos, Squadron Leader John Player crash-landed his Beaufighter. It was only a matter of time before the Luftwaffe intervened with a proper raid, and sure enough, on the night of 20 November, they finally struck hard, and the Beaufighter crews could do little about it. As we've seen, one of 255's pilots was killed and another injured, and numerous aircraft were destroyed or damaged. A couple of Beaus had got in the air, only to be shot at by naval guns, but by then the bombers had gone. Without a proper ground crew and parts, even lightly damaged aircraft, or those that picked up problems en route, were effectively out of action. Remarkably, after a further raid, the squadron was left without any serviceable aircraft and would fly no more patrols for a week.[11]

The raid marked a low point for 255, with the under-equipped squadron helpless in the face of an Axis aerial onslaught. Spitfire and Hurricane squadrons were despatched to forward bases like Souk Al Arab, and despite losses to attacks on their airfields, they at least had the chance to make up for this in the air – in fact, by the end of November, the six Spitfire squadrons had amassed 113 victories.[12] With 255 effectively crippled, the night raiders had it all to themselves, so an emergency message went out to the most successful nightfighter squadron in the Mediterranean – 89 Squadron. A detachment of six Beaus arrived in Algiers on 25 November, equipped with their old Mark IV radar, spare parts and mechanics. At the same time, twelve of 255's Beaufighter crews were despatched back to England to pick up new Beaufighters.

A couple of days later, there was further good news, when 'to everybody's great surprise a Flying Fortress arrived in the afternoon, filled to the brim with real "gubbins"!'[13] That evening, 89 Squadron quickly got into their stride and reminded everyone what a Beaufighter with 'gubbins' could do – on their second night of operations, the new arrivals intercepted two separate Luftwaffe bomber formations, shooting down five and damaging a couple more. Arthur Spurgin and John Etherton each scored two victories.[14] The arrival of the SS *Majola* and the squadron's ground crew, more AI sets and more new aircraft finally meant 255 Squadron was properly ready for operations. Three of 255's Beaufighters led by Squadron Leader John Player flew into the forward airbase at Souk Al Arab, just inside the Tunisian border, arriving on 6 December. Here they joined a small unit of 89 Squadron, who had just had another big evening, destroying four bombers. Under the newly established direction of Bone's mobile GCI, complete with the RAF's star controller, Squadron Leader John Brown, Player and Lammer flew standing patrols of eight hours twenty minutes, seeing nothing. However, the two other pilots, Jeffrey Hume and Mike Foster, both ambushed formations – Hume claiming two Heinkels and Foster three Heinkels destroyed.[15]

No. 255 Squadron was finally off the mark. Player and Lammer only had to wait until the following night:

Lammer: 'Range now 1500 feet, he is dead ahead and 30 degrees above, A.S.! 180.'

Player: 'Mmmmm'

Lammer: 'Up 200'

Player: [silence]

Lammer: 'Did you hear me say "up 200?"'

Player: 'YEEEEESSS'

Lammer: 'Can you see him?'

Player: 'YEEEEESSS'

Lammer's diary entry also noted this was a very special victory for the GCI operator, the experienced John Brown.

> 'It was a Heinkel 111, that was and incidentally it gave the Sultan of Sofley, our ace controller, Squadron Leader J. Brown, O.B.E, his hundredth Jerry destroyed. Congratulations on the first century!'[16]

The precision in Lammer's instructions – locating the enemy aircraft in three dimensions – illustrates well how centimetric radar represented a major step forward. Unlike the AI, a mobile radar unit had been prioritised in the invasion logistics plans, set up and protected by RAF's 2721 Field Squadron,[17] and was key to the aerial victories for 89 and 255 Squadron. The night wasn't over for Player and Lammer, as Brown vectored them on to three more aircraft, two of which were destroyed. Flying Officer Cox despatched a fourth bomber, a Heinkel He111, with Lammer noting, 'Nine bandits in two nights makes an auspicious beginning for the hitherto unfortunate 255th …'

The following day saw the Luftwaffe respond in the form of a strafing attack by a staffel of 'Jabo' Focke-Wulf Fw190s (newly arrived in the theatre) – although this time Beaufighters were spared, several Spitfires were destroyed. By this time, both air and ground crews were frequently employed building slit trenches around the airfield. If life at the forward airbase was hazardous, it was also sparsely equipped: 'Luxuries such as a dispersal hut or tent, aerodrome control officers and petrol bowser ... are evidently not known here.' And very uncomfortable. 'Billets for the aircrews in the village. These left much to be desired and large quantities of A.L.63 [the British Army's famous anti-louse powder, containing naphthalene, cresylic acid, pyrethrum and derris root] had to be used... In view of the previous night's experiences a deputation went off to see G/C Lees, the outcome of which was a wealthy Arab's house was secured for 89 Squadron and ourselves to share.'[18]

The new-found comfort was short-lived, as the unit moved to Setif aerodrome, with aircrew housed in a 'tented camp on the east side of the aerodrome'. Not missing out on the discomfort were the late arrivals, the remaining air and ground crew who had disembarked from SS *Majola*, then arrived at Setif by rail. 'They were all in a very unkempt condition having spent forty-eight hours in French cattle trucks marked "eight horses or forty men". Fortunately, there were no horses, but unfortunately there was a large accumulation of evidence of their recent presence, much to the disgust of all concerned. Hot meals had been organised for the weary prodigals ...'[19]

After a short lull in Luftwaffe activity, Dillon Kelly scored his first victory of the campaign on 15 December, accompanied by Lammer, although his Beau was struck by debris, stopping one of the engines about seventy miles from base.[20] During the crash landing, Kelly's Beau struck a parked Hurricane. The next night, it was Douglas Grieves' turn to get too close to his victim. 'Greaves opened fire on an He111 from a range of fifty feet and was made to fly through the curtain of fire and debris. Emerging the other side Greaves found his cockpit blacked out and according to his instruments, was doing a steep turn to starboard.' With his aircraft in an alarming dive, his radar operator Robbins declined to bale out, so Greaves removed one of his cockpit vision panels 'and contrived to scrape quite a lot of the newly acquired camouflage off the windscreen. Although the controls were exceedingly bad owing to the fact that the starboard aileron had been burnt off completely the pilot succeeded in flying the Beaufighter to Bone where he would have made a perfect landing had the flarepath been laid out. With only the moonlight to guide him, he struck a tent with one of the wheels, but even so the aircraft was a complete write off.'[21]

Both Greaves and Kelly would each score another victory before Christmas. The 89 Squadron detachment was also steadily adding to its scoring, with Arthur Spurgin shooting down the first four-engined bomber in the theatre on 21 December – a Piaggio P108, Italy's interesting but failed attempt to build a strategic bomber. Unfortunately, on the same night an engine failure cost the lives of Henry Mitchell and his co-pilot. Heavy rain would curtail further activities: the 'Aerodrome has become a huge sea of muddy water, orders were received that Beaufighters were not to take off…'[22] Despite the desultory surroundings, Christmas was celebrated with a choice of chicken, turkey or steak and kidney pudding plus one bottle of beer each, supplemented by some crude local wine. The Christmas hiatus marked the end of an intensive air battle, in which the punishment for logistical error could have been much worse.

No. 600 Squadron arrived in Maison Blanche on 7 December, led by Wing Commander Charles 'Paddy' Green, fitted with old AI Mark IV radar and having missed the worst of the Luftwaffe bombing. Another arrival in January was a new flight commander for 600 Squadron, 24-year-old Northern Irishman Frederick Desmond 'Des' Hughes, who had been reading law at Pembroke College, Cambridge, when the war began. He was posted to 264 Squadron flying Boulton Paul Defiants, arriving just in time for the start of the Battle of Britain. Unusually, he was already an ace before he flew the Beaufighter. He had scored his first two victories in daylight on 26 August, before the squadron was reassigned to night-fighting, and by the end of the Blitz in May 1941, he'd scored five victories to become one of the few Defiant aces,[23] winning the Distinguished Flying Cross to boot. He then switched to 125 Squadron where he switched to the Beaufighter, adding two more victories, before he got the call to head to Algeria, along with his radar operator at 125, Lawrence Dixon. The pair were quick off the mark, shooting down two Junkers Ju88s on 24 January. Hughes' new squadron had had a mixed war so far. No. 600 Squadron's 'real' war had started disastrously on 10 May 1940, when five of its six Blenheims were shot down in an attack on advancing German forces at Waalhaven. The squadron was reassigned to night-fighting, where it scored a modest seventeen victories over the next two years,[24] and like 255 Squadron, used the less reliable Merlin-engined Mark IIFs from late 1941. After a relatively quiet start, Green and Hughes would lead 600 Squadron through an extraordinary period of success.

Further reinforcements arrived in the shape of 153 Squadron, designated for both nightfighter and maritime escort roles. It had been formed as a nightfighter squadron in November 1918, far too late to see action, and had been promptly disbanded after the war. Twenty-three years later, the squadron was reformed as a nightfighter squadron at Ballyherbert airfield in Northern Ireland, coalescing around a flight of 256 Squadron's Boulton Paul Defiants. Beaufighters arrived to replace the Defiants in May 1942, but few opportunities for air combat. In late December, led by Wing Commander William Mosby, the squadron was despatched to Maison Blanche airfield in Algeria, to join up with 255, 600 and 89 squadrons. The first dozen aircraft arrived on 20 December, with three more arriving two days later. They were thrown into action immediately, with Flying Officer Kenneth Rayment shooting down a Junkers Ju88 on 24 December.[25]

While the New Year saw British First Army's progress towards Tunis stalled, and in some areas it had been pushed back from its furthest advances, the air force had come through a severe test and was now properly established for the battles to resume in the year ahead. The Luftwaffe had thrown everything into the battle and failed against inferior numbers of an RAF expeditionary force, suffering heavy losses in aircraft and particularly in experienced crew. The contribution at this stage of the nightfighter Beaufighters had been impressive – they had destroyed forty-nine bombers with just two aircraft lost on operations. Altogether, the eight weeks of Torch up to the New Year saw the Luftwaffe and Regia lose 411 bombers.[26]

The early months of 1943 didn't entirely go to plan for the Allies, but there was plenty of trade for the nightfighters, with 153 Squadron scoring fifteen victories in January, while 89 Squadron's Merv Shipard chalked up six more victories over Libya, the 'eastern front'. Shipard and his radar operator Doug Oxby had been one of 89 Squadron's original crews sent to the Middle East, and he would end his second tour with thirteen victories – highest-scoring Beaufighter ace in the Mediterranean. Interestingly, Oxby got another crack, flying with Mosquito ace Peter Green when he returned to operations in Britain, and participated in twenty-two victories[27] – the highest number of nightfighter victories of any individual aircrew member.

March saw significant breakthrough victories for the Allies, and thereafter it was only a matter of time for the Germans and Italians as they retreated to Tunis. Throughout this time, Beaufighters had tackled night-time enemy air attacks on Allied forces with some success. As we've seen, the last few weeks before the fall of Tunis, the Allies had launched Operation Flax – the deliberate targeting of daytime Luftwaffe and Regia Aeronautica air transport fleets, which had been employed flying in emergency supplies and evacuating wounded soldiers. By late April, losses were so high that the daylight flights were halted, with night flights ramped up instead. Beaufighter nightfighters were deployed, but achieving interceptions was generally difficult due to the short distance between the Ju 52s' Sicilian airfields and Tunis, hindering timely detection by the nearest coastal GCI radar bases at Monastir and Enfideville, which lay several miles to the south of Tunis.

On the night of 30 April, an air convoy of Ju52s was despatched from Tunis to bases further north in Naples, probably due to heavy Allied bombing attacks on the usual Sicilian bases. This was a much longer route which took the aircraft further west, into range of the RAF's new GCI radar station at Cap Serrat. That night, Flight Sergeant Alwyn Downing and his radar/observer Sergeant John Lyons had taken off on the early morning patrol from Bone airfield at 3.30, and after more than an hour of uneventful patrolling, GCI reported a contact and vectored them in on a formation of about a dozen Ju52s, at a location about thirty miles south of Calgiari in Sardinia.[28] Making out a single Ju52 in the dawn's grey light, Downing closed unobserved to within 150 yards and fired a two-second burst into his target, which burst into flames and dived into the sea. Lyons spotted three more flying in formation, so Downing closed in behind these, shooting down a second aircraft. Circling around on a third Junkers, an alert dorsal gunner opened fire, but to no avail, as Downing despatched this aircraft, then a fourth and finally a fifth, which exploded and crashed into the sea. Downing circled above the burning wrecks in the sea before heading home, having shot down five in the space of ten minutes.[29] This was the only time a Beaufighter crew achieved the status of 'ace in a day' – but they may even have scored more heavily. Luftwaffe records reported six aircraft shot down by fighters in the area near southern Sardinia (Downing's was the only fighter in the area), while one other went missing that night en route to Naples – it's plausible that this may have crashed into the sea unseen while taking evasive action in the dark, always a hazard when flying so low. Both Downing and Lyons were awarded the Distinguished Flying Medal and were also decorated by USAAF authorities. Six days later, in the Cap Serrat sector, another Beaufighter flown by Flying Officer Kendall caught two Ju52s as landing lights were switched on at El Aouina airfield, shooting down one, but his cannons jammed, meaning the second escaped with light damage.[30]

A few days after Kendall's ambush, Tunis fell and the Germans and Italians had been removed from North Africa. In just over sixteen months since arriving in Egypt, Beaufighter nightfighter squadrons had achieved 214 victories over Luftwaffe and Regia Aeronautica aircraft, mainly in the six months between Torch and Tunis falling. Only during the three-week period following the arrival at Maison Blanche, when 255 Squadron were left helpless without their AI 'gubbins', were Luftwaffe bombers allowed the freedom to be destructive at night. Coupling this decisive role by night with Beaufighter squadrons' myriad achievements by day, few other aircraft can match the contribution of the Beaufighter in winning the war in North Africa.

Chapter 12

Beaufighter Trauma

Long-range Instep Patrols, Bay of Biscay 1942–44

16 October 1942, Bay of Biscay

Three Junkers Ju88C-6s of V Gruppe, Kampfgeschwader 40, led by Leutnant Kurt Necesany were patrolling the grey, featureless expanse of sea that is the Bay of Biscay in late autumn. Their targets were the aircraft of RAF Coastal Command's anti-submarine squadrons, out and about in the bay hunting for U-boats. The Luftwaffe report somewhat lyrically described 'a spot grows out of the endlessness'.[1] The 'spot' is a 51 Squadron Armstrong-Whitworth Whitley, an ageing and obsolete bomber pressed into Coastal Command service, its previous black fuselage and undersides recently painted over with a pristine white finish. Unlike its sleek pursuers, the Whitley had a slightly comic, plodding appearance with its drooping nose-heavy gait and heavy bombardier's 'chin'. The three Ju88s attacked in series, machine guns and cannon blazing. Flight Sergeant R.J. Benn initially kept the Whitley on a straight course, relying on his front and rear gunners to get clear shots on the three Ju88s as they mounted their strafing pass.[2] On the Junkers' fifth strafing attack, the Whitley's starboard engine burst into flames and after a further attack, the Whitley plunged into the waves below, its depth charges detonating and triggering two great explosions. While the Ju88s circled the film of oil, the remnants, an unfortunate Vickers Wellington stumbled on to the scene. It too was destroyed, despite heroic manoeuvring and effective gunnery from the crew, leaving one Ju88 struggling home on one engine.

The Bay of Biscay had become the next great battleground for the Battle of the Atlantic, with 1942 seeing continued heavy losses to the Allied convoys, despite the Condor scourge and surface raiders being largely removed from the fray. There had also been increasing losses to the U-boats through the diligent work of naval corvettes and Coastal Command. Driving the success was technology – ever-improving ASW radar, Leigh Lights, Ultra intelligence, plus the scientific data analysis of Patrick Blackett's Operational Research Group, which achieved marginal gains through things like better aircraft camouflage and depth charge settings. There remained the 'Air Gap' – the heart of the Atlantic Ocean which remained out of effective range of the array of Coastal Command aircraft, the Whitleys, Wellingtons, Hudsons and Sunderlands scouring the oceans for U-boats. The extra-long range of the US-built Consolidated Liberator promised to resolve this, but famously Bomber Command got first dibs to feed Bomber Harris's insatiable desire to build a huge bomber force.

However, while the Air Gap remained, Coastal Command had settled on an area of sea where U-boats would be especially vulnerable – the Bay of Biscay. In the words of the soon-to-be head of Coastal Command, Sir John Slessor, 'This was the one place where we could be absolutely certain there would be U-boats to be found and killed.'[3] Eight U-boat flotillas operating in the Atlantic were based at Lorient, Brest, Saint Nazaire and La Pallice on the French coast facing into Biscay. Each had bombproof bunkers which numerous Allied raids failed to seriously damage. It meant lots of U-boats coming back and forth, often surfaced to conserve the battery power they used when submerged, so radar and Leigh light-equipped Wellingtons, Sunderlands, Whitleys and Liberators took on the attack.

However, they faced a deadly opponent – V Gruppe, Kampfgeschwader 40 (the anti-shipping wing). They had arrived in Bordeaux on 10 June 1942 and were equipped with the new Junkers Ju88C-6, a heavily armed *Zerstorer* (destroyer) version of the ubiquitous Luftwaffe medium bomber. It was a bigger aircraft than the Beaufighter, with a 20-metre wing span and an empty weight of ten tonnes, and was slightly slower with a top speed of about 310 mph.[4] Curiously, it was under-armed – it usually packed five 7.9mm MG17s and a single 20mm cannon, in a bizarre asymmetric arrangement in a solid nose, with three more MG17s in the dorsal and ventral positions. Crucially, this meant it struggled to bring down bigger aircraft quickly, and a well-flown bomber with strong defensive armament usually got to shoot back. Famously, a single Short Sunderland flying boat of 461 Squadron took on eight Ju88s on 2 June 1943, shooting down three and damaging others before reaching Cornwall and crash-landing.

Coastal Command and its Beaufighters were about to embark on their first major battle for air supremacy. In contrast to most air battles, it would be a long, relatively low intensity air battle fought over a vast stretch of sea – a game of cat and mouse, or more accurately dog, cat and mouse, where actually finding the enemy represented the main challenge. Neither side had the numbers to achieve annihilation of the other, so it became a battle of attrition.

V Gruppe arrived on the French coast at a significant moment. In mid-1942, U-boat losses to Coastal Command aircraft were not particularly threatening, but they were increasing. RAF aircraft had destroyed just four U-boats in the whole of 1941, but managed seven in the first six months of 1942, although none near the Bay of Biscay.[5] However, Coastal Command had stepped up operations, mainly with Wellingtons and Whitleys, aircraft deemed obsolete by Bomber Command, but which with their long-range and carrying capacity, made decent anti-submarine hunters. On 15 July, V Gruppe had its first victim – a Czech-manned Wellington which fell to the Ju88 of Hanny Passier.[6] Five days later, two more were shot down, although on this occasion defensive fire claimed one of the Junkers. Perhaps of more significance, the same month had seen the destruction of the first two U-boats in the bay.

With opportunity knocking at home, 248 Squadron and 235 Squadron had just sent most of their Beaufighters and aircrew to Malta to provide urgent maritime escort for the forthcoming Operation Pedestal (as covered elsewhere). On 20 July, the remaining units of 235 Squadron were sent from Norfolk to Chivenor in Cornwall and while encounters with the Junkers were initially fleeting, they did meet with Arado Ar196 floatplanes, a maritime reconnaissance plane. The single-engined Arados were slow, but highly manoeuvrable and packed a sting at both ends, with forward-firing 20mm cannon and a rear-facing MG17 fired by the observer. They weren't a match for the Beaus, and in two encounters in August, four were shot down without loss.[7] Unfortunately, this provoked a response, with a section of Focke-Wulf Fw190s from JG2 (aka *Richtofen*) commanded by the ace Oberleutnant Bruno Stolle, moved to guard the Cherbourg coastal area.[8] The so-called 'Butcher Bird', which combined brutal armament of two 20mm cannon and six machine guns with 400 mph pace, was the best fighter in the world for much of 1942, superior even to the Spitfire Mark V. Its significant speed advantage meant it could chase down the Beaufighter in most circumstances. Fortunately, the Fw190 had a limited radius of operations out into Biscay, even when carrying an external fuel tank. They could be avoided with careful mission planning. Alas, this was a lesson that would be learned the hard way.

The first Beaufighter encounter with V Gruppe's Ju88Cs came on 8 September, when two 235 Beaufighters witnessed a splashing column of water in the distance, and on exploring, spotted a Ju88 about four miles away. The splash was actually the final moments of a Lockheed Hudson as it hit the water, and as the Beaus pursued the Junkers, they saw a life raft with the Hudson crew scrambling aboard. The Beaus shot down the Junkers, killing its crew, while dropping a smoke flare that helped ensure the survival of the four Hudson crewmen (they were picked up by Germans). Elsewhere that day, there was another first, as Bruno Stolle shot down another of 235's Beaufighters in the first encounter between Fw190 and Beaufighter. The air battle in September saw Junkers destroying eight Coastal Command bombers with forty-eight crewmen killed and ten taken prisoner, but three Ju88s fell to 235 Squadron's Beaufighters[9] and two more U-boats were sunk by the bombers.

The battle continued as winter and poor weather and rough seas reduced opportunities on both sides. No. 248 Squadron's Malta detachment had returned and joined the fray, shooting down a Ju88 on 8 October, but Beaufighter successes would be rare during these weeks, and unfortunately marred by heavy losses to the Focke-Wulfs, with thirteen falling to their guns in the last two months of the year. A notable low point was 1 December, with both 248 and 235 Squadrons mauled by the Butcher Birds. The 248 Squadron logbook simply contains a handwritten note, 'Failed to return', by a flight of three Beaufighters who headed out on an early patrol.[10] The sole survivor of a flight of 235 Squadron noted being attacked by Arados, but didn't see what happened to the others – both were claimed by Fw190s. Luftwaffe records show the first of the Beau patrols was shot down 135 kilometres west of Brest, well within range of JG2 bases in Cherbourg.[11] There was no reason for their flight route to take them so close, and in future they wouldn't again, at least not for several months. By shifting the route tapes at mission briefing, the Focke-Wulfs were taken out of the battle.

Throughout the New Year, the Beaufighter would fight a series of air battles with the Ju88s, and while hard-fought and closely matched, they would usually come out on top. The first of these battles came on 29 January, when four 248 Squadron Beaufighters, led by Barbadian Flight Lieutenant Aubrey Inniss, pounced on a pair of Ju88s. The tag-team destruction of the bigger Junkers aircraft has echoes of killer whales attacking a bigger victim:

> 'Two Ju88 aircraft were sighted and immediately attacked. Aircraft D (Flying Officer Payne) attacked first with a long burst of cannon fire registering hits on starboard engine of E/A which at once caught fire. This attack was followed up by aircraft 'K' piloted by Sergeant D.A. Catrane which also got in long bursts of cannon fire. Enemy aircraft, which was now down at sea level, dived into the sea and was not seen again. While this action was in progress aircraft B and L (Inniss and Sergeant McLeod) respectively were attacking the second enemy aircraft. Aircraft B registered hits with long bursts of cannon fire, followed by aircraft L. After L broke away aircraft B delivered another burst of cannon fire and E/A was seen to crash on the water burning furiously, then appeared to disintegrate into burning patches.'[12]

The following day saw another battle, this time with losses even at two apiece, including the collision of a Beaufighter and a Junkers Ju88C, which both crashed into the sea. Among the casualties was a V Gruppe *Staffel Kapitan*. Ten days later, Squadron Leader David Cartridge led a flight of 248 Squadron Beaus in a successful battle with a flight of Ju88s, claiming three shot down without loss (actually just two were lost, although KG40 ace Dieter Meister also claimed two Beaus shot down, evidently mistakenly). These losses were acutely felt among V Gruppe's aircrew, an anxiety described as 'Beaufighter trauma'.[13] It also led to changes in tactics – while crews had believed the Ju88C was a good match for the Beau, it was decided that Ju88s needed to operate with at least a 2:1 advantage over the Beaus. Ju88s would generally be deployed in larger formations, meaning fewer missions and fewer interceptions. This helped even things, as shown when two of Bob Braham's 141 Squadron Beaufighters (based in Predannack before their intruder deployment) were lost when ambushed by superior numbers of Ju88s.[14]

In spring 1943, the new head of Coastal Command, Air Marshal John Slessor, ramped up the focus on the bay. The number of aircraft involved was greatly increased, with 264 Squadron the first of several Mosquito squadrons to join the fray. The Mosquito Mark VI just about matched the Beaufighter's armament with four cannon and four machine guns, but was 50mph faster than the Beau. Coastal Command was also switching to better anti-submarine aircraft. The Whitleys, which had been suffering the heaviest losses over Biscay, were replaced at 58 Squadron towards the end of 1942 by the much bigger and faster Handley Page Halifax. Even better, Consolidated Liberators were also arriving with 224 Squadron. The Liberator had the range to close the 'air gap', but in the air battle over Biscay, it had something else – not only lots of guns, but better guns: 50-cal (12.7mm) machine guns, which outranged the usual 7.7mm Brownings of the British-built bombers. Liberator gunners destroyed at least nine Ju88s. The Liberator was also difficult to shoot down – one USAAF aircraft being subject to no fewer than twenty-seven attacking passes by Ju88s before being finished off.[15]

By summer, 368 Coastal Command aircraft were operating in the bay.[16] There was one final addition to the legions of anti-submarine aircraft – the 'Rockbeau'. No. 236 Squadron of the North Coates strike wing had recently been equipped with rocket-carrying Bristol Beaufighters and was moved to Predannack to take part in the battle. The Rockbeau carried launch racks for eight rockets, which carried either a solid 25-pound solid armour-piercing warhead or a 60-pound high-explosive warhead. In practice, the AP warhead tended to be used against small ships and submarines, as they punched holes in metal hulls and superstructures. The Beaufighters could launch the rockets on an angled strafing pass, adding to the already terrific destructive power of the aircraft's guns. The Beaufighter didn't have the range or loiter time of the bigger bombers, but on 1 June, Flight Lieutenant Mark Bateman used the solid head rockets to damage a U-boat in the western Biscay. Some sources credit him with sinking the U418.

The tempo of the battle ebbed away in spring, with 248 Squadron reporting just a single contact with the Ju88s across April and May,[17] suggesting perhaps a deliberate strategy to avoid the Beaus. For the Germans, and particularly Admiral Donitz and the Kreigsmarine, it was a time of increasing alarm as U-boat losses surged, with 101 sunk in just the first five months of the year, of which Coastal Command aircraft contributed to half these losses. This included four in or near the Bay of Biscay in the first two weeks of May. U-boat crewmen gave a nickname to the bay – the 'valley of death'.[18] Something had to give, and the result was threefold. Firstly, Donitz withdrew his U-boats from the North Atlantic, where losses were worst. Secondly, he demanded a surge in V Gruppe sorties, and thirdly, he gave an ill-advised order that from 31 May, U-boats should surface and take on aircraft with their deck guns. While RAF losses to defensive anti-aircraft fire shot up, so too did U-boat losses. The U-boat order was rescinded two months later. However, V Gruppe's use of larger formations, in response to the Beaufighter patrols, had an unappreciated upside – it meant they were more able to 'finish off' the bigger anti-submarine aircraft. Sixteen Short Sunderlands were shot down between May and October,[19] compared with just one in the previous eight months.

The Ju88s were also given free rein to be much less discriminating in their attacks, and on 1 June they shot down two Wellingtons on a ferry flight to Gibraltar, followed by a Douglas DC3 airliner on a scheduled civil flight flying out of Lisbon, violating Portuguese neutrality. Luftwaffe intelligence had information there were Allied VIPs aboard, so Ju88s intentionally shot it down.[20] Among those on board was the great British actor Leslie Howard, star of *Gone with the Wind* and *First of the Few*. Just two days later, the Ju88s brought down an RAF Lockheed Hudson carrying tour-expired RAF personnel. Among the casualties was the legendary Beaufighter commander Robert Yaxley.

The bloody summer caused some alarm among RAF chiefs, and more Mosquito squadrons, along with 143 Squadron's Beaufighters, were drafted in. However, being new to the battle, they committed the cardinal sin of flying too close to the Cherbourg Peninsula. Four of a flight of six 143's Beaufighters were lost to the Focke-Wulfs.[21] The Luftwaffe combat report noted the Beaus were shot down just 120 km from Brest. Despite this bloody summer, the peak of V Gruppe's efforts coincided with the Allies' best month in the bay, with twelve U-boats destroyed in July, followed by four more in the first week of August.

The U-boat sightings and destruction then suddenly stopped. None would be destroyed in the next six weeks,[22] and the reason was new tactics, once again in response to the Beaufighters. Donitz basically moved the battle south. U-boat commanders adopted what became known as the Piening route (after U-boat commander Adolf Piening), where U-boats leaving Lorient and other ports hugged the French and Spanish coastlines (in doing so, violating Spanish neutrality). Close to the French coast, the Focke-Wulf Fw190s had established a powerful deterrent, so U-boats were safe. Only when well south of Biscay did the U-boats start to head out into the Atlantic. The ploy was time-consuming, and not risk-free, as Coastal Command started to operate closer to the Spanish coast later in the year – on 24 October, U566 was badly damaged and scuttled just north-west of Porto. This suited V Gruppe too, which could target ASW bombers who were forced further south looking for targets – and beyond the range of the Beaufighters. V Gruppe scored seventeen victories in Coastal Command's barren period of September and October.[23] However, the critical consequence of this tactical shift was that U-boat sinkings tipped below 100,000 gross registered tonnes in October,[24] just one sixth of that achieved in March.

The Beaufighters and Mosquitos continued to come out on top of the Ju88s on the occasions when they met. On 20 November, a dozen Ju88s escorting two large reconnaissance bombers – a Focke-Wulf Fw200 and the new and even bigger Junkers Ju290 – were intercepted by 235 Squadron Beaufighters and 151 Squadron Mosquitos. Both big bombers were destroyed, and two Ju88s were also claimed for no losses.[25] This clash also reflected a shift in priorities as the war slipped away from the Germany. With U-boats less of a threat, the Luftwaffe turned to protecting new anti-shipping squadrons, now carrying the deadly new '*wunderwaffe*', remoted-controlled guided missiles, Fritz X and Henschel Hs293. The first missions were carried out in Biscay, before KG40's new Heinkel He177s and KG100's Dornier Do217s were moved to the Mediterranean to help defend against the Allied invasion of Italy. As covered elsewhere, Beaufighters would play a significant role in battling this new threat.

Ultimately the remnants of what was V Gruppe (it was renamed *Zerstorergeschwader* 1) would be destroyed as a unit during the Normandy campaign, being disbanded soon after. However, their singular purpose – to defeat the RAF's anti-submarine campaign over Biscay – had failed much earlier, and a critical part of this was achieved by Beaufighters, which inflicted heavy losses and achieved psychological ascendency over V Gruppe – claiming thirty-five Ju88s for the loss of thirteen Beaufighters in head-to-head combat, a kill ratio approaching three to one.[26] During the battle, Coastal Command had its first two aces – 248 Squadron's David Cartridge and Aubrey Inniss, with both pilots ending up with eight victories for the war.[27] The work of Coastal Command's Beaufighters meant losses to the anti-submarine aircraft never reached unsustainable levels, and forced major operational changes which seriously undermined the U-boat campaign.

Chapter 13

Whispering Death

India and Burma campaign 1943–45

22 December 1942, Howrah district, Calcutta

On the longest night of what passes for winter in Calcutta, eight Mitsubishi Ki-21 'Sally' medium bombers from the 98th Sentai approached the southern district of Howrah, dropping eight tonnes of bombs, and in doing so marking a sinister first of the war.[1] The bombs missed their main target, the Howrah bridge, a key crossing point for Allied supply routes in eastern India, but hit a nearby fuel dump, causing quite an eruption which was seen across the city. Two cows were killed when a bomb landed within the grounds of a religious centre,[2] but there were no human casualties. Further raids over the next four days caused more serious civilian casualties. The raids, flying out of captured aircraft bases in western Burma, comprised of between three and ten medium bombers – tiny by the standards being set by the Luftwaffe and the RAF. In fact, the 'Sally' was scarcely credible as a strategic bomber, carrying a bomb load of just 2,250 pounds.

Yet these aircraft would probably come closer than Bomber Harris to proving Douhet's theory that strategic bombing could lead to a country's moral collapse. The bombs landed on the tinderbox that was British India in late 1942, following the swift and brutal humiliations of Hong Kong, Singapore and Malaya, and the long and painful retreat through Burma. It wasn't just disheartened British and Indian troops, Calcutta had received thousands of Indians fleeing Burma, survivors of a cruel trek in which vast numbers were lost on the trail through the mountains on the Burma/India border. The Japanese were winning this war and winning easily. The myth of European superiority had been crushed in full view of Asia's millions of colonial subjects, giving a bolt of energy to Indian nationalists. The Quit India movement was in full cry, forcing the Viceroy to incarcerate nationalist leaders, Gandhi and Nehru included, while thousands of captured Indian soldiers had signed up to serve the Japanese in Subhas Chandra Bose's Indian National Army. In Calcutta's Bengali hinterland was a further developing crisis – British scorched earth policy in the expectation of invasion, the loss of Burma's highly productive rice paddies and a major typhoon had resulted in a critical shortage of rice, which would balloon into a full-scale famine in early 1943.

The result was that the bombing sparked immediate, mass panic, and a huge exodus from India's biggest city, with numbers estimated between 350,000 and 1.5 million decamping,[3] mainly into the countryside, which was already starting to fill with the wandering destitute due to the emerging famine. The British Empire was losing control of their greatest possession, and it was clear a sustained Japanese bombing campaign had the potential to cause massive and uncontrollable upheaval, and perhaps even collapse of the Raj. It was very simple. The night bombers had to be stopped.

India in December 1942 wasn't without night defences – there were GCI stations, and as we saw in Malta a year previously, some squadrons of Hawker Hurricanes to fill the role of night-fighter as well as day-fighter. A Hurri flown by Squadron Leader Tony O'Neill had shot down a Japanese intruder on Christmas Eve,[4] but this perilous situation clearly needed Beaufighters. Once again, the call went to 89 Squadron, the original expeditionary nightfighter force in Egypt. And so eight Beaufighters, a mix of Mark ICs and VICs led by Squadron Leader Charles Clegg, took off from Edku in Egypt, and made its way via stops in Habbadiaya, Bahrain, Sharjah, Karachi, Jodhpur, and Allahabad, finally arriving at Dum Dum airfield near Calcutta, in the mid-afternoon of 14 January,[5] where the new unit met up with its newly promoted commander, Wing Commander Tony O'Neill, following his Christmas Eve victory. The following day, the detachment was declared operational under a new squadron number – 176 – and given a squadron motto, '*Nocte Custodimus*', 'We keep the night watch.' At 9.45pm, Flight Sergeant Maurice Pring's Beaufighter was scrambled in response to a GCI contact, and he soon picked up a flight of three Ki-21 Sallys about twenty miles to the south-east of Calcutta, aided by the light of the moon. Pring described what happened next:

> 'I drew very close to one bomber and my first burst set his starboard engine aflame, and I saw him break in half and go down. I then picked up the other two bombers and administered the same treatment to the nearer one, while some return fire came from the third bomber. As I saw the second raider on fire and going down, I attacked the third and gave him a hearty burst. Flames shot from the fuselage and I saw him crash. I could see all three Japanese aircraft burning below.'[6]

Pring had wiped out the flight in just four minutes, his three victories adding to three he'd previously scored in the Mediterranean. It was probably the most decisive clash of arms won by any British force over the Japanese in over a year of dismal defeats, and Pring would be feted as a hero by the local English language press, desperate for a hero after so much despondency and bad news. The 21-year-old was awarded the Distinguished Flying Cross and commissioned as a pilot officer, while his fresh-faced good looks would soon adorn RAF recruitment posters in India, alongside Indian airman Flying Officer Harjinder Singh. Four days later, it was the turn of the detachment's leading scorer, 28-year-old Australian Charles Crombie, who arrived in India an ace with nine victories. Crombie and his radar operator C.W. Moss set about a formation of three Ki-48 'Lilys' – slightly smaller but quicker bombers – claiming two destroyed and damaging the third – in fact just one Lily had been lost, but it was enough.[7] Thoroughly shaken by the Beau attack, two Lilys dived down to 150 feet in a desperate race to get home. Crombie's Beau was struck in the engine by defensive fire, so he initially ordered Moss to bale out, while he continued his attack. Unfortunately, the fire reached the fuel tanks, so with a wing ablaze, Crombie also hit the silk. This second destructive attack was enough to persuade the commander of 5th Hikodan (wing) to cancel all further nocturnal bombing attacks on Indian targets. Perhaps the panicked descriptions of the survivors had more impact on the Japanese commander than the silence of missing crews four days earlier. In just four days of operations, 176 Squadron had defeated the

Japanese night offensive and might just have prevented the implosion of British India. It would be nine months before the squadron scored another victory, a Kawanishi H8K flying boat off the coast of Ceylon.

The nightfighters arrived in the Indian theatre just as the first Beaufighter fighter-bomber unit was becoming operational. No. 27 Squadron had a fascinating service history going back to the First World War, acquiring the nickname 'Flying Elephants'. This was a nod to the squadron in 1916 being unique in being fully equipped with the Martinside Elephant, a huge single-seat fighter-bomber. The Elephant, like the Bristol Fighter, bucked the trend for small, light and manoeuvrable scout fighters, although unlike the Bristol Fighter, it wasn't very good, being slow and underpowered. After the Armistice, the squadron was despatched to the North-West Frontier, where it was involved in a pioneering, successful and morally questionable role, carrying out bombing raids on rebelling Waziri tribesmen in their mountainous strongholds in Afghanistan, a campaign known as Pink's War after Squadron Leader Richard Pink. The squadron stayed in the east, and was fatefully based in Butterworth, Malaya, flying Bristol Blenheims when the Japanese invaded in December 1941. Against the onslaught, numbers were quickly whittled down, and the tiny remnants of the squadron were disbanded in Java in February 1942. However, you can't kill a squadron and 27 Squadron was reformed just five months later with the express intention of operating Beaufighters, at Armada Road in Orissa (now Odisha state) to the west of Calcutta. The first Beaufighter arrived on 22 October, while crews arrived from Cairo's wastage pool, swapping the scorching desert heat for the stifling tropical humidity of eastern India. The full complement of sixteen aircraft was finally assembled by 21 December, under the command of Wing Commander Naish. Keeping all airworthy was a challenge, not helped by a lack of spares which would hinder operations for the early months of the squadron's deployment.

No. 27 Squadron had arrived in India at the same time as an attempted Allied counter-offensive into Burma, which made minor inroads into western Arakan. It predictably ground to a halt against expert Japanese defences, with the new Beaufighter squadron playing little part, if any, in proceedings. No. 27 Squadron's initial forays were focussed on the airfields from where the Japanese bombed Calcutta. The squadron's first operation, flying from

Dum Dum in Calcutta on Christmas Eve 1942, was a strafing attack by three Beaus led by Squadron Leader Bunny Horn on Toungoo airfield.[8] This was no milk run – Toungoo lay in central Burma, a round trip of over 1,000 miles, but the three Beaus returned safely, although with no clear results to report. A couple of days later a second raid was carried out on Heho airfield, but this was hampered by low cloud and cannon failure. The next few days saw a lot of cannon testing, as keeping the lethal weaponry fully operational would prove difficult in the heat and humidity.

On 9 January, the squadron moved up to Kancharpara airfield, much closer to Calcutta, and a month later, moved further west to Argatala. The airfield raids continued for a few more weeks, but on 9 February, 27 was given different targets. The previous day had seen the launch of Operation Longcloth, the first of General Orde Wingate's Chindit expeditions behind Japanese lines targeting enemy infrastructure. In support of this, a flight of four Beaufighters flew a 'Rhubarb' mission along the Chindwin and Irrawaddy rivers, targeting any river traffic.[9] The two rivers carried much traffic, with a variety of boats of different sizes, from small junks and sampans to bigger steamboats, being pressed into service by the Japanese for carrying troops or supplies. During this first attack, at least one vessel was left ablaze, with all Beaufighters returning safely. A second flight in the afternoon saw one of the Beaus returning with its main tail section shot through. The raid would set the tone for future Beaufighter missions in Burma: interdiction, the destruction or disruption of Japanese supplies and supply routes. This would mean a range of targets spread over a wide area which shifted over time: river transport on the Irrawaddy and Chindwin, Burma's railway system, Japanese supply dumps, and road traffic, but also continuing to target airfields. The one connecting feature was they were well behind enemy lines. Usually, Beaufighters sought targets of opportunity within pre-defined zones – a type of mission code-named 'Rhubarb' back in 1941. At this stage, there was no obvious chokepoint like the single track of the Kokoda trail.

Burma shared many of the difficulties of New Guinea. Most missions involved Beaufighters having to cross the Arakan mountain range twice, a natural, rugged barrier of jungle-lined peaks, reaching above 10,000 feet, and stretching five hundred miles from Nagaland in the north to the Chin

Hills in the south. Sometimes this meant a refuelling stop at one of the forward air strips in the shadow of the mountains, such as Dohazari, on the south-eastern edge of Bengal. The traverse of the Arakan meant a flight of about eighty miles across an area of rapidly changing weather, including violent thermals, wind shear and towering cumulonimbus clouds, with cliff-sided valleys and impenetrable forest facing any pilot looking to force-land a crippled aircraft. A damaged Beaufighter returning on one engine faced a daunting prospect – Bunny Horn and his very skilful navigator would be decorated for managing just this.[10] Yet it says much for the resilience of the Beaufighter that all manner of damaged aircraft made it home.

After clearing the Arakan, there was a speedy descent down to the 'deck', forest canopy permitting, for a low-level approach to the target-rich broad plains around the Chindwin and Irrawaddy rivers and Upper Burma's main cities of Myitkina and Mandalay, looking for targets to strafe with their cannon and machine guns. In this it was undoubtedly aided by the relatively quiet sleeve-valved Bristol Hercules, allegedly inspiring a nickname 'Whispering Death', of which more later. Targets further south, in the proximity of Rangoon or Prome, allowed a usually less stressful journey across the Bay of Bengal. On reaching the Burma plains, the Beaufighter still had plenty of fuel and all its ammunition, and very often struck a series of targets over the course of a couple of hours, as on 1 April's Rhubarb mission, which lists:

> 'E/A (enemy aircraft) with square wing tips and an inline engine, somewhat like a Messerschmitt 109' (perhaps a Kawasaki Ki-61 'Tony'?) … Buildings including a group of possible billets, a factory… a factory engine house, a 150-foot steamer, three motor transports on Taungup Road, one being hit; 'two probable resthouses shot up, outside one of these 20-30 horses and uniformed men were spotted… On the south side of Taungup hits were seen on huts and buildings gunned.' One of the four Beaus was hit by small arms fire on its port aileron, 'which became uncontrollable over Taungup but the a/c made base.'[11]

The whole mission, including a refuelling halt at Dohazari, had taken six hours twenty-five minutes, with all aircraft returned.

The Beaus usually operated in small units of two or four, and as well as the natural hazards, often faced small arms fire and anti-aircraft guns, particularly around air fields, consisting of 20mm and 12.7 mm heavy machine guns. Sometimes, they would encounter heavier batteries, as occurred on 19 February, when a flight of six Beaus set off to attack the base at Prome, a riverside town to the south of Mandalay, when Squadron Leader Illingworth's aircraft was hit by '3.7 ack-ack' (probably a misidentified 25mm Type 96 ack-ack gun) and was 'seen to crash and completely disintegrate'.[12]

On other occasions, the Beaufighters encountered Japanese Army fighters – usually Nakajima Ki-43 'Oscars'. These were highly manoeuvrable and could be deadly in skilful hands. However, as the Australians in New Guinea had already discovered, the Beau could match the top speed of the Oscar, and with its formidable forward armament, was usually able to deter or elude the Japanese fighters, with just nine lost to Oscars or other types in the whole Burma campaign. The first of these was another of 27 Squadron's Flight Commanders, Squadron Leader Statham, who appears to have been caught and rammed in the tail by the pursuing Ki-43.[13]

The arrival of the monsoon in May slowed down the tempo of operations, but didn't entirely curtail them, and focus shifted to attacking shipping off the Burmese coast, which avoided the now extremely hazardous crossing of the Arakan mountains. Even so, by late May, bad weather had forced several missions to turn back. A second Beaufighter unit, 177 Squadron, was being readied at Phaphamau airfield in north-west India, and became operational in August, ready for the end of the monsoon, with new Mark VICs and flying out of Feni airfield.[14] Like 176 Squadron, this was also a newly created squadron, with an equally evocative squadron motto, 'Silently into the midst of things' (used as the title of the squadron history penned by Canadian navigator Atholl Sutherland Brown). Learning from the experiences of 27 Squadron, the two squadrons would greatly increase both the intensity and effectiveness of operations. Within seven weeks of starting operations, 177 had flown 126 sorties, and the two squadrons had wiped out all large rivercraft on the Chindwin and Irrawaddy, chief amongst them being three large paddle-steamers, *Maha*, *Shwelan* and *Assam*. In that period, the squadron suffered its first loss, when a Beaufighter was seen 'to enter a cumulonimbus storm over the Chin hills', and was never seen again.[15]

With the failure of the Arakan offensive at the start of the year, the Fourteenth Army was now under the transformational command of General Bill Slim, who made a point of ruling out any early offensive while working to build his men's confidence in jungle warfare and to minimise casualties through disease. The RAF, under newly arrived Air CO Richard Pierse, focussed on building up the new 3rd Tactical Air Force. Pierce's build-up included squadrons of US-built Vultee Vengeance dive bombers and 'Hurribombers' who would pound the Japanese armies at the battle front, while the Beaufighters, with their superior range, sought out the supply routes well behind the lines. Beaufighter attacks would be supplemented by heavy bomber attacks on harder targets like bridges and factories, carried out by Wellingtons and B-24 Liberators. A third Beaufighter squadron, numbered 211, would become operational in December 1943, the trio of squadrons forming 901 Wing.[16] No. 211 Squadron was equipped with 'Rockbeaus', with rocket racks on wings, and would be tasked with attacking and destroying bridges in addition to other targets. Their CO was Irishman Patrick Meagher, formerly a Spitfire pilot, who brought his dogfighting skills to his new job and became the only Beaufighter pilot to 'ace' with five victories in the theatre.[17] Another new arrival was the CO for 27 Squadron, James Nicholson, Fighter Command's only Victoria Cross holder.

While Slim and his commanders were rebuilding the Fourteenth Army, the Japanese, whose 15th Army had dominated in Burma for nearly two years, had plans to go on the offensive. Their impetuous commander Renya Mutaguchi had planned the main U-Go offensive into the mountainous border region of Manipur, and a diversionary offensive, Ha-Go, through the Arakan towards Chittagong. Questions were raised about Japan's ability to keep such an offensive supplied. Mutagachi dismissed such concerns and High Command in Tokyo agreed. While Slim's Fourteenth Army would stand fast and take on the twin offensives by over 100,000 Japanese troops, the now more numerous Beaufighters stepped up their job of pounding the Japanese supply routes through central Burma, making a menace of themselves and disrupting the Japanese preparations.

One of their key targets was Burma's railway system, the main method of transporting troops, heavy weaponry and supplies to the front. During British rule, a substantial Burmese network of about 2,000 kilometres had been built using Indian labourers over the previous seventy years. The network was basically in the shape of a crucifix, stretching from Rangoon in the far south to Myitkina in the far north, with Mandalay forming the junction with Lashio in the Shan Hills to the east and Alon Monwa in the Chin Hills to the west. In October 1943, the Japanese had completed the Thai-Burma railway, linking the Burmese railway network to the Thai network and its shipping ports. This achievement had cost the lives of thousands of enslaved locals and Allied prisoners of war, victims of disease and the horrific brutality of Japanese guards. Beaufighter attacks focussed on locomotives and rolling stock, rather than the tracks themselves which were easy to replace, but maintenance huts and water towers were also hit. Burma's numerous railway bridges were also targets, although often tended to require attacks by heavier bombers, like the USAAF's B-24s and B-25s.

By December 1943, the Beaufighter attacks were causing real difficulties for the Japanese. On 5 December, a pair of Beaus, headed by 177 Squadron CO Wing Commander Philip Baldwin, patrolled the railway near Saigang to the north of Mandalay. They found no trains running, but numerous wrecked locomotives and rolling stock, derailed and to the side of the lines. They then reached a small 'flattened village' where they spotted two locomotives, 'camouflaged with scrim and rags', and mounted five strafing attacks, observing a number of strikes. Moving further on, they attacked three or four trucks on the main line, leaving them smoking, and finally attacked two locomotives in a siding, hitting one in the boiler, and causing 'a compact ball of white smoke'.[18]

Baldwin and others were able to confirm the Japanese were being forced to severely restrict running trains in daylight and were building makeshift camouflaged pens in railway sidings to try and protect locomotives by day. Running just at night meant a great reduction for the Japanese in terms of how much they could move, but worse than that, it didn't make the trains a whole lot safer, particularly during the dry winter months, when clear skies and moonlight enabled the Beaufighters to carry out remarkably destructive night raids. Given the distances and the terrain involved, and darkness multiplying the hazards involved in low level strafing work, these raids demanded quite remarkable flying and navigating skills from the crews, not to mention great courage.

On the night of 14 December, a pair of 177's Beaufighters, each carrying several small 40-pound bombs, took off about half an hour apart and headed for Thazi junction, south of Mandalay. Flight Lieutenant Harold Hunt's Beaufighter arrived at the designated area first, and having bombed a couple of trucks which had unwisely left their headlights on, Hunt then spotted a train pulling about twenty-five trucks, which include fuel tankers. According to the squadron records, Hunt strafed the train with cannon and machine guns:

> 'Fire started instantly, seemed to come from underneath loco. This fire spread rapidly to trucks. A series of minor explosions occurred and yellow flames seen to reach 40 to 50 feet high. A/c circled and made second attack, this time longer burst and flames burst up again. Flames also came from ground in the area for a length of 100 yards.'[19]

The fire was still blazing when the second Beau arrived, and the two aircraft would attack two more trains that evening, both returning safely to base in the early hours of the morning. Taking advantage of a spell of clear moonlit skies, 177 Squadron carried out nine consecutive nights of night raids like these, hitting other trains as well as truck convoys, with all crews returning safely.

If train attacks tended to occur at night, daylight patrols continued to target rivercraft. A typical example on 1 March saw a raid by four Beaus taking off at 7.20am, in which they made multiple attacks near Naunggyo with cannon and machine guns, damaging over sixty boats, and leaving twelve smoking or in flames.[20]

In an attempt to foil the Beaufighter river attacks, the Japanese took to stretching cables across the river between trees on either bank. These seldom troubled the Beaufighter – some of whom returned to base with cable wrapped around the wing – but did down Hurricanes. In 177 Squadron briefings, the mission maps into Burma marked no fewer than thirty-five points where Japanese had used these cables.[21]

With so many Japanese troops on the move, the Beaufighters also targeted troop encampments. It would be attacks on these that stimulated two of the enduring myths about the Beaufighter, the first of which was the Japanese conferring it the nickname 'Whispering Death', because of its ability to approach targets in near silence at low level – thanks to those sleeve valves. This appears to have unintentionally emanated from a journalist, Paul Chadburn, who flew on a mission with 27 Squadron's Charles Clegg, observing an attack, and produced an article for the *Parade Middle East* April 1944 edition, with the evocative title 'Death whispers over Burma'.[22] The other myth was that one Beaufighter caught a Japanese regimental parade in a jungle clearing, saluting Emperor Hirohito on his birthday, killing and wounding many men and scattering its horses, and cutting the pole of the raised flag in half. The story lacks specifics and isn't found in any squadron records, and appears to be an embellishment, possibly again of Chadburn's article, which describes a raid on a troop encampment, but with no Japanese or casualties so obviously visible.

After sixteen months of continuous action, 27 Squadron was withdrawn from the line in March to rest and rebuild, with tour-expired crews heading home. Just before being stood down, the squadron claimed its 200th locomotive destroyed. The squadron had flown 756 sorties with the Beau, sustaining eighteen losses, with thirty-two aircrew lost and three surviving as prisoners of war – a 2.4 per cent loss rate.[23] Given the dangers of their role, this was remarkably low, but it still meant half of the squadron's aircrew would be lost by their twentieth mission. Unfortunately, being shot down was usually fatal for both aircrew, simply because at low level, the opportunity to bale out was fleeting to non-existent. Those who did bale or crash-land could find themselves lost in impenetrable jungle with little to sustain them, and those captured faced Japanese brutality.

No. 27 Squadron's Paddy Sterling recalled what happened to the crew of a Beau which had been accidentally shot down by a USAAF P-38:

> 'Both pilot and navigator survived, though Chips (Flying Officer Chippendale) was shot through the body. Trig gave him what first aid he could, but after some misadventures the Japanese captured them. The Japanese were going to make them walk with Trig carrying Chips, but they were holding up the column so the Japanese put their

boots into Chips and killed him. We got Trig back from prison camp when Rangoon fell.'[24]

In another instance, downed Beaufighter crew Flight Lieutenant R.R. Williams and Flying Officer K.E. Herbert were captured, but neither survived after being involved in a hunger strike following a prisoner rebellion.[25]

Early 1944 finally saw the great Japanese offensive. It didn't get the best start, with the defeat of the diversionary Operation Ha-Go (a historic first Japanese Army defeat by the British of any kind) at the Battle of the Admin Box, while the logistics operation was constantly undermined by the continuing efforts of the Beaufighters in wrecking rail and river transport. Further east, Chinese forces along with British Chindits and US 'Merrill's Marauders' (another special forces unit) were threatening Myitkina. Nonetheless, Mutagachi's 15th Army was ready for U-Go in April 1944. Over 115,000 Japanese and Indian National Army troops were massed in the Arakan mountains for the invasion of India, with the great supply bases at Imphal and Dimapur as targets. To get this far, the Japanese had had to improvise – the RAF hadn't targeted the east-west Lashio branch line,[26] whose western terminus was in the southern Arakan, so the Japanese moved rail traffic on to it instead, which left a much longer trek to the front. However, on entering the mountains, much of the burden shifted from mechanised vehicles and rivercraft to animals: 30,000 cattle, 12,000 horses and 1,030 elephants,[27] as well as thousands of enslaved porters from Burma and Thailand. They were able to bring some heavy artillery, with guns up to 155mm calibre, alongside a tank regiment, employing the small Type 95 Ha-Go tank, although these were no match for Allied Lee-Grant tanks. However, to get so far with so many men, Mutagachi had also made a huge gamble – he took food rations to last just three weeks. They would rely on capturing 'Churchill rations'[28] – that is, Allied supply dumps. In essence it meant victory or death – by starvation. And by targeting railways, roads and rivers, the Beaufighters helped make sure it was the second option. By June and the arrival of the monsoon rains, the Japanese had failed to dislodge the Allies at Kohima and Imphal after bitter fighting and sustaining horrific casualties and began the long retreat back towards Burma. Defeat became the disaster. Thanks to the paralysis brought to Japanese logistics, there was no relief force, supplies, or any succour coming their way and they died in their thousands, with the Japanese suffering 90,000 casualties in the failed five-month campaign.[29]

The survivors limped back into northern Burma, and the Beaufighters picked up in the same vein as before. August saw sustained attacks on river craft on the Chindwin River, with Hurribombers, Wellingtons and US B-25s joining in too, destroying 500 rivercraft and seven motor launches. More aircraft arrived – with Torbeaus being brought in to equip anti-shipping squadrons 47, 22 and 217, the last front-line Beauforts making way. At this stage of the war, the Japanese were forced to try and supply the troops by sea and mounted a major convoy on 10 September which 211 Squadron found near Kalegauk Island (in the Andaman Sea, south of Rangoon), and attacked with cannon and rockets, despite being at the limits of their range. No. 177 Squadron followed up, including Atholl Sutherland Brown, who described events:

> 'We flew in loose formation down the coast at wave tops to avoid radar and likewise across the Gulf of Marteban which was like glass. In such conditions, flying into the sea is a hazard, but running out of fuel was a more serious one as the operation was at extreme range. We arrived off the island to find one coastal freighter stationary at sea. Attacks were made en passant to try to sink it but we continued around the lee of the island where six or seven ships were moored or beached. They opened up with flak as we dove towards them and the results were hard to confirm in the confusion of the melee except we had a number of direct hits.'[30]

However, despite the superlative performance of the Beaufighter in this theatre, Mosquitos were brought in to replace and supplement the Beaus at 47 Squadron, as well as to equip several new squadrons as the Allied air forces grew. The Mosquito had a fantastic and well-earned reputation in Europe, with its extra speed and general performance as a fighter-bomber clearly superior to the Beaufighter. However, this was Burma. A double tragedy on 20 October 1944 raised major concerns over the Mosquito's structural strength in the tropics – 45 Squadron's Squadron Leader Don Edwards'

Mosquito was observed to break up in the air after encountering stormy weather. The same day on a training exercise, the starboard engine nacelle of 82 Squadron's Flying Officer Parker's aircraft was seen to crumple upwards and break off, the plane then crashing in flames. All four crew were killed.[31] Suspicion fell on the plywood adhesives failing in the tropical heat and humidity, and Mosquitos were temporarily grounded. No. 47 Squadron's new Mossies were put on hold, and the squadron reverted back to using Beaufighter Xs. The reluctance to switch from Beaufighters to Mosquitos was still very evident several months later when 211 Squadron were converting, as the squadron record attested: 'The initial slight prejudice against wooden aircraft has been overcome, although it is evident that Mosquitoes cannot take punishment so well as Beaufighters.'[32]

1945 saw the continuing irresistible advance of the Allied army, with the Japanese in full retreat and offering plenty of targets. February saw 211 Squadron's busiest month, with seventy-seven sorties flown and numerous locomotives and motor vehicles hit, although they suffered three losses.[33] A Japanese convoy was caught on 4 February on the road into Meiktila with forty or fifty vehicles destroyed or damaged. Meiktila would be the next great victory for the Allies, falling on 1 March, and swiftly followed before the end of the month when Mandalay fell. This left Burma's southern capital Rangoon, for which Slim devised an amphibious assault, Operation Dracula, while elements of his army advanced down Burma's 'railway valley'. In preparation, four of the remaining Beaufighter squadrons – 22, 27, 177 and 211 – were moved to Charinga, near Cox's Bazaar and the coast just to the south of the Arakan. With the Torbeaus of 22 and Rockbeaus equipping the other squadrons, they formed a fully-fledged strike wing, but they would find few targets at sea, and missions consisted of patrols searching for targets in the central plains, a landscape filling with wrecked boats and vehicles, burned villages and wrecked bridges.

One Torbeau squadron to miss out on any action was 217 Squadron, still based in Ceylon, having been last to convert from Beauforts. Under the leadership of the experienced John Lingard, they had been preparing for a special mission: an attack on remnants of the Japanese battle fleet in Singapore harbour. A makeshift airbase was rolled out in the remote Cocos

Islands in order to bring Singapore into range of Torbeaus with special fuel tanks. Even this meant a highly dangerous 2,000-mile round trip across the Indian Ocean and the mountains of central Java. In April 1945, much to the frustration of the aircrews, this seemingly suicidal mission was cancelled.

On 30 April, a 211 Squadron Beaufighter piloted by Flying Officer Anthony Montague Brown was patrolling over Rangoon's waterfront and flew across the jail, then being used for Allied prisoners of war, spotting the sign 'Japanese gone' draped over the roof of one of its compounds.[34] Rangoon would be won with scarcely a fight. All that remained was the destruction of desperate pockets of retreating Japanese, who were pummelled by aircraft and advancing artillery, with thousands killed in the crossing of the monsoon-swollen Sittang River. Within a couple of weeks of Brown's jail discovery, the hard-working 177 and 211 Squadrons were withdrawn, with 177 disbanded and 211 converting to Mosquitos. In the case of 211 Squadron, they had flown 1,790 sorties, destroyed 223 locomotives and 612 motor transports, shooting down seven aircraft.[35] They had also suffered the highest losses, with thirty-eight Beaufighter operational losses in two and a half years of operations, and fifty-eight crew killed. Overall, the Beaufighter loss rate was about two per cent, astonishing given the risks they faced on deep penetration raids, day and night, over the Arakan mountains.

How to assess the Beaufighter's impact? Beau nightfighters made an extraordinary, decisive impact in just days of arrival, although thereafter their achievements were modest. They shot down a grand total of sixteen aircraft, not counting the accidental shooting down of a US B-29 Superfortress.[36]

Less easy to quantify are the achievements of the Beaufighter interdiction attacks – one can count the boats and trains and motor transports destroyed, but what do these numbers mean? Are they even accurate? What is very clear is that long-range interdiction was a key element in Slim's winning strategy from the start, and the evidence of its success was surely in the irrecoverable collapse of the Japanese logistics system which turned Japanese defeat into catastrophe on a par with that the Japanese had inflicted on the British earlier in the war. In short, Beaufighters played an essential role in the defeat of Japan in India and Burma.

Chapter 14

Nightfighter Paradise

Nightfighter operations, Pantelleria and Sicily, May to August 1943

Catania, Eastern Sicily, 11 August 1943

'Bill Pratley at the GCI put us into contact with a Ju88, which never saw us and was smartly put down in flames. Pratley then put us on to another Ju88, which did see us and tried to evade. Three of my cannons jammed but I was lucky enough to knock it down with a one-second burst from the fourth cannon and the machine guns, using a lot of deflection. We saw this crash and Laurie [Dixon] re-cocked the cannons. He had no sooner got back on his radar tubes when he picked up a third Ju88 without help from GCI. This one was happily wending its way home after dropping its bombs, Lawrie produced another copybook interception. I hit the Hun in the starboard engine, but it refused to burn. The top gunner sprayed tracer around us hitting the starboard wing and engine air-intake as he dived away. I pushed the nose hard down (propelling Laurie sharply up into his Perspex dome!) and gave a very long burst, hitting him hard. He crashed into the sea; this being witnessed by Paddy Green who had arrived to join the fray. Pratley then put me on to a fourth target and I was closing on AI radar when it flew into the 3.7 (37-millimetre calibre) AA barrage defending the airfield. I immediately received all the unpleasantness aimed at the Hun… I decided that discretion was very much the better part of valour and broke away...'[1]

As 600 Squadron's Des Hughes describes, the Beaufighter nightfighter working closely with ground control interception units, had become highly potent, and would play a critical role in the next stage of the Mediterranean war. Following victory in North Africa, Allied high command next focussed its efforts on Operation Corkscrew, the plan to pacify the tiny rocky island of Pantelleria. This tiny, rocky island, placed halfway between Tunis and Sicily, had been turned into a fortress airbase by the Germans and needed to be pacified before tackling Sicily and Italy. Most of the action over Pantelleria was conducted by the USAAF, with over a month of raids leading up to the amphibious landings on 11 June. Beaufighters weren't directly involved but did find plenty of trade with German bombers targeting Allied shipping and the Algerian ports of Bone, Oran and Djidelli. No. 153 Squadron, still operating out of Maison Blanche airfield, was notably successful in this interim period, with sixteen victories in just a fortnight after 12 May. Among its scorers were Englishman Leslie Stephenson, who shot down three Ju88s in one night on 23 May, becoming an ace as he did so, and Michael Wedgewood Benn, brother of the Labour politician, who shot down two on 17 May.[2] Pantelleria fell on 11 June, when the island garrison surrendered an hour before the British amphibious landings.

Next up was Operation Husky, the invasion of Sicily, and the first major step in freeing Europe from Nazi tyranny. Nightfighter Beaus were tasked with nocturnal protection of the invasion, and this required reorganisation. No. 600 Squadron were despatched to Malta, which would prove a very popular move among the aircrew, giving up the dusty, fly-blown tented airfields in Algeria. Des Hughes was particularly taken by the upgrade in hospitality, and Malta's miraculous recovery from its siege:

> 'The island was choc-a-bloc with ships, aircraft, equipment and men. The Luqa mess was full so we found ourselves most comfortably billeted in the Meadowbank Hotel in Sliema – a welcome improvement on our tented camps in Africa, particularly the grotty one at Bone. Everyone seemed to be still celebrating the end of the long siege. Good food and drink was plentiful and, to us newcomers at least, the

> fare and the service at the Union club (lobster thermidor, no less!) were remarkably luxurious for wartime. We were glad, too, to be able to buy decent bush-jacket uniforms and suede boots – we must have been a pretty scruffy-looking lot on arrival'.[3]

Also in Malta were the bulk of 108 Squadron (with a unit in Bu Amud in Libya), and 256 Squadron, a squadron equipped with new Mosquito XIIs led by Scotsman John Watson Allen, equipped with centimetric Mark VIII radar.

Left behind in Algeria were 153 Squadron – in July [4] they were moved a short distance to a newly rolled out US airfield at Reghaia, very close to Algiers. Naturally it was an impressive new runway but kept the same sub-optimal tented accommodation that characterised the Algerian airfield experience. Here they would operate alongside the newly arrived USAAF nightfighter squadrons – the 414th, 415th, 416th and 417th. All were in the process of converting from US-built Douglas P-70s (an aircraft type with a lot of aliases – also known as the A-20, DB-7, Boston and the RAF nightfighter, the Havoc) to Bristol Beaufighters, so 153 personnel would be on hand and able to advise. Another arrival in Algeria was a detachment of Beaufighters from Fighter Command's 219 Squadron in Britain, and while most of the action would be focussed on the Sicilian invasion, these aircraft would do a robust job of dealing with the more than occasional raids on North African ports over the next few months.

No. 153 Squadron may have got the rough end of the billeting arrangements, but they continued to get the lion's share of trade, with the Luftwaffe continuing attacks on Algeria's ports and the Allied convoys sailing through by night. On the night of 14 June, the Luftwaffe mounted a bombing attack on Bone harbour, with 153 intercepting and shooting down four Junkers Ju88s.[5] Such interceptions were important and successful in minimising damage to the numerous convoy vessels ferrying troops and equipment in readiness for the Sicilian invasion.

Operation Husky was launched on 10 July. This was the second great combined operation and involved US and British ground forces, a fleet of warships, supply ships and landing craft, paratroopers, gliders (disastrously) and a huge air umbrella. However, such a huge force was clearly vulnerable to Luftwaffe or Regia raiders at night, despite previous efforts to destroy or jam Axis radar systems. As a result, for the first time, the landing ships (LSTs) carried three mobile radar stations along with a full staff, with several plotting rooms for fighter direction in ships moored off the invasion beaches. The plan was to land these behind the first waves of troops and make these operational in time for nightfall on the night of the tenth. Among the first personnel to land at the British 'Bark' Beach, near Cape Pisarro, was Squadron Leader John Brown, the RAF's most successful radar operator of the war, who had guided Player and Lammer for his 100th victory as controller during the early days in Algeria. Unfortunately, on US 'Dime' Beach, the radar unit ran into a much more dangerous situation, and several RAF personnel found themselves under fire, and some would end up tending wounded among the US Rangers. Unfortunately, two RAF controllers, Squadron Leader Maurice Allen and Flight Lieutenant John Gray-King, were killed by an exploding mine.[6]

In spite of the difficulties, on the very first night of the landings, GCI radar units were in place and fully operational, and guided several successful interceptions. The first of these was a Beaufighter piloted by Michael Davison, who was vectored on to an unfortunate CANT Z1007bis at about 11pm. Seven Ju88s were lost that night, with the last claimed at 5.09 by 600 Squadron's John Turnbull, the first of many for the Australian.[7] The Mossies of 256 Squadron also opened their scoring. The next day saw a furious Axis counter-attack with raids throughout the day and following night. Just how dangerous the Luftwaffe's bombers could be was underlined the following afternoon, when the US freighter *Robert Rowan*, packed with munitions, was hit and erupted in a massive explosion. A large, tank-packed LST was also set ablaze by a fighter-bomber attack. The same night, 600 Squadron had its biggest night of the war so far, destroying five Ju88s and a CANT Z1007. The squadron CO Paddy Green scored twice, with another future ace, Francis Mellersh, getting off the mark. The 108 Squadron Beaufighter flown by Australian Robert Cowper got too close when shooting down a Ju88 and his Beau was hit by the debris. Both crew baled out, with Cowper safe, but his radar operator Pilot Officer Farquharson was lost.[8]

The following night was much better for 108 Squadron. CO Wing Commander Jasper Read led the way by destroying an He111 and a Ju88, with the squadron making five confirmed and three probable kills in the evening, with just a single aircraft falling to a 600 Squadron Beaufighter. Two nights later saw the Beaufighters' most successful of the campaign, with ten victories falling to the two squadrons. The COs of both squadrons had a particularly good night – Jasper Read shooting down two more Ju88s and Paddy Green claiming four Ju88s plus one damaged. Claims by the nightfighters amounted to thirteen enemy aircraft, against eleven recorded losses by the Luftwaffe.[9] The losses didn't stop the bomber raids, and while they achieved further damage to the anchored invasion fleet, including a torpedo strike which damaged the aircraft carrier HMS *Indomitable*, they were having tellingly little effect on the advancing invasion force, whether by day or by night. Field Marshal Kesselring, apprising the situation, would quickly give orders to pull his forces from the west of the island, and on 16 July, the Italians withdrew their air squadrons from the island.[10] The Axis tactical bomber force was rapidly being neutralised by the efforts of the RAF nightfighters.

Within less than three weeks, the parallel land campaigns led by the Allies' great rival commanders Montgomery and Patton had broken out of their respective beach heads and made advances north, with the British forces reaching Catania in the east while the US forces, which landed further west, had advanced rapidly against little opposition and had taken Palermo in the far north-west of the island.

By this stage, Sicilian airfields had been cleared for use by the Allies, and 600 Squadron had moved from Malta to Cassibile airfield, just to the south of Syracuse. Des Hughes recalled being very impressed by the lush and picturesque setting for the airfield, 'long and smooth and cut clean through a very large plantation of olive and orange trees',[11] although a problem was its proximity to the Allied anchorage near Syracuse, where nervous naval gunners regularly shot at Beaufighters as they took off, even hitting one aircraft. This was stopped after the irate Paddy Green and Des Hughes presented a 20mm Oerlikon shell which had lodged in the said Beau to the local naval commander.[12] While temperatures in the Sicilian summer soared, morale among the nightfighters was sky-high, with Hughes recalling the eagerness of pilots trying to get the plum patrol slots where trade was most likely.

A detachment of 255 Squadron, which had been left behind at Le Sebala airfield near Tunisia, was also flown into Sicily. Dakotas flew the ground crew into the captured airfield at Borrizzo, near Trapani on the west coast of Sicily. Left behind at Le Sebala were Wing Commander John Player and the squadron diarist and radar operator, Alfred Lammer, both of whom were tour-expired. 255's operations book, which on occasion doubled as a social diary, records they were given a farewell dinner and a 'Sing-song in the Airmen's mess' to send them on their way on 30 July.[13]

These reinforcements were needed, as the rapid acquisition of Sicilian territory greatly stretched the area to be defended at night by the Beaufighters and Mosquitos. The nightfighter force had achieved so much success by a strategy based on an uninterrupted, overlapping series of patrols, sometimes individual aircraft, in constant touch with a GCI station, so already in the air and able to respond immediately to any enemy contacts. Across the whole night, each of the squadrons would have at least one aircraft in the air, with the rest on stand-by before their patrol slot. On occasion, aircraft would be scrambled as enemy 'bogeys' had been picked up outside of a patrolled area. Such a system worked perfectly when the objective was defending the fleet anchorage and a relatively small beachhead, but coverage became stretched when defending the greater part of an island the size of Wales, particularly if the enemy attacked in numbers.

On the morning of 1 August, Luftwaffe bombers attacked the port of Palermo. The port had been in American hands for a few days, and was receiving supplies from a number of Allied ships – however, it lay at the extreme west end of Allied-held territory, as far from the landing beaches as could be. The bombing was accurate and relatively unhindered, with part of the docks and a British merchant ship destroyed, while an ammunition train and fuel dumps were also hit with spectacular results.[14] A single Beaufighter from 108 Squadron, having just been vectored on to a flight of friendly Wellingtons, then, tellingly, saw the flak above Palermo so turned to investigate, duly intercepting and shooting down a Junkers Ju88 using the onboard AI radar, not GCI vectoring.[15] The more locally based 255 Squadron had started flying patrols that night, but were alerted quite late – Flight Sergeant Cameron catching and shooting down a Ju88 about forty miles out to sea, about an hour after the raid. Luftwaffe records show that Cameron's victim was likely a Junkers Ju88C-6 nightfighter,[16] rather than a bomber. The Palermo raid showed the limits of rapidly set up expeditionary radar system in a fluid campaign – gaps were inevitable, and occasionally the enemy took advantage and inflicted major damage. This was a lesson which would come back to bite the Allies later on in Italy.

The Palermo raid didn't alter the momentum of the Sicilian campaign one jot, and very soon in August, German commanders were looking at evacuation across the narrow Straits of Messina, the closest point to Italy. The need to support the German rearguard actions and to maximise the chances of success in the evacuation meant the Luftwaffe came out in force. On 11 August, a force of Ju88s attacked RAF airfields at Lentini, to the south of Messina, destroying twenty Spitfires on the ground and killing several personnel.[17] It was here that Des Hughes, who'd missed out on posting a big score earlier in the campaign, shot down three Ju88s in one night, as described above, with his squadron colleagues shooting down two more.

On 17 August, the Germans and their Italian allies completed something they hadn't in Tunis – a successful evacuation of about 70,000 troops across the Straits of Messina, leaving the British Eighth Army and US Fifth Army in charge of their first big chunk of Europe. The five weeks of the campaign had seen the Beaufighter nightfighters achieve spectacular success – they had shot down eighty Luftwaffe bombers for just one aircraft shot down, one crash-landed, and one crewman lost. No. 600 Squadron had led the way with forty-four victories, with 108 Squadron scoring thirty-three – both notably ahead of the Mosquito-equipped 256 Squadron with twenty-three victories and two losses.[18] There was no denying the rampaging Scotsman John Watson Allen as the campaign's top scorer with thirteen victories in his Mossie, but no fewer than five Beaufighter pilots 'aced' during the campaign, with John Turnbull (nine), CO Paddy Green (eight), Des Hughes (five) from 600 Squadron, and 108 Squadron's Michael Davison and the CO, Jasper

Read (both seven).[19] The success of the Beaufighters and Mosquitos owed everything to the RAF's mobile radar units which came ashore under fire, and established a highly effective radar defence system within hours of landing. The RAF nightfighting efforts undoubtedly saved many ships and hundreds of lives from the start and throughout the campaign, and played a woefully under-rated part in the island's invasion.

Chapter 15

Strike Wings

Anti-shipping operations, English Channel & North Sea 1942-45

20 November 1942, Dutch coast

Twenty-six Beaufighters of 236 and 254 Squadron lined up for their first shipping strike from North Coates airfield in Lincolnshire. Their target was a small convoy including the freighter *Schiff 49* and several flak ship escorts, which were making their way along the Dutch coast towards Rotterdam. Of the Beaufighters, the fourteen 236 Squadron aircraft were standard Mark VICs, there for flak suppression with regular armament plus two 250-pound bombs, while the 254 Squadron aircraft were the new Torbeau Mark XIs, with ten carrying torpedoes and two joining 236 in flak suppression duties.[1] This was the first Coastal Command trial for the 'strike wing', pioneered by Patrick Gibbs in the Mediterranean, in which anti-shipping operations were conducted by three units – the ship-destroyers, usually torpedo-armed; anti-flak – using their cannon and sometimes bombs, to suppress the anti-aircraft guns, and top cover, who dealt with interfering fighters.

Things started to unravel early. One of the Torbeaus failed to even make the runway with a 'faulty selector gear' when taxiing.[2] The remaining twenty-five Beaus flew south to circle over Coltishall, where they were scheduled to join their Spitfire escorts. They didn't show up after a short while, so the impatient Wing Commander Howard Fraser ordered the formation to make a start, flying east across the North Sea at wave-skimming height. Evidently, this abrupt move not only meant there would be no top cover, but it also caught four of the anti-flak formation by surprise. They too got left behind, eventually turning back to base. Another Beau developed engine problems, joining the lengthening list of early returns. As they drew towards their target, the anti-flak aircraft led by Fraser headed up to 2,000 feet, while the nine Torbeaus rose to 175 feet for their torpedo run. At this point, a formation of Focke-Wulf Fw190s intervened, and with no top cover escorts, got among the anti-flak Beaus, shooting down one and damaging two others. The remaining anti-flak Beaus set about the flak ships, running the gauntlet of heavy fire (which at least deterred the Fw190s), but two more were lost, including Fraser. Unfortunately, the convoy had been sailing very close to the coast, which meant shore batteries extended the shooting gallery for the Beaus, and several more of the anti-flak aircraft were badly damaged. The Torbeaus then attacked, hoping to catch the broadsides of the freighters by attacking at right angles to the path of the anti-flak Beaus. While the Torbeaus escaped casualties, the result was a terrific anticlimax, as several torpedoes hit the shallow sea bottom and exploded early, the remaining ones missing their targets. No freighters were lost, and while the anti-flak unit had sunk a small armed tug, three Beaufighters had been lost and six crewmen killed, with two more crash-landing and several others returning riddled with holes.[3]

In short, a fiasco. With Fraser killed, 236 Squadron needed a new CO, and Squadron Leader Neil Wheeler, who had scarcely finished his training on the Beaufighter, was called over to North Coates to take up the new role of Wing Commander, his first task to work out what went wrong. He had no experience in anti-shipping – he had been flying photo-reconnaissance Spitfires out of Heston.[4] However, the Cranwell-trained 26-year-old proved to be the right choice. Perhaps the PRU background, work which focussed on gathering photographic detail, was good preparation, as Wheeler was meticulous in exploring the November raid's failure – the missing fighter cover, using torpedoes in shallow waters and the poor co-ordination of attacks.[5] The North Coates strike wing was created – with 236 and 254 Squadrons joined by 143 Squadron. Over the next few months, the squadrons practised incessantly, even doing practice attacks on the battleship *King George V* and destroyers. There would also be occasional reconnaissance sorties, but no strike wing activities for the Beaufighter until April.

This hiatus was disappointing for the outgoing Joubert, but his focus on creating an effective strike wing would bear fruit. While Germany was nowhere near as dependent as Britain on shipping for vital supplies, it had one critical maritime supply route: to and from occupied Norway and neutral Sweden, source of vital raw materials for the German war effort – up to 10 million tons of high-quality iron ore each year, as well as being Germany's only source of nickel.[6] This fed into spiralling demand in the German war economy for aircraft, tank, guns and shells, particularly from 1943 onwards, as Albert Speer belatedly began to energise the German war economy. Any reduction of this inflow had the potential to drastically impact a German war machine which was already having to make major compromises as the war went on. Just how vital supplies through Norway were might be gauged by the fact that Norway was occupied by over 200,000 German troops,[7] more than Rommel had at any point in North Africa. Norway also retained a fighter wing, Jagdgeschwader JG5, which would be equipped with the superb Focke-Wulf Fw190 from late 1942.

German convoys were much smaller than their Allied counterparts, and from the start much more heavily protected. Another aspect was that Germany did not possess a large number of merchant ships, often relying on Swedish, Norwegian and Dutch vessels. They not only couldn't afford to lose their valuable cargoes but couldn't afford to lose the ships themselves. The *Reichskommisar Schifffahrt* in Hamburg listed just 506 vessels of all types available in the whole of north-west Europe.[8] Usually, freighters were outnumbered by escort vessels, often improvised flak ships – converted tugs or sloops, which bristled with anti-aircraft weaponry of different calibre – 105mm, 88mm, 37mm and often 20mm quad turrets. Occasionally, rocket launchers were carried, cable mines and even small barrage balloons. Crudely improvised they may have been, but against low-level air attacks, the flak ships were lethal.

The ore convoys plied short routes – from the main ore-loading port of Narvik, it took just three days' sailing to reach German and Dutch ports, during which time they could hug the coast within the range of shore-based fighters and anti-aircraft batteries from bases in northern Norway down to Kiel and Rotterdam. Norway's coastline was particularly helpful for this, with thousands of small islands and steep-sided fjords – the Skaergaard – providing a helpfully discreet route for merchantmen until they reached the Skagerrak and the opening to the Baltic. Up to this point in the war, Coastal Command's anti-shipping squadrons had been woefully ineffective,[9] and aerial mines tended to be more cost-effective. However, with strike wing tactics developed in the Mediterranean, and the great potential of the Beaufighter, now capable of carrying torpedoes, there was clearly a chance to reverse this trend.

The North Coates strike wing's first raid under new management was on 18 April 1943. Wheeler led a formation of ten Torbeaus from 254 Squadron and twelve anti-flak Beaus from 143 and 236 Squadrons and made their rendezvous with an escort of Spitfires and Mustangs. The target was a convoy of eight freight ships and eight escorts. The anti-flak Beaus took on and strafed the flak ships, leaving three seriously damaged. The Torbeaus hit the biggest of the freight ships – the 4,906-ton *Hoegh Carrier* – with three torpedoes, sending it to the bottom.[10] This time, there were no losses among the Beaufighters. A raid eleven days later was even more successful, with three ships sunk, including two freighters which totalled 9,181 tonnes, and one of the escorts.[11] However, just two days later, disaster struck. On 1 May, thirty-one Beaufighters were sent on a search and attack mission to find the light cruiser *Nurnberg* and three destroyers off the coast of Norway. Unfortunately, the area lay outside of the range of escort fighters, breaking one of Wheeler's key principles. Sure enough, they ran into the Norway-based JG5's Focke-Wulf Fw190s and Bf109s. The Beaus jettisoned bombs and torpedoes and employed corkscrewing dives to try and shake off the lethal German fighters. Five were shot down, in one of the worst days for Beaufighter losses.[12] The next strike, on 17 May, with escort service resumed, was much more successful, with three ships sunk, including a 3,000-ton merchant vessel, and no losses.

April had seen the arrival of a new weapon for the RAF, the 3-inch rocket projectile, another bright idea traced back to Lord Tizard's various research groups. Consisting of a warhead, a tube containing cordite propellant and four small stabilising fins, there were two versions – one which carried a 25-pound solid steel head, and another, a 60-pound high explosive charge.[13]

No. 236 Squadron's aircraft were fitted with rocket rails for carrying eight rockets, four on each wing – the first Rockbeaus. Its first use was actually in the Bay of Biscay against a U-boat which was possibly successful (and covered elsewhere). The benefit of the rockets is that they could be launched in a strafing dive, adding considerably to the weight of fire, and unlike a torpedo, there was no slow, vulnerable attack run, and a single aircraft had eight chances to hit. The downside was a rocket strike was less likely to be lethal than an 1,800-pound torpedo.

The strike wing debut for the Rockbeau was against a large convoy of five Swedish merchant vessels, seven flak ships and five minesweepers.[14] They fired 176 rockets, and along with cannon and machine guns caused some damage and casualties on several flak ships. However, 254 Squadron's Torbeaus started their attack late and ran into heavy flak, with two shot down and four badly damaged, while the freighters turned towards their torpedoes, which duly missed.[15] The choreography was amiss, but the other factor was the rockets didn't do their job – several of the high explosive-tipped rockets failed to detonate, leaving undamaged flak ships and unperturbed gunners to turn their guns on to the Torbeaus. Generally, the high explosive rockets were much less effective than the solid warhead ones.

The incoming chief of Coastal Command, John Slessor, was impressed by the virtuosity of the wing, commenting, 'Each of these so-called strikes was a carefully planned, highly organised and hard-fought action.'[16] However, he was less impressed by the results for effort spent, and for a while the strike wing's future was in question. However, evidence from the Ministry of Economic Warfare showing the disruption of shipping reaching Rotterdam won the day.[17] A new strike wing was formed in November at Wick in northern Scotland consisting of 404 (Royal Canadian Air Force) Squadron, and 144 Squadron, which had recently switched from Hampdens to Torbeaus earlier in the year. Prior to forming the Wick strike wing, 404's Beaufighters had seen some action – on 28 July, they had shot down four Blohm und Voss Bv138 trimotor flying boats.[18] The Wick wing's first official strike was 22 November in which they destroyed a Norwegian merchant ship and damaged two others.

Before the year closed out, 254 Squadron's Torbeaus were engaged in a particularly significant mission – attacking an Italian blockade runner,

Pietro Orseolo, which had been taking a range of munitions, machinery and various materials and chemicals to Japan, and returning with thousands of tons of natural rubber from Japan's recent conquest, Malaya. German industry could produce synthetic rubber of low quality which could be improved by blending with natural rubber. *Pietro Orseolo* needed to be intercepted before it reached the deep-water docks of northern France. As a result, Torbeaus linked up with 248 Squadron in Predannack who would take on the anti-flak role, taking time away from their Biscay patrols. No. 183 Squadron's Typhoons would provide fighter cover, as the wing's route would take them close to Cherbourg and the deadly Focke-Wulf airfields. This temporary Biscay strike wing wouldn't have the first attack on the vessel; in fact, it had been shot up by Typhoons and Mosquitos two days previously. Photo-reconnaissance aircraft observed the ship with escorts, near the port of Concarneau in southern Britanny, so the new strike wing set off on 22 December. The Torbeaus planted two torpedoes into the *Piedro Orseolo*, leaving it crippled – it actually didn't sink until the next day, by which time it had been towed into shallow water, and its precious cargo of rubber was saved.[19] It proved to be among the last of the blockade runners – as Donitz decided to cancel further runs, leaving Germany to manage shortages of essential raw materials.

The early part of 1944 saw Coastal Command set up further strike wings, and some movement between bases according to where shipping was being found and attacked. The 'Anzac strike wing' was formed in March in Leuchars, in central Scotland, with 455 (Royal Australian Air Force) and 489 Squadrons (Royal New Zealand Air Force). With very slim pickings off the Norwegian coast, the Anzacs would move south within weeks to Langham on the north Norfolk coast. The other wings continued to find targets on the coast of Holland.

D-Day meant the strike wings would be deployed on a new mission. They would have the task of guarding the flanks of the huge invasion fleet from what remained of the Kreigsmarine. This specifically meant dealing with threats from E-boats, mini-submarines, destroyers and torpedo boats, all of which could cause carnage if let loose among troop carriers and landing craft. The threat was very real – on 28 April, during a training exercise off Slapton Sands in Devon, E-boats had sunk three troop carriers, killing at least 749 US servicemen. The strike wings were thus deployed at the edges of the invasion – the west flank defined by a line between Weymouth and St Malo, covered by the Wick wing, relocated to Davidstow Moor in Cornwall. The east flank was left to the handily placed North Coates and Anzac wings. All the aircraft of both wings now sported new paintwork, black and white invasion stripes. First action was on 19 May, when the Davidstow Beaufighters caught two torpedo boats and four small minesweepers rounding Brest near Ushant Island. The Beaus carried high explosive rockets, which once again disappointed, mainly falling short of their targets, and little damage being done. The small flotilla put up a powerful flak barrage and brought down one of 144 Squadron's Beaufighters, and damaged others.[20]

It was a disappointing rehearsal, and the only one the strike wings would get in the run-up to D-Day. On the afternoon of the invasion, the call came for the Davidstow wing, with reports of three destroyers, which included two modern, large and heavily armed Narvik class destroyers, *Z24* and *Z32*, weighing 2,600 tonnes each and a third smaller ex-Dutch destroyer *ZH1* heading north towards Brest (and just a few hours sailing to the invasion beaches). This time, fourteen Beaufighters were carrying armour-piercing rockets, sixteen were anti-flak, and fighter cover was provided by 248 Squadron – who had switched Beaufighters for Mosquitos following their great success in the battle over Biscay. The raid was perfectly conducted, with multiple rocket hits on the *Z24* and *Z32*, and both were left in a distressed state, with multiple holes, some flooding and fires breaking out. Despite the powerful ack-ack of the destroyers, no aircraft were lost, with one of the escorting Mosquitos shooting down a Ju88 to boot. The destroyers limped into Brest, surviving another attack in the early hours, and spent thirty-six hours being feverishly patched up.[21] They eventually did join the action on 9 June, much too late to affect the course of the invasion, and were mauled by British and Canadian destroyers, *ZH1* being sunk, and *Z32* badly damaged and run aground,[22] where it was subject to a further attack by the Davidstow wing. *Z24* survived to become the first destroyer to be sunk on the open sea by a strike wing rocket attack on 24 August, when it was targeted by the Langham wing, something noted by the Royal Navy. An accompanying torpedo boat *T24* was also sunk.[23]

The North Coates wing had a less dramatic D-Day, destroying two small 'harbour defence' vessels on 8 June. However, they despatched three E-boats and an R-boat on 13 June.[24] The wing was back with business as usual on the 15 June, when they attacked a large convoy just off Schiermonnikoog, northernmost of the Dutch Fresian islands. This attack combined the North Coates and Langham wings, and would be led by Wing Commander Tony Gadd. Gadd had worked with torpedoes since his early career at Gosport, flying alongside Patrick Gibbs as a Beaufort pilot at 22 Squadron. He was probably the most experienced torpedo pilot in the RAF, counting 1,150 torpedo drops in his career (albeit mostly not in combat).[24] With Mustangs overhead, twenty-four anti-flak Beaus shot up the eight flak vessels, before the twenty Torbeaus looped around to attack the freighters. No aircraft were lost, while multiple hits were recorded on the two freighters and both were sunk (weighing in at a combined 12,000 tonnes).[25] The raid, for the first time, stirred public attention, with Gadd being interviewed by the BBC (and later awarded the Distinguished Flying Cross), and a month later a cameramen accompanied a strike wing as it flew into action.

The mayhem of a strike mission was particularly vividly described by 144 Squadron's Philip Brett, as a Torbeau pilot following in the anti-flak Beaufighters. On 21 July 1944, he was part of an operation which brought together 144 and 404 Squadrons flying out of Langham and Strubby (in Lincolnshire):

> 'Our leader, Squadron Leader Robin Burwell, held 144 back, aiming to brings us into the ships just as the anti-flak aircraft completed their work. On his order – Attack, Attack – we spread out as briefed, choosing individually the biggest targets we could find and setting our travelling light torpedo sights accordingly. The other squadrons had caused havoc. There was smoke everywhere on the sea and in the sky. Explosions were occurring along the whole length of the convoy. I came in like a good new boy, doing just what I had been told. I was aware of a sort of sparkling curtain between me and my target and

> the pretty tracer curving gracefully towards us, but I was concerned only with speed and height and the need to wait until the ship grew large. My torpedo gone, I could at last ram open the throttles and take violent evasive action as I climbed through the flak from my target and the surrounding escort vessels into the safer sky beyond. As we circled the scene of the attack there were still bursts of heavy flak everywhere above the convoy. Some of the aircraft seemed to be having a second go. Many of the ships below were enveloped in smoke and steam and several were blazing.'[26]

While the careful choreography of the strike was observed successfully, nobody could actually tell what had happened in the smoke and noise, and it took a couple of days for RAF intelligence to determine what actually happened, which confirmed that Brett's torpedo struck home, and the 4,160-tonne Finnish-owned freighter *Orient* was sunk, as well as an escorting minesweeper. Amid the mayhem, the strike wing attacks were attacking commercially owned boats manned by civilians from occupied countries, and obviously many would be killed or wounded. One symptom of this was that Swedish insurers stopped insuring merchant vessels sailing to German ports.[27]

The success of D-Day and the Allied invasion of France meant a major reorganisation of strike-wing deployments. France and its U-boat bases were rapidly being lost to the Kreigsmarine, releasing aircraft from Biscay. Finland's peace with the Soviet Union meant their former German allies fell back into Norway, meaning the loss of Finnish and Swedish ports in the Gulf of Bothnia as alternative supply routes for ore convoys. This meant all iron ore came out of northern Norwegian ports, with convoys sailing at night, and attempting to hide in the cover of the fjords by day. If before, Coastal Command could erode and reduce ore supplies, they now had the opportunity to sever this lifeline for the German war machine. Could this be a war-winning strategy? Probably not by itself, but the Beaufighter once again would cause consequential damage to the German war effort, contributing to its total defeat just months later.

Under the guidance of its new head, with the controversial Sholto Douglas having replaced the excellent John Slessor, Coastal Command set up new Scottish strike wings at Banff and Dallachy. These were led by the feted fighter ace (and newspaper heir) Group Captain Max Aitken, who had become an ace in a Hurricane in the Battle of France, before scoring several victories as a Beaufighter nightfighter pilot, both over England and over the Aegean with 46 Squadron.[28] At Banff, Aitken was handed the command of the former Biscay patrol squadrons 236 and 248, along with 143 (from North Coates) and 144 (most recently at Strubby). However, only 144 would retain the Beaufighter, with the other three squadrons having converted to Mosquito FBVIs, and in the case of 248, this included the new 'Tse-tse' Mosquito XVIII with 57mm Molins cannon. Dallachy, in as much as they were a separate wing, had three squadrons of Beaufighters (the Anzac pair, 455 and 489, the Canadian 404 Squadron, while in addition 144 Torbeaus were shared with Banff wing). Another occasional element were the Mustang squadrons providing fighter escorts, 19 and 65 Squadrons – more generally the Mosquitoes provided fighter cover too.

Banff wing operations began in September 1944, with the first operation on 6 September, led by 144 Squadron's new CO Tony Gadd, although the mission would be aborted following bad weather. The new Norwegian operations would demand different tactics to the attacks off the Netherlands. The ore convoys sailed at night, finding shelter within the numerous steep-sided fjords, which meant they were difficult to find or attack. However, the convoy captains also realised they could sail with impunity in the first couple of hours after dawn, as an assembled wing took time to form in the early light and cross the North Sea. The RAF came up with an ingenious solution – an RAF Vickers Warwick from RAF Drem would drop a series of marker flares, flame floats and drift lights on a large area of sea a few miles west of Stavanger at about 4 a.m. The strike wing took off in the darkness at about the same time, and headed for the flare-lit area, which they reached in dawn's early light, and formed up ready for the attack.[29] The 'Drem system' was a success first time out on 9 October, with a 2,000-tonne freighter and an escort vessel sunk for no losses. As winter approached and the nights lengthened, the Drem system became less effective. Nonetheless, by the end of 1944, the Banff and Dallachy wings had sunk thirty-three ships weighing over 46,000 tonnes.[30] The cost at this stage had been remarkably low, with the loss of just two aircraft for every three ships sunk – but this was not to continue.

On 9 February, two 489 Squadron Beaufighters on the morning reconnaissance had spotted two separate flotillas in the fjords near Bergen in southern Norway – the Narvik class destroyer *Z33* and flak ship escorts and a group of five freighters, all over 2,500 tons. The air group commander, Sturley Simpson, had decreed that the destruction of one of Germany's few remaining destroyers should be prioritised above the convoys that were the raison d'etre of the whole strike wing's existence.[31]

In the early afternoon, thirty-two Beaufighters took off from Dallachy, from 404, 144, 455 and 489 Squadrons, led by Australian Wing Commander Colin Milson, a veteran of Beauforts in the Mediterranean, and escorted by RAF Mustangs. They found the destroyer in the Forde Fjord, a long but narrow S-shaped fjord, shielded by precipitous cliffs on either side. Snow lay on the cliff tops and in hollows, while shallower parts of the fjord had frozen over.[32] There was just one plausible attack route to be followed by every Beaufighter, whether anti-flak or Rockbeaus, while the narrowness of the fjord restricted the number of Beaufighters that could enter at any one time, with the rest milling around waiting their turn. Two years of learning the importance of precise strike wing choreography was cast aside with hasty improvisation. Each Beaufighter had to fly along the same length of the narrow steep-sided fjord, running the gauntlet of shore batteries, before meeting an arc of minesweepers and flak ships at a jutting promontory into the fjord, behind which, and unsighted, lay the heavily armed destroyer. This was Light Brigade stuff, and if that wasn't enough, just as Milson led the first flight to enter the fjord, the Focke-Wulfs arrived and a furious air battle broke out between Fw190s, Beaufighters and Mustangs.[33]

The losses were the worst for any single operation involving Beaufighters. The Canadian 404 Squadron bore the brunt, losing six aircraft with eleven aircrew killed, mainly to anti-aircraft fire in the fjord. Another 455 Squadron Beau was shot down with both crew lost, while two aircraft from 455 and 144 Squadron ditched in the fjord, their crews surviving. In the case of the 144 Squadron aircraft, this had been badly damaged in combat with Focke-Wulf Fw190s, and after a descent which saw the aircraft crashing through a pine forest, the aircraft came to rest just off shore in the neighbouring Hoydels Fjord. Both the pilot, Percival Smith, and his badly injured observer, Spike Holly, were rescued by a local Norwegian family, whose actions undoubtedly saved Holly's life (he sought and befriended his rescuers after the war).[34] Five Focke-Wulfs were shot down, including Staffel leader Rudi Linz, a seventy victory ace, who Holly is believed to have hit with his Vickers machine gun. The destroyer was lightly damaged, as were several escorts. On what became known as 'Black Friday', many of the twenty-three surviving Beaufighters made it back to Scotland despite heavy damage, once again, a great testament to the aircraft's strength.

As the war barrelled towards its inevitable conclusion in the spring of 1945, opportunities for the strike wings increased, and of course the ore supply was squeezed as the Germans started to run out of ships and their war situation generally fell apart. It has been estimated that by February 1945, Germany was receiving just half a million tons of ore shipments (annualised), when it had been 8.5 million tons the previous year.[35] However, the continued operations inevitably led to unfortunate incidents where the strike wing attacked vessels subsequently found to be carrying passengers, such as the Norwegian ferry *Austri* on 22 February, mistakenly attacked and destroyed, with at least thirty innocent passengers killed and many wounded.[36] The last few weeks of the war saw the action shift closer to Germany, mounting attacks in the Kattegat and Baltic, and continued into May 1945 almost oblivious of the terminal collapse of the Reich. On 3 May, the North Coates and Dallachy wings attacked two convoys near Kiel, and between them destroyed five vessels and two escorts which weighed in at over 25,000 tons, with the last loss of a Beaufighter and crew. The following day, the North Coates Beaufighters sank four U-boats, four days after Hitler's death.[37] With this last strike, all wings were finally stood down.

Even with the severe losses of Black Friday, the Banff and Dallachy wing Beaufighters suffered no worse a loss rate than the Mosquitos. By the end of the war, forty Beaufighters had been lost against forty-seven Mosquitos, including six which had been damaged and flown on to 'Brighton', code-name for Sweden, where the aircraft were interned. The Mosquito clearly had better performance, particularly when tackling Focke Wulfs, but the

Beau's resilience evidently got it back home, across the North Sea, more often when damaged. Its air-cooled Hercules engines could take much more damage and keep running, while the Mosquito's water-cooled Merlins were vulnerable with a single hit to the radiator.

Both types performed supremely well in the most dangerous of tasks, and despite the additional hazards posed by the fjords chosen by the Germans to shelter and hide their ships, the loss rate dropped to about 1.1 aircraft per sinking. By the end of the war, the combined Banff-Dallachy wings had destroyed seventy-eight ships for the loss of eighty-seven strike aircraft. This included fifty freight vessels and six U-boats, totalling 113,666 tons, of which the Dallachy wing sank one-third of the freighters and forty per cent of the tonnage.[38] All told, UK-based strike wings sank 244 ships weighing in at about 305,000 tons. It still meant heavy losses in terms of air crew – Roy Conyers Nesbitt estimated that over sixty per cent of all aircrew who flew in the strike wings would be killed in action.[39]

Chapter 16

The Gates of Hell

Long-range Aegean Operations 1943–44

26 April 1943 Gambut, Libya

A flight of four of 227 Squadron's Beaufighters took off from the dusty, tent-lined Gambut airfield in eastern Libya. Their mission: a sweep over the islands of the southern Aegean Sea, once the gateway to Classical Greece and Byzantium, cradles of civilisation where Europe met Asia, Christianity met Islam, and theatre for some of the most fabled battles in history: Troy, Salamis, Thermopylae, Preveza, Gallipoli, and just two years previously, the Allied defeat in Crete. Nowadays, the islands have become the most alluring of holiday destinations, islands of stunning beaches, crystal-clear seas and historic ruins. Beaufighter crews coined a different description: the gates of Hell.[1]

In charting their flight north, the Beaufighters carefully bypassed the heavily defended Luftwaffe airfields of Crete before reaching the Aegean Sea beyond. They were led by their experienced CO, the New Zealander Russell Mackenzie. Their mission was an offensive sweep over the Dodecanese, a chain of twelve islands in the southern Aegean, which lay about 400 miles away, and meant the Beaufighters would be looking for targets of opportunity at the outer limits of their effective range. This was the fifth day of such operations, and one of the aircraft soon turned back with smoke billowing through the cockpit. A second of the Beaus had other mechanical difficulties and dropped out of sight of the others. It failed to return to base and was posted 'missing'. Mackenzie and the remaining Beaufighter, flown by Flight Sergeant Harvey, carried on, finding a 'large schooner' which Mackenzie strafed first, seeing some strikes hit. Unfortunately, the following Harvey pulled out of his strafing run too late, hitting the schooner's mast and tearing off part of the wing. The stricken Beaufighter was too low to recover and dived into the Aegean, with neither crewman surviving. Mackenzie's lone Beaufighter continued its sweep, and found a smaller schooner, which the determined Kiwi blasted into oblivion, before turning for home. Six weeks later, the two crew of the missing Beau reported in at Gambut. They had turned their misfiring Beau towards neutral Turkey, where they'd been briefly interned, before the pair worked their way back to their squadron.[2]

This patrol highlighted the high price of conducting operations at arm's length in the eastern Mediterranean. This was compounded by the usual problem with 'sweeps' – the first hurdle was finding meaningful targets. With the Aegean Sea being a strategic backwater, and with so many Axis ships lost in previous months, supply of the island garrisons was done through small vessels – caiques, some with engines, some with sails, often being described as schooners. Some of these might have little military value or be innocent non-combatants like fishermen trying to ply their trade in a war zone – it was difficult to tell from the cockpit of a Beaufighter. As a result, despite the heroic efforts of the pilots and the potency of their aircraft, the costs on some missions quite markedly outweighed any results, like 25 April.

As we've seen, 227 Squadron had seen much action in the escort and flak suppression role for Gibbs' Beauforts in Malta, but in February they had been reassigned to Egypt, to regroup under their new commander Mackenzie. The Kiwi had proven one of the most successful of 89 Squadron's nightfighter pilots, scoring four victories over Alexandria in the summer of 1942. A further victory with 227 made him an ace.[3] At Edku in Egypt, 227 were reunited with 252 Squadron, which had continued with both convoy patrols and army close support operations in Egypt throughout 1942 and the first part of 1943, missing out on all the action in the western Med. This was about to change. From April both squadrons would start offensive sweeps flying out of Gambut over the Aegean Sea. As 227 Squadron's flight records state, 'The business of the squadron was to search around the Aegean for caiques with which the Axis was supplying the island garrisons.'[4] Ultimately, these Beaufighter operations marked the revival of Churchill's strategic interest in the Balkans and Greece, the famed 'soft underbelly of Europe'.

Many islands in the southern Aegean were occupied by garrisons comprised of thousands of Italian troops, notably Rhodes and the biggest of the Dodecanese archipelago, namely Cos, Samos and Leros. With very few German troops present and the Italian war effort reeling from defeat, it seemed to be ideal for the Allies to make incursions with relatively small forces. Beyond the islands and Greece, the Balkans were essential for the German war effort, with Romania possessing the only natural oilfields accessible to Hitler. The first Beaufighter operation over the Aegean had taken place on 21 April, when four Beaufighters from 227 Squadron did an exploratory patrol over the Aegean.[5]

The Germans and Italians responded to the Beaus' attacks by mooring vessels in harbours with flak defences, and with the creation of five armed caiques – numbered GA41 to GA45 – which while they flew the Greek flag, housed some very heavy and up-to-date anti-aircraft armament, including 88mm and 37mm ack-ack guns and quad 20mm gun turrets. The result was while the summer saw some successes, it also saw mounting losses for the Beaufighters, with the two squadrons losing fifteen aircraft in three months.[6] The biggest success had been 252 Squadron's raid on the seaplane base at Preveza, when at least four seaplanes were destroyed and seven were damaged, and the fuel dump blown up.[7]

In early September came Operation Accolade, the British occupation of the Dodecanese islands in the southern Aegean Sea. The campaign completed a personal trilogy of ill-conceived if well-intentioned fiascos in the eastern Mediterranean by Winston Churchill. Triggered by Italy's surrender on 8 September, the plan was to seize several of the Dodecanese islands and secure the surrender of the Italian garrisons on the islands. Unfortunately, the key assumption underpinning the venture – that of limited German resistance – was badly flawed, as Hitler was determined to seize anything Italian-occupied. In August, a whole German division had landed on the biggest island of Rhodes, which quickly defeated the occupying garrison. This probably should have stopped the plan dead, but the British went ahead in taking the other islands, notably Kos, Samos and Leros. The air support plan bore the fingerprints of the new AOC Middle East, Sholto Douglas, who'd taken over from Tedder at the start of 1943. Over the next two months, the battle consisted of the Germans prising the islands back from a small British force (about 5,200 men in all) and their new, and often reluctant Italian allies. The Luftwaffe had Cretan and Greek airfields close to the islands and over 350 fighters and bombers available, including ninety Bf109s.[8] The Luftwaffe was for the last time in the war, in any theatre, able to assert clear air superiority.

The two Beaufighter squadrons already operating over the islands, 252 and 227, were moved to Cyprus in August, marginally closer to the islands, based initially at Limassol. In the early stages of the battle, the Beaus would provide escort for small convoys ferrying in troops and supplies.[9] In addition, they were charged with attacking enemy ships and airfields and providing air cover for the various Royal Navy units in the region. All these critical roles had to be done at the limit of the Beaufighter's effective range where the Luftwaffe had considerable numbers of Bf109s. There were some successes, with attacks on a range of small vessels – barges, coasters, Siebel ferries, caiques, converted torpedo boats and some small freighters. Such losses didn't significantly disrupt German progress, with Cos falling on 3 October, taking with it the only Allied airbase at Antimachia, where two ill-fated flights of Spitfires (6 SAAF and RAF's 74 Squadron) had fought bravely until literally bombed out of existence. Nonetheless, despite the intensity of operations, casualties among the Beaus were initially relatively light. The worst incident came when a Beaufighter taking off from Limassol on the short trip to a bigger new airfield at Lakatavia swung on take-off and crashed into a stationary Beau. All four crew, plus another pilot being carried as a passenger, were killed.[10]

As the fighting continued for Samos and Leros, more Beaufighters were brought in – a small unit of converted nightfighters from 46 Squadron, then 47 Squadron's Torbeaus arrived at Gambut, offering strike capabilities. In October, overturning Eisenhower's initial refusal to offer US assistance, help arrived from the US 12th Air Force, with a flight of B-25H Mitchells joining the anti-shipping effort. These were the latest of 'Pappy' Gunn's gunships, originating from his work alongside the Beaus in the New Guinea campaign, which carried formidable forward armament including a 75mm cannon.[11] There was also an all-too-brief appearance by elements of the 1st and 14th Fighter Group's Lockheed P-38 Lightnings, who operated for three days in early October, enjoying a 'Stuka party' in which they claimed sixteen victories, including a remarkable seven by Major William L. Leverette (there was overclaiming here, as just eight Ju87s were actually lost).[12] The Lightning, the twin-engined 'forked-tailed devil', was faster and more manoeuvrable than the Beaufighter, with equal range, and was a match at low altitudes for the Bf109. A longer deployment might have made a real difference over the Dodecanese in a way the Lightning rarely did elsewhere in Europe (its high-altitude performance wasn't competitive). However, US commanders were clearly unimpressed by the abrasive AOC Sholto Douglas, so much that they blocked his proposed appointment to South-East Asia Command,[13] and this disharmony might have had consequences here. As it was, from 10 October until the final fall of Leros on 16 November, Beaufighters were the only Allied fighters providing any kind of air cover in a theatre which was in easy range for three Bf109 fighter gruppes. The consequence over the last month of the battle was that Beaufighter losses finally started to spiral upwards.

On 5 November, six 227 Squadron Beaufighters on an offensive sweep near Rhodes ran into a flight of Bf109s. The Beaus turned east, and opened their throttles and, manoeuvring violently, attempted to get away, but the Bf109s, jettisoning their drop-tanks, hauled them in and picked off the Beaus one by one, with four sent crashing into the Aegean in flames.[14] In tactical terms, the Beaus had committed a cardinal sin of air combat, by turning away from attackers, scrubbing off speed so they would be more easily caught, and showing their tails, rather than persisting with a head-on pass, where their cannon could have broken up the Bf109 attack. All eight crew were lost. To cap a black day for the Beaufighters, 47 Squadron lost two of its Torbeaus to flak in an attack on a small convoy, although all four crew survived to be taken prisoner of war, including 47's CO, Johnny Lee-Evans.[15]

The following day, 47 Squadron would lose its stand-in CO, Charles Ogilvie, in a similar strike mission on troop-carrying barges. Ogilvie was last seen being chased by a Bf109, but he and his navigator would turn up back at base just before Christmas, minus the plane. Such was 47 Squadron's loss rate that several tour-expired instructors would be drafted in, including Stanley Muller-Rowland, arriving at Gambut on 13 November.[16] Even Muller-Rowland would be forced to ditch on his first mission back in action, after sustaining damage in an attack on Junkers Ju88 bombers, he and his navigator being rescued from the Aegean by a friendly Greek fisherman. On 16 November, in the last hours of the battle for Leros, 47 Squadron's seven remaining Torbeaus and one 603 Squadron Beaufighter would mount a final mission in support of the beleaguered British troops, attacking a Siebel ferry/landing craft and barges. Despite the heavy flak and attacks by Bf109s and Arado Ar196s, the ferry erupted in flames. Three of the Beaus were shot down, with just one survivor from the three crews. That evening, 47 Squadron were down to just a single airworthy Beaufighter, having lost eight aircraft in ten days.[17]

With the fall of Leros, 3,500 British and Allied troops went into captivity. The Beaufighter squadrons had played an heroic role in proceedings, but operating at such long-range in skies dominated by the Luftwaffe's shore-based fighters was asking too much. Much as the army deployed was too few and too lightly armed to take on a German division, the air force planning had underestimated the enemy. Not for the first time, Sholto Douglas had presided over an ill-thought-through plan. Over the campaign, Beaus shot down fourteen aircraft, destroyed multiple small vessels and helped destroy several larger ones, but suffered twenty-nine aircraft lost, including forty-two aircrew killed.[18]

However, the Beaufighter's mission in the Aegean continued. Obviously alerted to future British incursions, German troops were poured into the Greek islands to replace Italian forces, and these had to be supplied somehow. Sideshow it may have been, but occupying the islands involved thousands of troops who could have been deployed on the main fronts in the east and Italy. It also continued to tie down a small Luftwaffe air group, despite the overwhelming demands of the Defence of the Reich, with German cities now being pummelled around the clock and rocketing attrition among Luftwaffe fighter pilots.

As a result, after the loss of Leros, the four Beaufighter squadrons stayed put in Libya and Cyprus, and continued in their mission to destroy any ship or boat movements between the islands of the Dodecanese, but also further afield, to the inner islands of the Aegean as well as Crete (which unsurprisingly had the largest German garrison, involved in a particularly brutal partisan war). In this, the Beaufighters continued to work with USAAF B-25 Mitchells. On 18 November, a sweep by Beaus and B-25s across Paros and Naxos included an attack on a two-masted caique, 'Hits scored with 20mm, near misses from 75mm shells. Caique left leaning with 40-degree list. Men jumping over side during attack.'[19] As the year closed out, and adverse weather tended to limit operations, 603 and 252 Squadrons were taken off ops to convert to a new weapon, underwing rockets, following their successful use by Coastal Command's Beaufighters. Both the 60-pound high explosive warhead and the 25-pound armour-piercing warhead were employed, and against small vessels like the caiques and Siebel ferries encountered in the Aegean, the rockets would prove to be highly effective.

However, the hazards remained the same – on the first sweep of the New Year, 47 Squadron ran into Bf109s and one of the Torbeaus was shot down. On 13 January, 227 Squadron, now commanded by 272 Squadron legend John Buchanan, mounted a successful attack which saw three patrol boats destroyed, although one of the Beaus had to ditch and its crew were taken prisoners. Losses mounted over January and February, with a flight from 252 Squadron being hit near Leros by Bf109s and losing three Beaus, the sole surviving Beau managing to elude his pursuers in heavy cloud.[20] On 16 February came the sad loss of the inspirational John Buchanan. He had led four Beaufighters into an attack on an armed dredger in the Argolic Gulf, further to the west than usual operations. Buchanan's aircraft was struck by flak, and he was forced to ditch. Tragically, an aircraft mechanic who'd come on the sortie as a passenger was drowned when the aircraft quickly sank. However, John Buchanan was observed by the other three crews sitting on a floating oil tank, 'twiddling the ends of his moustache and giving the V-sign'.[21] He would be joined by his navigator, Reg Howes, who had recovered a dinghy dropped by one of the circling Beaus. Unfortunately, by the time they were picked up, Buchanan would be dead through exposure and thirst, although Howes survived the ordeal.

Despite the losses, the Beaus attacks were hurting, and with supplies running short in Crete, German High Command put together a heavy escort for one of the largest vessels left in the Aegean, the 5,343-ton *Lisa*, packed with heavy guns and essential supplies, which set out from Piraeus on 21 February. The size of the target prompted a major effort from the four Beaufighter squadrons – and this time the Torbeaus were key. Twenty-two Beaufighters set out, six 252 Squadron Beaus missed the rendezvous, leaving six Torbeaus, two flak suppression Beaus and eight flying top cover, to do battle – accompanied by four B-25s. The Beaus and B-25s clashed with the escort, including Ju88s, Bf109s and Arado Ar196s, with three enemy aircraft shot down for the loss of three Beaus. The six Torbeaus dropped their fish, there was a large explosion, and intelligence later reported the freighter was destroyed.[22] A couple of weeks later, a single 603 Squadron Beaufighter flown by Flight Lieutenant Pringle, on a night intruder patrol in poor weather, found a German torpedo boat, the 970-ton TA15 (a converted old Italian destroyer). Attacking with high-explosive rockets, Pringle observed three fires break out, setting the ship ablaze before it was destroyed in a huge explosion.[23] Perhaps encouraged by this spectacular rocket success, and mindful of there being so few large targets that warranted torpedo attack, the RAF withdrew 47 Squadron's Torbeaus, which were redeployed in India. Another change was that 227 Squadron, one of the bastions of the RAF's maritime strike wings in the Mediterranean, would start to be subsumed in several bites into 16 Squadron, of the South African Air Force.

On 31 May, the Germans attempted once again to break the blockade of Crete. This time, they scraped together three merchant vessels – all mere minnows of less than 2,500 tonnes in registered weight, with a large flotilla of torpedo boats and armed 'UJ-boats', and the usual air cover. Ultra signals warned the Allies, and the following day, a powerful initial wave of Marauders and Baltimores caught the convoy just thirty miles from its destination at Heraklion. The effect of these more conventional bombers was limited to a single hit, but the arrival of a second wave five minutes later, consisting of twenty-two Beaus from 252 and 603 Squadrons, would prove more dramatic. No. 252 Squadron's Beaus swept in first, with their leader Wing Commander Meharg being struck by flak immediately and being seen to dive into the sea.[24] Blasting away with 20mm cannon, machine guns and a mix of armour-piercing and high-explosive rockets, the Beaus left all of the merchant vessels ablaze, two escorts sunk and a third damaged. Of the flaming hulks, two were towed to Heraklion, one was abandoned and all (including the damaged torpedo boat) were sunk within the next week as follow-up bombing raids on Heraklion harbour and a submarine finished things off. Losses were heavy – four Beaus shot down or crash-landed, but remarkably Meharg and his navigator survived to become prisoners, along with three other crew members from the other Beaus, while another managed to find friendly hands.[25] The convoy's evisceration was a major blow for the beleaguered German garrison.

The rest of the summer saw continuing strikes and several further successes. On 30 August, the capture of the Ploesti oil fields in Romania by advancing Soviet forces meant the main rationale for occupying the Dodeconese and other Greek islands was gone, and the Germans made the decision to evacuate the islands. This was a task made so much more difficult by the scarcity of sizeable boats, after so many had been sunk over the previous months. By this stage of the war, the Bf109s had been withdrawn from the Aegean, and while there was still plenty of flak, air cover was left to the Arado floatplanes, and Beaufighter losses became rarer. Operations continued into September for 252 Squadron, with their new CO, Dennis Butler, and 603 Squadron. The shipping that remained was hunted down, and if not destroyed, tended to be left as flaming, shell-holed hulks.

This was a feature of the combined cannon/machine-gun/rocket attack – it caused immense damage, injuries, riddled, shredded hulls and superstructures, and often fires on the upper deck of the target boat, but it was unusual for the boat to sink. The effect was the same – often the vessels were abandoned or scuttled while still afloat, or the hulk simply sunk later. One of the larger vessels was the 1,900-ton *Schiff 50* (aka *Drache)*, a much-adapted and prolifically renamed minelayer-cum-flakship-cum-troop carrier. It survived one Beaufighter attack at sea without too much damage, only to be attacked again in port at Samos by 252 Squadron and destroyed, with the captain and ten crew killed.[26]

With so few boats to lift troops from the islands, the Germans once again turned to air transports. This time, the Luftwaffe concentrated on nocturnal evacuation flights, as Allied fighters, including long-range RAF Mustangs, were dominant by day. In response, the RAF set up a special flight of nightfighters drawn from 46 Squadron – a long-standing Beau squadron which had shifted back and forth between night and daylight roles. However, there was a further key element – HMS *Ulster Queen*, which had begun life as a ferry sailing back and forth across the Irish Sea. It was impressed into the navy early in the war and fitted out with an impressive array of anti-aircraft guns. In late September 1944, it was fitted with a GCI radar station and radar controller and stationed off the coast of Crete. Once again, the trio of GCI-AI-Beaufighter clicked with immediate results. 'Immediate' being an understatement. With the *Ulster Queen* in position, the first four Beaus flew up to Gambut in the late afternoon of 26 September, and each took off on a solo patrol at ninety-minute intervals and headed for a location to the north of Crete, where about eighty minutes after take-off they would establish radio contact with 'Landmark', code-name for the GCI controller on *Ulster Queen*. Roy Butler and his AI operator Ray Graham was the second aircraft up, contacting Landmark at 2150 hours. Within two hours, Butler, Graham and 'Landmark' had destroyed a large Dornier Do24 flying boat and two Junkers Ju52s, one of these the floatplane version. Butler just made it home on the fumes of an empty tank.[27] The third patrolling Beau claimed another Ju52 a couple of hours later. Over the course of the next seven nights before *Ulster Queen* was withdrawn, 46 Squadron's Beaus performed with stunning efficiency. On his third patrol, Roy Butler racked up his fifth victory to become an ace. The eight Beaus flew twenty-six sorties and shot down sixteen Luftwaffe aircraft without loss – one kill for every 1.63 sorties.[28] Remarkably, two of the victims were Junkers Ju88/188 nightfighters, sent to intercept and destroy the Beaus.

The net result of the actions of the strike squadrons and the nightfighters in the Aegean over 1944 was to help enforce a highly effective blockade of the Greek islands. The attempted evacuation of the Greek islands was only partial, and over 18,500 German troops and 4,000 Italian Fascist loyalist forces were left stranded and useless in the eastern Mediterranean, all subsequently surrendering to British forces,[29] with the first of the islands taken in October 1944.

In eighteen months of operations, 138 Beaufighters had been lost and 107 aircrew killed in highly dangerous operations where the target was often of asymmetric value – the state-of-the-art fighter-bomber with highly trained crew tackling leaky old caiques, schooners and barges. Long-range plus ground attack is always the recipe for high losses, and sure enough, most Beaus were victims of flak, but distance also killed, with nearly twenty-nine per cent of losses due to mechanical failure, accident or unknown reasons – more than twice the losses inflicted by Bf109s.[30] The all-arms Dodecanese campaign had been a costly and very avoidable failure for the British, and for once, Beaufighters were part of the defeat. However, there was redemption – just four squadrons would go on to win a stunning aerial victory, by achieving a blockade of a large army of experienced German soldiers. In winning, the Beau had shown itself an immensely versatile weapons platform, morphing tactics and attaching new weaponry and machinery as the tactical situation changed – starting with strafing and bombing, then introducing the Torbeaus, then the rockets and finally, the AI-equipped nightfighters. In the theatre of Achilles and Troy, Greek triremes and Ottoman galleys, Mustapha Kemal and the Anzacs, the Beaufighter had written a new epic in war.

Chapter 17

Italian Denouement

All Beaufighter units, Italy and the Balkans 1943-45

Strait of Bonifacio, 9 September 1943

Italy had surrendered, declaring its Armistice on 8 September, just one day before Allied landings started at Salerno. The Allies had demanded the main warships of the Regia Marina were handed over, and Admiral Carlos Bergamini led a flotilla out of La Spezia harbour (in northern Italy), the two battleships, the 45,000-ton Italian flagship *Roma* and her sister ship *Italia*, along with several cruisers and destroyers, initially heading to the Italian-held port of Maddalena in Sardinia. When word arrived that the Germans had occupied the port, Bergamini changed course to head for the Allied-held port of Bone in Algeria. All the while they were being tracked by the Luftwaffe reconnaissance aircraft. While passing through the Strait of Bonifacio, between Sardinia and Corsica, they sighted a squadron of unidentified aircraft which Bergamini assumed were RAF escorts. They had earlier been covered by a patrol of 52 Squadron Martin Baltimores, one of which would take the last photo of the magnificent *Roma*.[1]

In fact, these aircraft were much more sinister – eleven Dornier Do217Ks of III Gruppe/ Kampfgeschwader 100, each aircraft armed with a Fritz X bomb under each wing. Fritz X was a lethal new invention – a remote-control glider bomb which weighed in at 1,200kg – among the very first precision-guided weapons to be used in war, and the first of Hitler's *wunderwaffe*, the 'wonder weapons' which he believed would bring victory for the Reich. Sitting on board the Dorniers, the bomb aimers used a Kehl radio transmitter to send messages to steer the Fritz X as it descended.

They had been used previously on a couple of occasions without significant results, but Allied intelligence was unaware that it was operational. The first wave of Dorniers struck at 3.30 in the mid-afternoon, one Fritz X just missing the *Italia* and damaging its rudder, then fifteen minutes later, when the second wave attacked, Feldwebel Heinrich Pelz fired off a Fritz X and guided it for a flight of forty-one seconds into the side of the *Roma*, holing it and flooding the engine rooms.[2] Five minutes later, from another Do217K, Feldwebel Eugen Degan steered a second Fritz X into the *Roma*, setting off a chain reaction and a mighty explosion in the ship's magazines. A total of 1,393 sailors went down with her, including Admiral Bergamini. It was the first battleship lost exclusively to air attack since the sinking of *Repulse* and *Prince of Wales* off Malaya over twenty months earlier.

The explosion that ripped through the *Roma* marked the end of Mussolini's Italian Empire in dramatic fashion. It also illuminated the ruthlessness of the Nazi regime, sending a message to the Allies that the Germans were still far from finished, and were still capable of inflicting painful blows. Plus of course, the whole calculus of the war shifted once again. By falling back onto internal lines of supply, the Germans had removed the pain of maritime supply routes in the Med. It meant a whole set of new problems for the Allies to resolve, and for the Beaufighter squadrons, it would mean ever more dangerous assignments, all over the Mediterranean.

In the interval between the fall of Tunis and the Sicilian campaign, there had been changes for the new strike squadrons. The Bristol Beauforts of 39 and 47 Squadrons were finally retired from service. Their replacement? The new Beaufighter TFX, the 'Torbeau'. They were joined, as a short-term measure to support this conversion, by a third TFX-equipped squadron from Coastal Command, 144 Squadron, to form 328 Wing. No. 144 Squadron had been based at Tain, near Inverness, and had used Handley Hampdens for the first three years of the war. The squadron had not been having a good war – within a month of hostilities starting, a flight of five of the squadron's Hampdens had been massacred by Bf109s during a raid on Heligoland.[3] In 1942, with its Hampdens converted to carry torpedoes, the squadron was also involved in a failed mission to the Arctic port of Murmansk to provide aerial escorts for Convoy PQ18. Five of the Hampdens were lost en route.[4]

Fortunately, on its return to Britain, 144 converted to Beaufighters, before its assignment to the Mediterranean in June.

The new wing was based at the unbecomingly named Protville 2, little more than a tented encampment with two runways which had been rolled out by US engineers to the north-east of Tunis. It also hosted US Havoc nightfighter squadrons, which would soon switch to Beaufighters. The conversion course for 39 and 47 Squadron's Beaufort crews included pilots being accompanied at the controls of a Beau by 144's pilots, while Beaufort navigators got trained up on using the wireless and attending to the rear gun in addition to their main job.[5] The Torbeaus could double up the roles of torpedo bomber and flak suppression with just half the crew of a Beaufort. However, they would find slim pickings left in the Mediterranean.

Their first Torbeau mission was successful, sinking a merchantman which had been towing six barges. However, 144 Squadron got off to a rocky start, one Beau crashing into the sea, watched by Jack Howe: 'The leader, Flying Officer Eric Muller-Rowland was flying at very low level, when I think his propellors clipped the sea. He suddenly pulled up before crashing into the water.'[6]

Muller-Rowland survived (he would prove to be a highly effective Torbeau pilot), but his navigator was lost. Two more Beaus had a minor collision as they circled the stricken Beau. However, some success followed over the next few days – Squadron Leader Lee-Evans shot down a Heinkel He115 floatplane and sank a submarine hunter. In early July, with the run-up to Operation Husky, the amphibious invasion of Sicily, the three squadrons of Torbeaus sat on standby for several days awaiting the intervention of the Italian fleet that never came. With landings completed, they were let off the leash to search for more targets in nearby Sardinia, where the impending fall of Sicily triggered some fevered movements to and from this now vulnerable island.

Jack Howe described one of these attacks on 23 July:

> 'We found the target near Civitavecchia but saw only one of the destroyers. The torpedo Beaufighters climbed to 150 feet for their drop and the anti-flak team climbed to 500 feet. Flight Sergeant Hamer shot down one of the flying boats (an escorting Dornier Do24)

> and we tackled the destroyer, which appeared to be in the lead. We dived steeply and aimed at the destroyer's stern where the depth charges were likely to be positioned. We hoped for a lucky strike with the cannon, which would cause an explosion. Intense flak was encountered, which meant we had distracted attention from those attacking with torpedoes. In fact, it seemed that we had attracted too much because there was the proverbial large bang and we took a hit in the nose of the aircraft, which was badly damaged. I was hit in the legs but we managed to complete our attack.'[7]

Jack made it back to base, but his war in the Beaufighter was done. Three days later, 144 Squadron's short tour was over, and by way of a parting shot, they shot down a pair of Me323 Gigants. In these first few weeks as a wing, the Torbeaus had sunk eight vessels weighing in at about 18,000 tonnes with the loss of twelve aircraft.

With the invasion of Italy, the Torbeaus of 39 and 47 Squadron remained focussed on the to-ings and go-ings between Corsica, Sardinia and mainland Italy. And as before, the success of RAF strike squadrons, this time working in unison with US 12th Air Force B-25 Mitchells, had greatly restricted sea evacuations, with the result that the Germans were forced once again to use air transport convoys to evacuate their troops out of Corsica. With the main air force efforts focussed on supporting the expanding bridgehead in southern Italy, it would be Torbeaus from 39 and 47 Squadrons and Malta-based Mark VIs from 272 Squadron who would once again have the task of dealing with the transporters. On 23 September, the Torbeaus struck first, when a patrol from 39 Squadron encountered and destroyed what would be identified correctly as three Savoia SM82s in Luftwaffe markings (they belonged to Transportgeschwader 1's 'Savoia Staffel').[8] In the afternoon, 39 and 47 Squadron were involved in two more interceptions of transporters, claiming three Ju52s and another SM82 destroyed and two more damaged. One Beaufighter was lost to defensive fire, and another crash-landed at Protville – 39 Squadron's Flying Officer Neil Cox, having shot down two Ju52s on his first mission in a Beaufighter.[9]

Proceedings followed at first light the next day with successive flights from 39 Squadron intercepting four transport formations. Among them was Neil Cox, having dusted himself off after the previous day's crash:

> 'Orders were given that our attacks should be head on against JU52s so as to reduce/eliminate the effectiveness of the machine guns fired by the soldiers from the open port holes of the aircraft. At about 1630 hours off the east coast of Corsica near Bastia we came across a formation of fifteen Ju52s flying low over the sea. Our leader manoeuvred the formation to carry out a low-level head-on attack. The contact being head on was very brief. One moment we were firing our cannons at the oncoming enemy aircraft and the next we whizzed past their formation. Afterwards, I made a wide right-hand circuit and spotted three more Ju52s in formation heading south-west. I climbed up to 1,000 feet on their port side and turned in to make a stern attack on their leader. At approximately 450 yards I opened fire and saw hits and broke off my attack at 200 yards to make a slight turn to the left to engage the port aircraft. I fired one long steady burst at him, closing in to about 50 yards, when he exploded in flames... Very shortly afterwards Bill [Spearey, Cox's navigator] saw this aircraft and the leader's aircraft, whose starboard engine was pouring out black smoke, crash into the sea.'[10]

Unfortunately, at this point, Bf109s intervened, and after a lengthy chase in which Bill Spearey was badly wounded, Cox crash-landed for a second day running, this time at sea, dragging his navigator to safety in the dinghy. Cox had shot down four Ju52s in two days, crash-landing on both occasions.

No. 39 Squadron's Beaufighters shot down eight Ju52s that day, with four Beaufighters shot down or ditching, yet even this would be upstaged by 272 Squadron, who had 'the finest day in the squadron's history', when they attacked three waves consisting of fourteen Ju52s, shooting down nine without loss to themselves – with Canadian Rodney Phipps scoring four. Raising the day's total to twenty was 603 Squadron, who claimed three

Ju52s.[11] This magnificent day in the Beaufighter's history was the final day where German troops and supply ships would have to run the gauntlet in the western Mediterranean. With no more Ju52s or freighters to attack, 328 Wing's job was effectively done for now. The Torbeaus would be needed elsewhere as Churchill's latest sideshow got underway in Greece.

While the Torbeaus headed elsewhere, nightfighters would be more heavily involved in Operation Avalanche, the invasion of Italy, with 600 and 255 Squadrons operating out of northern Sicily, ready to tackle night raiders over the main invasion beaches at Salerno. With the main landings taking place on the morning of 9 September, the Germans launched 158 sorties overnight against the invasion fleet, inflicting some damage, with a cruiser, a large transport and six landing craft hit.[12] Beaufighters of 255 and 600 Squadrons weighed in along with 23 Squadron's Mosquitos, with the Luftwaffe suffering eighteen bombers shot down.[13] No. 600 Squadron's Alwyn Downing shot down two of seven bombers claimed by Beaufighters. On this occasion, many victories were achieved with 'freelance' patrols over the fleet – without the aid of GCI.[14] Over the next week, the two squadrons shot down twenty-two bombers as German bombers continued to attack the Allied fleet. On the night of 12/13 September, 600 Squadron shot down five, identifying their victims as Ju88s and He111s, but in fact, two of the aircraft were Dornier Do217Ks of Kampfgruppe KG100, armed with Fritz X missiles. These had attacked the fleet the previous day, hitting US cruiser *Savannah* and Dutch gunboat *Flores*, and would later hit and badly damage the veteran British battleship *Warspite*.[15] However, despite heavy casualties on *Savannah*, they hadn't prevented successful landings at Salerno.

In Réghaïa, Algeria, 153 Squadron's nightfighters were adjusting to the drudgery of being 'convoy stooges' – flying lengthy patrols from late afternoon through to dawn, often three to four hours in length, keeping a watchful eye out over the convoys coming through the Straits of Gibraltar, the essential supply line for the Allies in Italy. The patrols tended to be done by individual or paired Beaufighters, directed by one of a string of GCI stations now situated along the northern coast of Algeria and Morocco. The Beaus would shift bases between Oran, Tahar and Réghaïa,[16] and they would share duties with newly established Free French squadrons, operating

Spitfire Vs and P-39 Airacobras. Here too, the new threat loomed of German bombers with guided bombs, flying out of southern France.

On 26 November, Convoy KMF26, an eleven-strong convoy formed from troopships coming from Bone in Algeria with supply ships from England and headed towards Italy. In the late afternoon, three Beaufighters from 153 Squadron were scrambled to intercept a large formation of Luftwaffe aircraft, in the Gulf of Bougie (modern-day Béjaïa). The formation included at least fourteen of Kampfgruppe KG40's new Heinkel He177s along with He111s and Dornier Do217s. This was the first mission for this much-delayed strategic bomber in the Med, and each carried two Henschel Hs293 remote-controlled missiles, which had seen some action in the Bay of Biscay. The Hs293 had been developed in parallel to Fritz X with two crucial differences – it had a rocket-powered launch, meaning it could be deployed from greater range (although still reliant on the bomb aimer's eyesight) and the warhead contained high explosive, for attacking unarmoured freighters and troop carriers.

No. 153 Squadron's Beaufighters were joined in the melee by a flight of Beaus from the US 414th Fighter Squadron, Spitfire Vs from the Free French Group de Chasse (Fighter Group) 1/7 and US Bell P-39 Airacobras in one of the last major air battles over the open seas of the Mediterranean. The heavily armed Beaufighters were particularly lethal, with 153's Pilot Officer Froggatt gunning down two, while Flight Sergeant Boulton shot down a third and damaged two others. No. 414 Squadron's 2nd Lieutenant Francis B. Clark shot down a fourth. Unfortunately, 153's new CO Leslie Stephenson failed to return, presumably hit by defensive fire. The French Spitfires also scored heavily, and KG40's He177s suffered dreadful losses – seven were shot down or ditched, while two staggered home only to crash-land at their Bordeaux base, one crashing with all crew killed.[17] However, the aircraft of Hans Dochtermann got through to the convoy and launched its missiles, one of which struck SS *Rohna*, an 8,600-ton liner packed with nearly 2,000 US GIs. Despite the rescue efforts of nearby ships, 1,015 US GIs and 119 crewmen were killed. As on other similar occasions with such great losses in a shipping disaster, the Allies suppressed all news and information about the *Rohna*'s loss, much as they would the following year following the Slapton Sands disaster. It is a myth that the secrecy stopped the Germans finding out about the loss (they later sent aircraft to strafe survivors),[18] but their own losses led to the He177 wing being suspended from daylight operations. This decision, in no small part forced by the Beaufighter's attack, would seriously diminish the threat from one of the Luftwaffe's deadliest weapons during the invasion of Europe.

Back in Italy, after weeks of intense action over Salerno, October and November had been quiet for the two nightfighter squadrons, against a background of sweeping advances northwards for the Allies, including taking the key airfields of Foggia. The Beaufighters were moved into bases in southern Italy, with 255 at Gottaglie (on the 'heel') and 600 at Montecorvino, where they would remain until early 1944. In the nine weeks after the landings, up to the start of December, there was far less 'trade' from German raiders, and the two squadrons chalked up just eight victories.[19] Unfortunately, Allied air commanders interpreted the lack of activity the wrong way. On the afternoon of 2 December in Bari, Desert Air Force chief, Air Marshal 'Mary' Coningham, creator of the Desert Air Force, at a press conference made a remark which would come back to haunt him. 'I would consider it as a personal insult if the enemy should send so much as one plane over the city.'[20] A few hours later he would eat his words, as the Luftwaffe launched a raid on Bari's port by 105 Junkers Ju88s, assembled by Kesselring from units in Italy and the Balkans.

Bari was packed with Allied merchant vessels and was unfathomably lit up to assist unloading for the Monte Cassino offensive. A vessel carrying munitions was hit early on, erupting in a huge explosion which destroyed several nearby vessels, the flames lighting up the targets for subsequent waves of aircraft. By the end of the raid, twenty-nine vessels displacing over 60,000 tonnes were destroyed along with most of their cargoes. Worse than that, the US Liberty ship *John Harvey* was hit. It was carrying a secret consignment of mustard gas, which was released into harbour waters, unknowingly poisoning hundreds of seamen escaping the inferno.[21] Fortunately, US surgeon Dr Stewart Alexander recognised the mustard gas symptoms and saved many lives as a result.

But where were the Beaufighters? Just two of the bombers were shot down by Bari's flak defences, with nightfighters entirely absent during the raid. An enquiry pointed out that radar defences had been jammed by the Luftwaffe dropping düppel – thousands of foil strips (the Allies had used it earlier in the year with devastating effect over Hamburg, calling it 'window'). However, this was just one element of a bigger failure. The Allied invasion force was reliant on mobile expeditionary radar, and long-range radar masts providing early warning don't appear to have been in place and working. These would have picked up düppel concentrations and alerted fighter controllers to an approaching air formation. However, the only radar stations in place so close to an advancing battlefront were the RAF's mobile GCI stations, which could precisely vector fighters on to bombers, but as seen with the Palermo raid, were short-ranged and could leave gaps in radar coverage, particularly facing the sea. Squadron records show that the earliest GCI pick-up of the raiders showed them twenty miles away from Bari[22] – scarcely five minutes of warning before they reached the target, too late for scrambling aircraft to intercept. Without early warning, the RAF needed to have patrols in the air – which they had, but they were in the wrong place. No. 255 Squadron was patrolling the Port of Naples, well to the west of Bari, which, with its proximity to Salerno, had seen several Luftwaffe raids; 600 Squadron had aircraft patrolling further north around Foggia's airfields,[23] a base for an increasingly large Allied air fleet. Both were clearly vital Allied bases which needed protection. Only at 1930 hours, with Luftwaffe bombs starting to fall, did either squadron react to Bari. No. 255 Squadron's Pilot Officer Nicholas was one of three Beaufighters scrambled:

> 'Scrambled to 8,000 feet on 360 degrees for raiders over Bari. Number of bandits not given. On approaching Bari, flak and flares seen over that port. Broadshirt CGI swamped by window. Nav/Radio [Pilot Officer Carter] had many contacts all over the tube seen to be windows and ignored. Instructed to patrol east and west about fifteen miles north of Bari at 10,000 feet and freelance. At about 2000 hours, a contact was obtained at four miles range ... The bandit was taking

violent evasive action with changes of height from 8,000 to 12,000 feet and 80-degree turns. Visual obtained between 1,000 and 1,500 feet. Thought to be a Do217 by position of four exhaust stubs. Chase had lasted ten minutes, closed to 700 feet when enemy aircraft suddenly peeled off to port and visual and contact were lost … Raid appeared to be over when aircraft reached Bari.'[24]

No. 600 Squadron had one aircraft respond, Squadron Leader Angus Horne, who was patrolling over Foggia when he observed flak over Barletta, which lies to the north of Bari. He then noted a 'Huge explosion in target area at 1955 hours – pillar of smoke up to 10,000 feet.'[25] The flak died down a few minutes later, before he was vectored on to an enemy bomber about eight miles away, which was able to elude him.

The key issue, more important than the use of düppel, was that the RAF's nightfighters in Italy were hopelessly overstretched. After Sicily, the two Mosquito squadrons had been moved back to Malta, supporting Algeria-based Beaufighter squadrons with convoy patrols. There were just two Beaufighter squadrons in southern Italy, and they couldn't be in three places at once. What is unfathomable is how, with so many merchant vessels tied up in Bari port unloading in floodlights, there was no adjustment to the regular patrol plans. Perhaps Coningham and the RAF commanders were simply too complacent, fixated on the state of the Luftwaffe's retreating air forces in Italy. Perhaps. However, the Bari bombing, along with the *Roma* and *Rohna* sinkings, while having little bearing on the Italian campaign, underlined that the Luftwaffe was still highly dangerous if given an opening. Beaufighters would need to be deployed wisely.

By early 1944, the ground campaign in Italy had become thoroughly bogged down in poor weather and mountainous terrain around Monte Cassino, and a second amphibious landing was carried out at Anzio beginning on 23 January, meaning another large Allied fleet to protect. This once again would pitch Beaufighters against Luftwaffe's guided missile-carrying bombers from the KG40 and KG100 anti-shipping wings, and both 600 Squadron and 255 Squadrons would have considerable success. They would be joined in this by the US 414th Nightfighter Squadron, flying out of Borgo in Corsica. Over seven days, the Beaus claimed fourteen bombers destroyed and several damaged. Among these were missile-equipped Heinkel He177s, with 255 Squadron's Flight Sergeant Scollan and 600 Squadron's Alwyn Downing both shooting down two in a single night.[26] No. 600 Squadron's total passed 100 victories with just two losses in combat since their arrival in Tunisia. More importantly, shipping losses at Anzio were very limited.

With Rome falling on 4 June and most of the few remaining Luftwaffe units rushed west following D-Day, there would be few more opportunities for the Beaufighter nightfighters to score during the rest of war in Italy, despite the agonies for the army around Anzio and Cassino. Both 255 and 600 Squadron Beaufighters continued to fly night patrols, but found themselves increasingly vectored on to bogeys, only to discover an Allied aircraft with its IFF signal turned off. The long list of nearly shot down aircraft included Wellingtons, Liberators, Bostons and a puzzling number of Martin Baltimores,[27] most likely aircraft flying missions across the Adriatic as part of the 'Balkan Air Force' where they supported Tito's partisans.

The nightfighters were also roped into intruder missions to Zagreb, Sarajevo and Skopje in Yugoslavia, where they supported the efforts of the two new South African Beaufighter squadrons, 16 and 19. These were difficult and dangerous raids with increasingly few meaningful targets as the war headed towards its conclusion. The frustration of No. 255 Squadron's CO is clear in his report: 'The situation in Yugoslavia is generally complicated by moving Russian battle lines and Partisan troops and it does not appear at present a very happy hunting ground for a squadron that wants to see some returns.'[28] Both 255 and 600 were also tasked on several occasions with attacks on shipping and barges in the Adriatic, with 255 Squadron crews even asked if they would cough up crews for the maritime experts of 272 Squadron. The great No. 272 Squadron also faced the problem of running out of targets, although they would achieve one more big success in the destruction of the 51,062-ton cruise liner *Rex* in the port of Trieste on 7 September.[29] Even 272 would soon be faced with sustaining losses for diminishing returns when tackling the remaining smaller, heavily armed vessels still afloat. The war was running out for the Beaufighters based in Italy.

Both 255 and 600 Squadrons would start switching to Mosquito XIXs at the end of the year. No. 600 Squadron went on to achieve 180 victories in the war,[30] all but two with Beaufighters, making them the highest scoring nightfighter unit of the war, including 163 of these in the Mediterranean. No. 255 Squadron had managed seventy-eight in the same time span, being less heavily involved in Sicily, but they had the satisfaction of having the RAF's best footballing side in Foggia, beating 256 and 272 Squadrons and the Royal Signals in successive games.[31] No. 153 Squadron, left guarding the Straits in Algeria, didn't make it to the end of the war, the squadron being wound up in October 1944.

The Mediterranean was the key theatre for the Beaufighter, even above its achievements in Home Defence, Coastal Command, India and the Pacific. It was a theatre where Beaufighter crews pioneered new roles for itself which would be employed to the full elsewhere, and where they faced their biggest challenges, particularly in Italy, where the value of their work was great, particularly over Salerno and Anzio landings, when air cover at night was essential. However, the war against the Germans never ceased to present hazards, and punished complacency with incidents like the *Roma*, Bari and the *Rhohna* tragedy. These serve to highlight a theme that runs throughout the story of this magnificent aircraft, which is that the Allies could have done even better with more Beaufighters.

Epilogue

The Beaufighter's service didn't end with Second World War. Unsurprisingly the greatest war of all spawned lots of little wars, and the RAF and her Beaufighters would see action for a few years more. As freedom for Greece was secured, Beaufighters found themselves thrown into the anti-communist counter-insurgency in Greece in early 1945 – with remarkable success[1] thanks to excellent army intelligence which reduced non-combatant casualties. The defeat of Communist ELAS insurgents in Greece can be seen to mark the first 'hot battle' of the Cold War. The Beaufighter would also see action in Malaya in ground attack operations in Malaya, flying with 45 Squadron until 1949, and four Beaufighters smuggled out of Britain saw action with Israel in the Israel-Palestine War in 1948. Other Beaufighters served in more peaceful circumstances for the air forces of Portugal, Turkiye and Dominican Republic. These instances aside, Beaufighters were generally scrapped or the aviation equivalent of being put out to grass, serving as target tugs in the RAF and RAAF through the rest of the 1950s. The last operational flight was on 12 May 1960.[2]

The Bristol Aeroplane Company struggled to match the Beaufighter. It produced a less successful successor, the Brigand, but with Roy Fedden leaving the company in 1942, and Leslie Frise in 1945, to join the much smaller Percival Aircraft Co., there was a changing of the guard. Bristol's magnificent Centaurus engine would power the final generation of British piston-engined fighters – the Hawker Tempest V and Sea Fury – albeit too late for the war. However, the over-reach and collapse of the Bristol Brabazon project was followed by the failure to break into the commercial aircraft market as the jet age arrived. The gorgeous Bristol Britannia was the very last aircraft produced in any numbers before Bristol became one of the nationalised companies that formed the British Aircraft Corporation in 1963, meaning the Bristol DNA was in Concorde, the Tornado, the Eurofighter and various Airbus airliners, and today Bristol's main Filton site forms the largest aerospace site in the country,[3] including a factory owned by Roy Fedden's longtime rivals Rolls-Royce.

The remarkable and unappreciated fact about the Beaufighter is that it was present and making a real difference at almost all the great turning points in all theatres of the war. It even contributed significantly to the gargantuan German catastrophe at Stalingrad. In doing so, it caused huge destruction – it amassed over 1,240 air-to-air victories, with sixty-nine Beaufighter aces led by Jon Braham, John Cunningham, Moose Fumerton and Merv Shippard (only the Spitfire and Hurricane equipped more RAF aces). They destroyed hundreds more on the ground, in addition to at least 800 locomotives, thousands of motor vehicles and small water craft, and participated in the destruction of over 200 ships.[4]

The story of the Beaufighter is one of Allied air forces learning how to fight the new war that Hitler had inflicted on the world, and how the brilliant foresight of Dennis Barnwell, Leslie Frise and Roy Fedden provided the aircraft which perfectly fit a range of unforeseen tactical demands. In doing this, it became the first true multi-role combat aircraft, an aircraft built as a weapons platform which would be the precursor for classic warplanes like the Mosquito, F4 Phantom, Grumman Tomcat and Panavia Tornado, all sharing the critical attributes of the Beaufighter – competitive speed, twin engines, two crew members and hefty basic armament. Even today, fifth-generation fighters like the F-35 are designed to carry out multiple tactical roles, even if digital technology allows the crucial second crew member to be based remotely. The Beaufighter's story is also central to the development of radar – the critical trio of aircraft, airborne intercept radar and ground control, which clicked to astonishing effect in the most stressful of settings. The remarkable successes achieved by the nightfighter Beaufighters, with among the most one-sided 'kill ratios' of any warplane in the Second World

War, were interleaved by dramatic failures where the tightly knit system was disrupted or not fully in place, such as at Maison Blanche and Bari.

So why is the Beaufighter's contribution so forgotten while other aircraft, the Spitfire, the Hurricane, the Lancaster and the Beaufighter's 'rival' the Mosquito are still feted to this day? Perhaps one reason is despite the excitement and sheer exhilaration of actual Beaufighter missions captured on film, cinema has almost totally ignored the Beaufighter. There is a brief appearance in the 1957 classic *Ice Cold in Alex* and most recently, Damien Parer's film footage from a Beaufighter over the Bismarck Sea is incorporated into a biopic about Australia's greatest war cameraman. Unfortunately, in cinematic terms, the more photogenic Mosquito got the gig with *633 Squadron*, whose fatal mission, with Mosquitos flying at low level down a flak-infested fjord to hit a vital target (a rocket fuel factory not a destroyer), can only have been inspired by the Beaufighters' Black Friday attack of 9 February 1945. This would later inspire George Lucas's Star Wars finale with X- and Y-wing fighters running the gauntlet down a narrow defile under heavy fire. The Mosquito stole the glory, a reflection of its own prodigious achievements, but as we've seen, the Beaufighter in many ways got there first and in a real sense, helped change the direction of the war.

Sadly, no Beaufighters have flown for a number of years, but one hopes that either or both of the two current restoration projects at Duxford and in New South Wales can get this magnificent aircraft back into the air. This could finally spur the proper recognition of this genuine war-winning plane and its heroic crews.

Appendix 1

Beaufighter squadrons of the Second World War

About fifty squadrons used Beaufighters in combat during the Second World War, with various training units on top of that. Remarkably, Beaufighter crews made claims for 1,240.83 enemy aircraft shot down, a much higher figure than generally realised. This has been gleaned by laboriously cross-checking using a range of sources. The figure puts the Beaufighter just behind the Mosquito (1,275 victories) with the two top RAF scorers unsurprisingly the Hawker Hurricane and the Spitfire. However, the vast majority of Beaufighter victories (seventy-seven per cent of them) were over Luftwaffe bombers and transport aircraft, with the Junkers Ju88 the top victim (comprising about thirty-five per cent of Beaufighter kills). The bulk of claims by Spitfires, Hurricanes and high-scoring USAAF aircraft were against fighters – Bf109s, Bf110s, Fw190s and such like. As this book has shown, the losses of bombers and transporters really hurt – the Luftwaffe struggled to make good throughout the war.

An important note is that the air victory figures are 'confirmed victories' (by the Allied forces) and not confirmed losses by Axis forces. There is often a discrepancy between claimed victories and actual losses, although notably much less so with actions fought at night, where there is even scope for underclaiming, as may have occurred with Alwyn Downing's 'ace in a day' night interception. Of course, air-to-air victories were only a part of the mass of destruction the Beaufighter inflicted on the Axis forces, some squadrons also tallied the destruction of locomotives, motorised vehicles, rivercraft, aircraft on the ground, and some of these figures are given here. Shipping losses caused by the RAF's strike wings were also tallied. Yet in some cases, while evidence of actual destruction was lacking, the tactical impact of the Beaufighter's attacks were clearly seen in the disintegration of enemy armies, most notably in Burma and New Guinea.

	Dates of use	Command / location	Aerial kills & other results	Notable aircrew
16 SAAF	Apr 43 – Jun 45	Ground attack, strike, Italy, Balkans	0 vics	
19 SAAF	Aug 44 – Jul 45	Ground attack, strike, Italy, Balkans	0 vics	Don Tilley, Steve Stevens
22 RAAF	Jan 45 – Aug 46	Ground attack, strike, Indonesia	0 vics	
25	Sep 40 – Oct 42	Fighter Command, UK	19 vics (plus 3 with Blenheim, 37 with Mosquito)	Micheal Herrick
27	Dec 42 – Feb 46	Ground attack, strike, India, Burma	See 901 Wing data	James Nicolson VC
29	Sep 40 – May 43	Fighter Command, UK	34 vics (plus 2 with Blenheim, 49 with Mosquito victories)	Guy Gibson, 'Bob' Braham
30 RAAF	Sep 42 – Aug 45	RAAF, New Guinea, Indonesia	0 vics	'Blackjack' Walker, Ron 'Torchy' Uren
31 RAAF	Nov 42 – July 46	RAAF, Darwin, Indonesia	20 vics (plus 54 on ground)	Charles Read, Reginald Gordon
39	Jun 43 – Dec 44	Torbeau squadron, Italy, Greece	18 vics	Derek White
45	1946 – 1949	Ground attack, Malayan Emergency	0 vics	
46	May 42 – Nov 44	Night and day fighter (Mediterranean)	52 vics	Roy Butler
47	Jun 43 – Apr 45	Torbeau squadron, Mediterranean, Burma	7 vics	Johnny Lee-Evans
68	May 41 – Jul 44	Fighter Command, Air Defence GB, UK	43.5 vics (plus 6 Mosquito)	Miroslav Mansfeld
89	Sep 41 – Mar 45	Fighter Command, DAF, UK, Egypt, Malta, Algeria, Burma	141.33 vics	'Moose' Fumerton, Merv Shippard
93 RAAF	May 45 – Aug 46	Indonesia, Malaysia	0 vics	

	Dates of use	Command / location	Aerial kills & other results	Notable aircrew
96	May 42 – Oct 43	Fighter Command, UK	0 vics (plus 5 Defiant / Hurri, 23 vics and 181 V1s in Mossie)	
108	Mar 43 – May 45	Nightfighter, Egypt, Algeria, Malta, Sardinia	36 vics	'Jasper' Read
125	Feb 42 – Feb 44	Coastal defence	1 vic (plus 29 and 5.5 V1s in Mosquito)	
141	Jun 41 – Nov 43	Nightfighter, UK, 100 Group	22 vics (plus 12 Defiant and 34 Mosquito)	'Bob' Braham
143	Aug 42 – Oct 44	Coastal Command (North Coates wing)	6 vics (plus 6 Mosquito), see strike wing stats	
144	Jun 43 – May 45	Torbeaus, Algeria, Banff, Dallachy strike wings	3 vics (plus 2 Mosquito), see strike wing stats	
153	Oct 41 – Sep 44	Night/day fighter, Mediterranean	65 vics	Kenneth Rayment, Leslie Stephenson
176	Jan 43 – Aug 45	Nightfighter, India, Burma	12 vics	Maurice Pring, Charles Crombie
177	May 43 – Aug 45		0 vics, see ground attacks	Atholl Sutherland Brown
211	Oct 43 – May 45	India, Burma	7 vics	Pat Meagher, Stuart Muller-Rowland
219	Sep 40 – Jan 44	Fighter Command, UK	66 vics (plus 1 Blenheim, 62 Mosquito)	Arthur Hodgkinson
227	Aug 42 – Dec 43	Maritime fighter, strike wing, Mediterranean	46 vics	Dallas Schmidt
235	Dec 41 – Jun 44	Coastal Command	16 vics (plus 8 with Blenheim, 12 with Mosquito), see strike wings data	

	Dates of use	Command / location	Aerial kills & other results	Notable aircrew
236	Oct 41 – May 45	Coastal Command (North Coates wing)	3 vics (plus 4 with Blenheim), see strike wing data	
239	Sep 43 – Jan 44	Fighter Command, UK	0 (58 with Mossie)	
248	Jul 41 – Jan 44	Coastal Command, UK and Malta	21 vics, 23 on ground (plus 1 with Blenheim, 12 with Mosquito), see strike wing data	David Cartridge, Aubrey Inniss
252	Dec 40 – Dec 46	Coastal Command, Desert Air Force	38 air and 26 ground	Bill Riley
254	Jun 42 – May 45	Coastal Command (North Coates wing)	See strike wing data	Bill Sise
255	Jul 42 – Feb 45	Nightfighter, UK, Mediterranean	86 vics (plus 9 with Defiant)	John Player, Alfred Lammer
256	May 42 – May 43	Nightfighter, UK	1 vic (plus 7 with Defiant, 35 with Mossie)	
272	April 41 – April 45	Maritime, Mediterranean	100 (air) and 85 (ground)	Gordon Yaxley, John Buchanan
307 (Polish)	Aug 41 – Jul 44	Nightfighter, UK	12 vics (plus 2 Defiant, 16 Mosquito)	
404 RCAF	Jun 43 – May 45	Coastal Command Davidstow, Banff wings	See strike wing data	Ken Gatward
406 RCAF	June 41 – April 44	Nightfighter UK	14.5 vics (plus 39 with Mosquito)	George Lawrence
409 RCAF		Nightfighter UK	9.5 vics (plus 53 with Mosquito)	
414 NFS USAAF	May 43 – Feb 45	Nightfighter Algeria, Italy	9 vics	
415 NFS USAAF	July 43 – Apr 45	Nightfighter, Tunisia	11 vics	Nathaniel Linsay
416 NFS USAAF	June 43 – Dec 44	Nightfighter, UK, Algeria, Corsica, Belgium	4 vics	

	Dates of use	Command / location	Aerial kills & other results	Notable aircrew
417 NFS USAAF	June 43 – March 45	Nightfighter, Tunisia, Italy	9 vics	Robert Hamilton
455 RAAF	Dec 43 – May 45	Anzac / Dallachy Wing	See strike wing data	Colin Milson
456 RAAF	Sep 41 – Dec 42	Fighter Command	4 vics (plus 36 with Mosquito)	
489 RNZAF	Mar 43 – May 45	Anzac / Dallachy Wing	See strike wing data	John Dinsdale, Derek Hammond
600	Sep 40 – Feb 45	Nightfighter, UK, Algeria, Malta, Sicily, Italy	178 vics (plus one each with Blenheim and Mosquito)	Des Hughes, Paddy Green, Alwyn Downing
603	Feb 43 – Dec 44	Mediterranean	9 vics (plus 241 with Spitfires)	
604	Sep 40 – Apr 44	Nightfighter, UK	92 vics (plus 1 with Blenheim, 41 with Mossie)	John Cunningham, Jimmy Rawlings
1435 Flight	Mar – Jun 42	Nightfighter, Malta	19 vics	Gill Hayton
Fighter Interception Unit	Sep 40 – Jan 44	Nightfighter and Home Defence	4 vics (plus 1 with Blenheim, 17 with Mosquitos and 86.5 V1s with Tempests)	Glyn Ashfield, Rory Chisholm

Appendix 2

Gazetteer of Outstanding Beaufighter aircrew

	Nat.	Squadrons	Aerial vics / other results	Notes
Aitken, Max	Eng	68, 46	6 (of 14.2)	Wing CO, Banff Strike Wing
Bartlett, Maurice	Eng	272	1.8	Died in accident, 1.1.42, Egypt
Benn, Michael Wedgewood	Eng	108	2	Brother of Tony Benn, politician
Berry, Joseph	Eng	255	3 (plus 59.5 V1s in Tempest)	Post-Beau, highest V1 scorer, KIA 2.10.44 (Belgium)
Bobeck, Ladislaw	Cze	68	5	
Boyd, Archibald	Eng	600, 219	10	
Braham, Jon 'Bob'	Eng	29, 141	19 (of 29)	Leading Beaufighter scorer
Bretherton, Bruce	Aus	255	6 (of 8)	
Buchanan, John	Eng	272, 227	11.16	Top daylight Beau ace, KIA 16.2.44 (AA, Aegean)
Campbell, Gillian Lorne 'Punch'	Eng	272	2 (plus 6 on ground)	
Cartridge, David	Eng	248	8	Top scoring Coastal Command ace
Chisholm, Roderick 'Rory'	Eng	604	7 (of 9)	
Churchill, Richard	Eng	144		Great Escape survivor (d.2019)
Coate, Ern	Aus	272	9.5	
Crawford, Hector 'Heck'	NZL	143, 252, 272	1 (plus 0.5)	KIA 6.2.42 Martuba (Libya)
Crew, Edward	Eng	604	8 (of 12.5 plus 21 V1s)	
Crombie, Charles	Aus	89, 176	11	
Cunningham, John	Eng	604, (85)	16 (of 20)	First Beaufighter ace
Daniel, Edward	Eng	1435 fl	7 (and 4 V1s)	KIA 5.7.44 (V1 explosion destroyed his Tempest, England)
Downing, Alwyn	Wal	600	12	'Ace in a day', 29.4.43

	Nat.	Squadrons	Aerial vics / other results	Notes
Edwards, Henry	Eng	89	7	
Fumerton, Robert 'Moose'	Can	89	14	Top Malta nightfighter ace
Gadd, Tony	Eng	144		Strike wing leader and Olympian bobsleigh
Gatward, Ken	Eng	236, 404		Led Champs Elysee raid
Geddes, Keith	Eng	604	5	Scottish rugby international
Gordon, Reginald Lloyd	Aus	31 RAAF	6	KIFA
Green, Charles 'Paddy'	Eng	600	9 (of 11)	CO, 600 Squadron
Gregory, 'Sticks' (r/o)	Eng	141	(17)	Bob Braham's r/o.
Hammond, Derek	NZl	272,489	1	
Hayton, Gill	NZl	1435 fl	7	
Herrick, Michael	NZl	29	1 (plus 6)	KIA 16.6.44 Denmark (Mosquito)
Hodgkinson, Arthur	Eng	219	8 (of 12)	KIA 10.7.43, Sicily
Horn, Ernest 'Bunny'	Eng	27		Leading Burma intruder
Hughes, Desmond 'Des'	NI	125, 600	11.5 (of 18.5)	
Inniss, Aubrey	Bar	248	7.5	Top Barbadian ace
Kinmouth, Michael	Eng	89	7	
Lammer, Alfred (r/o)	Aut	255	(5 as r/o)	R/o and 255 diarist
Lee-Evans, Jonny	Eng	47		POW 5.11.43, Aegean
Lingard, John	Eng	143, 217, 252, 272	0.5 (plus 1)	Torbeau commander, Ceylon
Linsay, Nathaniel	USA	US 415	2	First US Beaufighter pilot to score a victory
Lyon, John	Eng	600	(12)	R/o for Downing, KIA 31.1.44, Anzio
Mansfeld, Miroslav	Cze	68	6.5 (of 8.83 plus 2 V1s)	
MacKenzie, Russell	NZl	89, 227	5	
Meagher, Patrick	Ire	211	5 (of 9)	CO, 211 Squadron
Mellersh, Francis	Eng	600	7 (plus 1 in Mosquito and 39 V1s)	Son of First World War flying ace
Morris, Douglas 'Zulu'	SAf	406	4	

	Nat.	Squadrons	Aerial vics / other results	Notes
Mottram, Tony	Eng	272		CO, 272 Squadron, Davis Cup and Wimbledon tennis
Muller-Rowland, Stanley	Eng	47, 236		KIA 3.10.43, North Sea
Muller-Rowland, John Stuart	Eng	211	2	
Nicolson, James	Eng	177		Battle of Britain VC winner, KIFA 2.5.45, (Liberator)
Oxby, Doug	Wal	89	13 (of 22)	Highest scoring nightfighter navigator
Pepper, George	Can	29	6	KIFA 17.11.42, Detling
Phipps, Rodney	Can	272	5.5	
Pike, John	Eng	248		Coastal Command
Pike, Thomas	Eng	219	6	
Pring, Maurice	Eng	89, 176	6	KIA 5.12.43, Calcutta
Rankin, Ronald	Aus	272	5.53	
Rawlings, Jimmy (r/o)	Eng	604	(17)	Cunningham's r/o
Rayment, Kenneth	Eng	153	5	Co-pilot, Munich air disaster
Read, James 'Jasper'	Sco	89, 46, 108	10	CO, 108 Squadron
Rees, Stewart	Aus	600	6	
Reeves, Nevil	Eng	89	9 (of 14)	
Riley, William 'Bill'	Ire	252, 272	5.33 (of 8.66)	KIFA 16.7.42 (collision on ops), Egypt
Schmidt, Dallas	Can	227	8.5	
Shippard, Mervyn	Aus	89	13	
Shore, Ross	Eng	227		Malta strike wing leader
Smith, Albert	Can	252, 272	5	
Spurgin, Arthur	Aus	89	5	
Stevens, Steve	SAf		SAAF 19	Balkan Air Force. Noted autobiography
Topham, Johnny	Eng	219	9 (of 13)	
Turnbull, John	Can	125, 600	12.5	
Uren, Ron 'Torchy'	Aus	RAAF 30		30 Squadron RAAF
Watson, Anthony	Eng	272	6.83	
Walker, Brian 'Blackjack'	Aus	RAAF 30		CO, 30 Squadron RAAF
Wheeler, Neil	Eng	236		CO, North Coates strike wing
Wight-Boycott, Mike	Eng	219, 29	4 (of 8)	
Yaxley, Robert Gordon	Eng	252, 272		CO, 272 Squadron KIA Bay of Biscay 3.6.43 (Hudson)

Appendix 3

Coastal Command Strike Wings

Wing	Squadrons	Merchant vessels sunk	U-boats sunk	Escorts and others sunk	Total est. tonnage
North Coates	236, 254, 143 (all Beaus)	29	6	79	117,853
Davidstow (also Wick, Strubby)	144, 404	10		14	44,220
'Anzac Wing' (Leuchars, Langham)	455, 489	9		12	26,499
Portreath	235, 248	1		6	2,740
Banff	143 (M), 235, 248, 144 (B)	33	5	19	68,535
Dallachy	144, 404, 455, 489 (all Beaus)	17	1	3	45,130

Appendix 4

South-East Asia 901 Fighter Bomber Wing summary

Squadron	Sorties	Locomotives destroyed	Other	Crew lost (KIA, POW)	A/c lost
27	756	200	Hundreds of small boats and craft. Several a/c on ground	35	18
177	1830	266	282 motor transports, 273 boats and barges, plus 2,189 small rivercraft destroyed or damaged, 1 a/c destroyed.	48	28
211	1790	223	612 motor transports, 'prodigious numbers' of river boats and craft. 25 a/c destroyed (6 in the air)	58	38

Appendix 5

Specifications and performance summaries of operational Beaufighter marks

	Power plant	Power output / hp	Loaded weight / lbs	Top speed / mph	Armament
Beaufighter IC/IF	Hercules III, X, XI	2 x 1,400	21,120	323	All 4 x 20mm, 6 x 7.7mm
Beaufighter IIF	Merlin XX	2 x 1,250	21,077	337	
Beaufighter VIC/VIF	Hercules XI	2 x 1,600	21,322	333	
Beaufighter XI	Hercules XVII	2 x 1,735	21,000	330	
Beaufighter TF10	Hercules XVII	2 x 1,735	25,400	330	Torpedo-carrying
Beaufighter DAP 21	Hercules XVIII	2 x 1,735	25,400	330	Torpedo-carrying

Endnotes

Chapter 1 – Conception

1. C.H. Barnes, *Bristol Aircraft since 1910*, pub.1964, 3rd edition, Putnam Press, p13
2. Ibid, p16
3. Ibid, p14
4. Ibid, p20 / p80-89
5. Ibid, p109, letter of Major Vere Bettington, No.48 Squadron, 13 May 1917
6. Ibid, p108
7. Sir Roy Fedden, *First 25 Years of Bristol Engine Development*, Aeronautical Journal vol 65, issue 605, May 1961
8. C.H. Barnes, *Bristol Aircraft since 1910*, pub.1964, 3rd edition, Putnam Press, p211-229
9. Ibid, p201-203
10. K.J. Meekcoms, E.B. Morgan, *The British Aircraft Specifications File,* Air Britain (1994)
11. C.H. Barnes, *Bristol Aircraft since 1910*, pub.1964, 3rd edition, Putnam Press, p257-258
12. Sir Roy Fedden, *Correspondence*, Aeronautical Journal, vol 75, issue 724, April 1971
13. Barnwell's note supporting Type 142 proposal, 9 July 1935, quoted C.H. Barnes – *Bristol Aircraft since 1910*, pub.1964, 3rd edition, Putnam Press, p266-267

14, 15, 16. Ibid, p34-35

17, 18. Ibid, p283-289

19. Ian White, *The History of Air Intercept Radar and the British Nightfighter 1935-1959,* p8-9
20. C.H. Barnes, *Bristol Aircraft since 1910*, pub.1964, 3rd edition, Putnam Press, p290-291
21. Chaz Bowyer, *Beaufighter, the Untold Story of a Wartime Icon*, quoting Leslie Frise, Sapere Press, p7

22. Sir Roy Fedden, *First 25 Years of Bristol Engine Development*, Aeronautical Journal vol 65, issue 605, May 1961
23, 24. Frank Nixon, *Aircraft Engine Developments of the Past Half Century*, Aeronautical Journal vol 70, issue 661, Jan 1966, p7-8

Chapter 2 – Birth of the Beau

1. C.H. Barnes – *Bristol Aircraft since 1910*, pub.1964, 3rd edition, Putnam Press, p290-293
2. Philip J.R. Moyes, *Bristol Beaufighter I – II, Profile Publications Aircraft* Number 137, pub. 1966, p4
3. Bill Gunston, *Combat Aircraft of World War 2,* 1st edition 1978, Salamander Books (source of various aircraft specifications)
4. John Cunningham (quoting his radar operator Jimmy Rawlings), *Night Fighter*, 1957, Collins
5. Phil Zimmer, *The Mighty Beau*, Warfarehistorynetwork.com
6. Roy Conyers Nesbit, *The Strike Wings*, Pen and Sword 1984, p203
7. Ian White, *The History of Air Intercept Radar and the British Nightfighter 1935-1959,* p21
8. Frank Nixon, *Aircraft Engine Developments of the Past Half Century*, Aeronautical Journal vol 70, issue 661, Jan 1966, p7-8
9. Jeremy Howard-Williams, *Night Intruder, A Personal Account*, Sapere Books, p41
10. Bill Gunston, *Combat Aircraft of World War 2*, 1st edition 1978, Salamander Books, p85 (source of aircraft specifications)

11, 15. Calculation based around specifications for fire rate and projectile weight of various weapons – Hispano Mk I, Browning 7.7mm, MG17 machine gun and MG FF cannon. Beaufighter 12.08 kg / second, Bf110C 5.14 kg/s; Battle & Blenheim 250 g/s

12. John Terraine, *The Right of the Line*, Hodder and Stoughton 1985, p128
13. Ibid, p134
14. Alastair Horne, *To Lose a Battle: France 1940*, Macmillan 1969

Chapter 3 – Nightfighter

1. Ian White, *The History of Air Intercept Radar and the British Nightfighter 1935-1959*, p5
2. Ibid, p35
3. Bill Gunston, *Combat Aircraft of World War 2*, 1st edition 1978, Salamander Books (source of aircraft specifications).
4. Jon 'Bob' Braham, *Scramble*, Greenhill Books 2021 (original 1961), p29-30
5. Ian White, *The History of Air Intercept Radar and the British Nightfighter 1935-1959*, p285

6. National Archives, NAO Air 27 record 341-14
7. Ian White, *The History of Air Intercept Radar and the British Nightfighter 1935-1959*, p50-51
8. Jon 'Bob' Braham, *Scramble*, Greenhill Books 2021 (original 1961), p34-35
9. Christopher Shores and Clive Williams, Aces High, Grub Street 1994, Harrow LAM victories credited to Patrick Burke (p159) and Dennis Hayley-Bell (p319)
10. White, *The History of Air Intercept Radar and the British Nightfighter 1935-1959*, p87
11. Ibid, p70
12. www.historiccoventry.co.uk/blitz website (archived) Coventry's Blitz article
13. Ian White, *The History of Air Intercept Radar and the British Nightfighter 1935-1959*, p89
14. Ian White, If you Want Peace, Prepare for War (Squadron History of 604 Squadron), 2004 (online), p23-45.
15. www.smithsonianmag.com/ air space magazine (website), Cat's Eyes
16. Jeremy Howard-Williams, *Night Intruder, A Personal Account*, Sapere Books, p41
17. White, p287
18. Ibid, p89
19. NAO AIR 41/17 'Air Defence of Great Britain, Vol III'
20. White, p88 As above
21. Jon 'Bob' Braham, *Scramble*, Greenhill Books 2021 (original 1961), p48-49.
22. John Foreman, *RAF Fighter Command Victory Claims, Part 1 (1939-41)*, pub.2012, Red Kite Publishing.
23. www.smithsonianmag.com/ air space magazine (website), Cat's Eyes
24. White, p83. As above
25. www.rafmuseum.org.uk website, article The Blitz, the Hardest Night.
26. Basil Collier (quoting Sholto Douglas) The Defence of the United Kingdom, pub.1957, HMSO.
27. Williamson Murray, *Strategy for Defeat: the Luftwaffe 1933-45*, Pickle Partners (original edition 1983)

Chapter 4 – Convoy Stooges

1. John Pimlott, *Illustrated History of the German Air Force in World War 2*, Motorbooks International
2. Leo McKinstry, *The Cinderella Boys*, John Murray 2023, p53

3, 4, 5. NAO AIR 27 1508-1

6. Leo McKinstry, *The Cinderella Boys*, John Murray 2023, p63
7. Christopher Shores and Clive Williams, *Aces High*, Grub Street 1994, p519
8. www/Aces.Safarilovioorg/ website, *Luftwaffe Wartime Aerial Victory credits* (against Beaufighter)
9. Christopher Shores and Clive Williams, *Aces High*, Grub Street 1994, p168

10, 11. NAO Air 27 1496/24
12. NAO Air 27 1496/24 and 1446/23
13. www/combinedops.com/vaagso, website detailing mission
14. NAO Air 27 1443-25
15. Leo McKinstry, *The Cinderella Boys*, John Murray 2023, p125
16. Ibid, p120-121
17. Ibid, p122-23
18. NAO Air 27 1496-28
19. Andrew D. Bird, *A Separate Little War*, Grub Street, 2008, p11-12
20. C.H. Barnes, *Bristol Aircraft since 1910*, p299-300
21. NAO Air 27 708-26
22. NAO Air 27 1496-33
23. Graham Pitchfork, *Beaufighter Boys*, Grub Street 2019, p47
24. Leo McKinstry, *The Cinderella Boys*, John Murray 2023, p141

Chapter 5 – Rogue Warriors in the Sky

1. NAO Air 27/1508/2
2. Christopher Shores, Giovanni Massimello and Russell Guest, *A History of the Air War in the Mediterranean, 1940-1945, Volume One: North Africa* (2012), Grub Street, p456
3. Christopher Shores and Clive Williams, *Aces High*, 1992, Grub Street, p519
4. NAO Air 27/1508/3
5. Christopher Shores, Giovanni Massimello and Russell Guest, *A History of the Air War in the Mediterranean, 1940-1945, Volume One: North Africa* (2012), Grub Street, p470
6. Ibid, p499
7. Ibid, p506
8. John Terraine, *The Right Side of the Line*, Hodder and Stoughton 1985, p344-45
9. Tedder, *Quietly in Command*, Vincent Orange, Routledge 2006
10. Christopher Shores, Giovanni Massimello and Russell Guest, *A History of the Air War in the Mediterranean, 1940-1945, Volume One: North Africa* (2012), Grub Street, p559
11. Ibid, p594
12. John Terraine, *The Right Side of the Line*, Hodder and Stoughton 1985, p343
13. NAO Air 27, 1577-11
14, 15. Text supporting Yaxley's DFC award, quoted *London Evening Gazette*, 17 October 1941, p6033
16. NAO Air 1577-19
17. Roy Conyers Nesbit, *The Armed Rovers*, Pen and Sword 2012, p51
18. Ibid, p48
19. NAO Air 27, 1577-19

20. Roy Conyers Nesbit, *The Armed Rovers*, Pen and Sword 2012, p51
21. Ibid, p55
22. Christopher Shores, Giovanni Massimello and Russell Guest, *A History of the Air War in the Mediterranean, 1940-1945, Volume One: North Africa* (2012), Grub Street, p937-939
23. Tony Spooner, *Supreme Gallantry, Malta's Role in Allied Victory*, John Murray 1996

24, 25. NAO Air 27, 1577-19

26. Roy Conyers Nesbit, *The Armed Rovers*, Pen and Sword 2012, p53
27. Christopher Shores, Giovanni Massimello and Russell Guest, *A History of the Air War in the Mediterranean, 1940-1945, Volume One: North Africa* (2012), Grub Street, p1020
28. Text supporting Yaxley's DSO award, quoted *London Evening Gazette*, 12 December 1941, p7051
29. Roy Conyers Nesbit, *The Armed Rovers*, Pen and Sword 2012, p57
30. Roy Conyers Nesbit, *The Armed Rovers*, Pen and Sword 2012, p55-56

Chapter 6 – Mediterranean Night Terror

1. Christopher Shores, Brian Cull and Nicola Malizia, *Malta: The Spitfire Year*, Grub Street, 1991, 57-59
2. Ibid, p65
3. Ibid, p67

4, 5, 6. NAO Air 27 729-2 / 3

7. *The Cliffs* website the cliffs.com.mt, *The Historic Importance of the Dingli Radar, one of the landmarks of Dingli Cliffs*
8. Christopher Shores and Clive Williams, *Aces High*, Grub Street 1994, p113
9. H.L.de Zeng, D.G. Stanket, E.J. Creek, *Bomber Units of the Luftwaffe 1933-45*, vol II, Ian Allen
10. James Holland, *Fortress Malta, An Island under Siege 1940-43*, Orion 2003, p215
11. Christopher Shores, Brian Cull and Nicola Malizia, *Malta: The Spitfire Year*, Grub Street, 1991, p109
12. Ibid, p112
13. Ibid, p118, 129
14. Ibid, p273
15. Christopher Shores and Clive Williams, *Aces High*, Grub Street 1994, p271-272
16. *London Gazette* (online archive), supplement No.35502, p1381
17. Shores, Massimello, Guest, Olynyk and Bock, *A History of the Mediterranean Air War, volume 2: North African Desert*, count of victories
18. Christopher Shores, Brian Cull and Nicola Malizia, *Malta: The Spitfire Year*, Grub Street, 1991, p367
19. Ibid, p592

20. Ibid, 372
21. NAO Air 27 729-14/16 Count of sorties and victories
22. Christopher Shores, *Duel for the Sky*, Grub Street 1999, p165
23. Christopher Shores, Brian Cull and Nicola Malizia, *Malta: The Spitfire Year,* Grub Street, 1991, p439
24. Ibid, count of victories
25. Ibid, p651
26. Ibid, p582
27. Ibid, p592
28. Ibid, count of victories

Chapter 7 – Night Defender and Intruder

1, 2. Martin Middlebrook and Chris Everitt, *The Bomber Command War Diaries*, 1985, Viking Books
3. Ian White, *AI Radar and the British Night-Fighter*, Pen and Sword 2007, p117
4. Jeremy Howard-Williams *Night Intruder, A Personal Account*, Sapere Books, p24
5. Ibid, p37
6. Ibid, p39
7. Ian White, *AI Radar and the British Night-Fighter*, Pen and Sword 2007, p147-149
8. John Foreman, *RAF Fighter Command Air Combat Claims*, part 2 (1941-43), count of victories
9. Ian White, *AI Radar and the British Night-Fighter*, Pen and Sword 2007, p113
10. Jeremy Howard-Williams *Night Intruder, A Personal Account*, Sapere Books, p61/62
11. Ian White, *AI Radar and the British Night-Fighter*, Pen and Sword 2007, p117
12. A.C. Grayling, *Among the Dead Cities: Was the Bombing of Civilians a Necessity or a Crime,* Bloomsbury, p50-52
13, 14, 15, Ian White, *AI Radar and the British Night-Fighter*, Pen and Sword 2007, p119-120
16. Bill Gunston, *Combat Aircraft of World War 2,* Salamander, 1979, p26-28
17. NAO Air 27 1791/22
18, 19, Ian White, *AI Radar and the British Night-Fighter*, Pen and Sword 2007, p119-120
20. H.L. de Zeng, D.G. Stankey, E.J. Creek, *Bomber Units of the Luftwaffe, 1933-45,* volume 1, p24
21, 22, Ian White, *AI Radar and the British Night-Fighter*, Pen and Sword 2007, p182
23. Martin Middlebrook and Chris Everitt, *The Bomber Command War Diaries*, 1985, Viking Books p272, 281
24. Ibid, p123, 172

25. Peter Hinchliffe, *The Other Battle: Luftwaffe Night Aces versus Bomber Command,* Castle Books, 2001, p69
26. Martin Middlebrook and Chris Everitt, *The Bomber Command War Diaries,* 1985, Viking Books p219
27. Williams / Shore, *Aces High,* Grub Street 1992, p382-383
28. Mark Huxtable, *Mosquito claims for enemy aircraft,* Mossie.org website
29. Howard-Williams, p79
30. Norman Franks, *RAF Fighter Command Losses Volume 1, 1939-41,* 2nd edition, Midland Publishing 2008, p47
31. Jon 'Bob' Braham, *Scramble,* 1961, Frederick Muller Ltd, recent edition Greenhill Books, p136
32. Ibid, p142-143
33. Ibid, p146-147
34. John Spooner, *Nightfighter Ace*, Sutton Books 1997
35. Middlebrook and Everitt, *John Foreman Fighter Command Air Combat Claims Part 3, 1943-45*, p487-488
36. Martin Middlebrook and Chris Everitt, *The Bomber Command War Diaries,* 1985, Viking Books p409 and p445
37. Martin Middlebrook and Chris Everitt, *The Bomber Command War Diaries,* 1985, Viking Books p716-783 Squadron records

Chapter 8 – Il Flagello di Dio

1, 2. Christopher Shores, Giovanni Massimello and Russell Guest, *A History of the Air War in the Mediterranean, 1940-1945, Volume Two: North African Desert* (2012), Grub Street, p459-468
3. Roy Conyers Nesbit, *Armed Rovers,* Pen and Sword Books, p12
4. Patrick Gibbs, *Torpedo Leader* (2002), Grub Street, p74-78
5. Ibid, p65
6. Ibid, p58
7. NAO Air 27 1577/19
8. Christopher Shores, Giovanni Massimello and Russell Guest, *A History of the Air War in the Mediterranean, 1940-1945, Volume Two: North African Desert* (2012), Grub Street, p473
9, 10. NAO Air 27 1577/21
11. Christopher Shores, Giovanni Massimello and Russell Guest, *A History of the Air War in the Mediterranean, 1940-1945, Volume Two: North African Desert* (2012), Grub Street, p513
12. Ibid, p531
13. Patrick Gibbs, *Torpedo Leader* (2002), Grub Street, p161-162
14. Ibid, p252
15. Ibid, p257

16. Christopher Shores, Giovanni Massimello and Russell Guest, *A History of the Air War in the Mediterranean, 1940-1945, Volume Two: North African Desert* (2012), Grub Street, p1288
17. Patrick Gibbs, *Torpedo Leader* (2002), Grub Street, p263
18. Ibid, p265
19. Ibid, p267
20. Ibid, p271-273
21. James Holland, *Fortress Malta, an Island under Siege*, Orion, 2003, p315-139
22. Christopher Shores, Brian Cull, Nicola Maliza, *Malta: The Spitfire Year 1942*, Grub Street, 1991, p456
23. Max Hastings, *Operation Pedestal*, William Collins, p29
24. Shores, Cull, Maliza, p474
25. Max Hastings, *Operation Pedestal*, William Collins, p183
26. Ibid, p186-187
27. Christopher Shores, Brian Cull, Nicola Maliza, *Malta: The Spitfire Year 1942*, Grub Street, 1991, p494
28. Ibid, p493
29. Ibid, p495

30, 31. NAO Air 27, 1496/39

32. Max Hastings, *Operation Pedestal*, William Collins, p268-269
33. Roy Conyers Nesbit, *Armed Rovers,* Pen and Sword Books, p82

34, 35. Ibid, p84-85

36. Ibid, p86-89
37. Ian Playfair, F.C. Flynn, C.J.C. Molony and T.P. Gleave (2004) *The Mediterranean and Middle East: British Fortunes reach their Lowest Ebb (September 1941 to September 1942).* History of the Second World War United Kingdom Military Series. Vol. III (Uckfield 2004)
38. Christopher Shores, Giovanni Massimello and Russell Guest, *A History of the Air War in the Mediterranean, 1940-1945, Volume Two: North African Desert* (2012), Grub Street, p1321
39. Roy Conyers Nesbit, *Armed Rovers,* Pen and Sword Books, p89
40. Christopher Shores, Giovanni Massimello and Russell Guest, *A History of the Air War in the Mediterranean, 1940-1945, Volume Two: North African Desert* (2012), Grub Street, p1333
41. Clive Williams and Christopher Shores, *Aces High*, Grub Street 1994, p515
42. Roy Conyers Nesbit, *Armed Rovers,* Pen and Sword Books, p93
43. Roy Conyers Nesbit, *Armed Rovers,* Pen and Sword Books, p137-151
44. Roy Conyers Nesbit, *Armed Rovers,* Pen and Sword Books, p151

Chapter 9 – Aussie Battler

1, 2. George Turnbull Dick, *Beaufighters over New Guinea, 30 Squadron RAAF 1942-43*, Royal Australian Air Force Museum 1993, p6

3. Ibid, p8
4. Ibid, p9
5. Stephen Eather, *Flying Squadrons of the Australian Defence Force,* Aerospace Publications 1995
6. George Turnbull Dick, *Beaufighters over New Guinea, 30 Squadron RAAF 1942-43,* Royal Australian Air Force Museum 1993, p15-16
7. Doug Gillison, *Official Histories – Volume 1* Royal Australian Air Force 1939-42, Australian War Memorial, 1962, chapter 29, p616
8. George Turnbull Dick, *Beaufighters over New Guinea, 30 Squadron RAAF 1942-43,* Royal Australian Air Force Museum 1993, p22-23
9. Peter Fitzsimons, *Kokoda*, Hodder Australia 2004, p389
10. Ibid, p395
11. Ibid, p364
12. Karl James, *The Track*, Australian War Memorial 2009
13. Jay A. Stout, *Savage Sky, Emerald Hell: The U.S, Australia, Japan and the Ferocious Air Battle over New Guinea*
14. George Turnbull Dick, *Beaufighters over New Guinea, 30 Squadron RAAF 1942-43,* Royal Australian Air Force Museum 1993, p34
15. George C. Kenney, *The Saga of Pappy Gunn*, Duell, Sloan, Pearce 1959, p31-36
16. George Turnbull Dick, *Beaufighters over New Guinea, 30 Squadron RAAF 1942-43,* Royal Australian Air Force Museum 1993, p23
17. Doug Gillison, *Official Histories – Volume 1* Royal Australian Air Force 1939-42, Australian War Memorial, 1962, chapter 30, p631

18, 19. George Turnbull Dick, *Beaufighters over New Guinea, 30 Squadron RAAF 1942-43,* Royal Australian Air Force Museum 1993, p24

20. Ibid, p38
21. Peter Fitzsimons, *Kokoda*, Hodder Australia 2004, p395-398
22. George Turnbull Dick, *Beaufighters over New Guinea, 30 Squadron RAAF 1942-43,* Royal Australian Air Force Museum 1993, p32
23. Ibid, p35
24. Ibid, p51
25. Ibid, p32
26. Peter Fitzsimons, *Kokoda*, Hodder Australia 2004, p364
27. George Turnbull Dick, *Beaufighters over New Guinea, 30 Squadron RAAF 1942-43,* Royal Australian Air Force Museum 1993, p51-52, quotation from Australian *Sun* newspaper
28. Ibid, p57
29. Peter Fitzsimons, *Kokoda*, Hodder Australia 2004, p365
30. George Turnbull Dick, *Beaufighters over New Guinea, 30 Squadron RAAF 1942-43,* Royal Australian Air Force Museum 1993, p109
31. Ibid, p82-83
32. Ibid, p84-85

33. Garrett Middlebrook, *Air Combat at 20 feet*, Authorhouse 2004
34. Official Histories, volume 1, chapter 32, p696
35. Gregory C. Gilbert, *Battle of the Bismarck Sea*, Air Power Development Centre, 2013, p65
36. Graham Pitchfork, *Beaufighter Boys*, Grub Street 1992, p194
37. Archive record sourced by Jim Turner, 30 RAAF Association archivist and author.
38. Steve Eather, *Flying Squadrons of the Australian Defence Force*, Aerospace Publications 1995, p66
39, 40. Doug Gillison, *Official Histories – Volume 1* Royal Australian Air Force 1939-42, Australian War Memorial, 1962, chapter 30, p648-653
41. ADF Serials website, *Australian and New Zealand Military aircraft serials and history*, Beaufighter A19, aircraft A19-29, A19-45, A19-58
42. Quotation sourced by Jim Turner, archivist for 30 Squadron Association
42. ADF Serials website, aircraft A19-40; Shores and Williams *Aces High*, Grub Street 1994, p293
43. Stephen Eather, *Flying Squadrons of the Australian Defence Force,* Aerospace Publications 1995, p66-67
44. Beaufighter DAP A8 count
45. Ibid, Beaufighter DAP A8, aircraft A8-85
46. Ibid, Beaufighter DAP A8 and A19 listing

Chapter 10 – The Bloody Flax

1. Christopher Shores, Giovanni Massimello and Russell Guest, *A History of the Air War in the Mediterranean, 1940-1945, Volume Two: North African Desert* (2012), Grub Street, p477
2. Ibid, p487
3. Ibid, p488
4. Robert Forsyth, *To Save an Army*, Osprey 2022, p32-38
5. Ibid, p40
6. Fritz Morzik, German Air Force Air Lift Operations, p146-183
7. Forsyth, p41
8, 9. Fritz Morzik, German Air Force Air Lift Operations, p121-145
10. Christopher Shores, Giovanni Massimello and Russell Guest, *A History of the Air War in the Mediterranean, 1940-1945, Volume One: North Africa*, p774 (E-book)
11. Ibid, p948
12. Ibid, p950
13. Ibid, p959
14. Fritz Morzik, German Air Force Air Lift Operations, p121-145
15. Murray Williamson, *Strategy for Defeat: The Luftwaffe 1933-45*, Quantum, 2001, p242 (E-book)

16. Roy Conyers Nesbit, *Armed Rovers*, Pen and Sword, p177-178
17. Murray Williamson, *Strategy for Defeat: The Luftwaffe 1933-45*, Quantum, 2001, p241 (E-book)
18. Shores, Massimello and Guest, *A History of the Air War in the Mediterranean, 1940-1945, Volume One: North Africa*, p94 (E-book)
19. Fritz Morzik, German Air Force Air Lift Operations, p121-145
20. NAO Air 27 1577/35
21. Ibid
22. Ibid
23. Roy Conyers Nesbit, *The Armed Rovers, Pen and Sword*, p161 (E-book)
24. NAO Air 27 1577/35
25. Christopher Shores and Clive Williams, *Aces High*, Grub Street 1994, p156
26. Shores, Masimello and Guest, p323-325
27. Shores and Williams, Aces High, Grub Street 1992, p535-536
28. Roy Conyers Nesbit, *Armed Rovers*, Pen and Sword, p169-170
29. Murray Williamson, *Strategy for Defeat: The Luftwaffe 1933-45*, Quantum, 2001, p241 (E-book)
30. Robert Forsyth, *To Save and Army*, Osprey 2022, p106-112
31. Murray Williamson, *Strategy for Defeat: The Luftwaffe 1933-45*, Quantum, 2001, p227-228 (E-book)
32. Robert Forsyth, *To Save and Army*, Osprey 2022, p115-116
33. Ibid, p118-122
34. Ibid, p140-141

35, 36. Morzik, p184-200

37. Shores, Masimello and Guest, p631-635
38. Roy Conyers Nesbit, *Armed Rovers*, Pen and Sword, p194-195
39. Roy Conyers Nesbit, *Armed Rovers*, Pen and Sword, p197
40. Shores, Massimello, Guest, Olynyk and Bock, *A History of the Air War in the Mediterranean, 1940-1945, Volume 3: North Africa*, Grub Street, 2016, p1149-1159 (E-book).
41. Ibid, p1207-1218

Chapter 11 – Mud, Gubbins and Glory

1. Alfred Lammer, NAO Air 27 1521-20 (255 Squadron appendices)
2. Shores, Massimello, Guest, Olynyk and Bock, *A History of the Air War in the Mediterranean, 1940-1945, Volume 3: North Africa*, Grub Street, 2016, p1149-1159 (E-book)
3. NAO Air 27 1518-14
4. Battle of Britain Monument website, *The Airmen's Story: Alfred Lammer*

5, 6. NAO Air 27 1518/43

7. Bobby Oxspring, *Spitfire Commander*, Kimber 1984, p131-132

8, 9, 10. NAO Air 27 1521/20 (Lammer's Squadron diary)

11. NAO Air 27 1518/43
12. Shores, Massimello, Guest, Olynyk and Bock, *A History of the Air War in the Mediterranean, 1940-1945, Volume 3: North Africa*, Grub Street, 2016, p1149-1159 (E-book), Count of recorded victories
13. Alfred Lammer, NAO Air 27 1521/20
14. Shores, Massimello, Guest, Olynyk and Bock, *A History of the Air War in the Mediterranean, 1940-1945, Volume 3: North Africa*, Grub Street, 2016, p343 (E-book)
15. NAO Air 27 1518/45
16. Alfred Lammer, NAO Air 27 1521/20
17. NAO Air 29/76/4
18, 19. Alfred Lammer, NAO Air 27 1521/20
20. NAO Air 27 1518/45
21. Shores, Massimello, Guest, Olynyk and Bock, *A History of the Air War in the Mediterranean, 1940-1945, Volume 3: North Africa*, Grub Street, 2016, p503 (E-book)
22. Alfred Lammer, NAO Air 27 1521/20
23. Christopher Shores and Clive Williams, *Aces High*, Grub Street 1994, p156
24. Ibid, p342
25. NAO Air 27 1027-29
26. Shores, Massimello, Guest, Olynyk and Bock, *A History of the Air War in the Mediterranean, 1940-1945, Volume 3: North Africa*, Grub Street, 2016, p1149-1159 (E-book), count of recorded victories
27. *Daily Telegraph* Obituary, Wing Commander Douggie Oxby, DSO, DFC, DFM 12.4.2009
28. NAO Air 27 2061-18
29. Shores, Massimello, Guest, Olynyk and Bock, *A History of the Air War in the Mediterranean, 1940-1945, Volume 3: North Africa*, Grub Street, 2016, p1283-85 (E-book)
30. Shores, Massimello, Guest, Olynyk and Bock, *A History of the Air War in the Mediterranean, 1940-1945, Volume 3: North Africa*, Grub Street, 2016, p1314-5 (E-book)

Chapter 12 – Beaufighter Trauma

1, 2. Chris Goss, *Bloody Biscay*, Crecy Publishing, 1997, p37
3. John Terraine, *The Right Side of the Line*, Hodder & Stoughton, 1985, p409
4. Chris Goss, *Bloody Biscay*, Crecy Publishing, 1997, p29-30
5. U-boat.net website, U-boat.net/fates/losses/1942 (and 1943)
6. Chris Goss, *Bloody Biscay*, Crecy Publishing, 1997, p30
7. Ibid, p26
8. Ibid, p35
9. Ibid, p245

10. NAO Air 27 1496/48
11. Aces Safarik website, www.aces.safarikovi.victories-germany-ww2-claims-beaufighter
12. NAO Air 27 1496/49
13. Chris Goss, *Bloody Biscay*, Crecy Publishing, 1997, p51
14. Jon 'Bob' Braham, Scramble, *The Memoir of Britain's Most Decorated Fighter Pilot*, 1961, Frederick Muller Ltd, recent edition Greenhill Books, p121
15. Chris Goss, *Bloody Biscay*, Crecy Publishing, 1997, p94
16. Leo McKinstry, *Cinderella Boys*, John Murray, 2023, p191
17. NAO Air 27 1496/32 and 34
18. U-boat.net/maps/Biscay.htm
19. Chris Goss, *Bloody Biscay*, Crecy Publishing, 1997, p238-239
20. Ibid, p74-75
21. Ibid, p110
22. U-boat.net/fates/losses/1943
23. Chris Goss, *Bloody Biscay*, Crecy Publishing, 1997, p238-239
24. Ibid, p145
25. Numbers triangulated from various sources, including Goss and NAO Air 27 papers
26. Christopher Shores and Clive Williams, *Aces High vol 1*, Grub Street 1994, p168 and 351

Chapter 13 – Whispering Death

1. Bryn Evans, *Air Battle for Burma*, Pen and Sword 2016, p84
2. *Second World War People's War*, BBC online (archived), account of Mrs Katyan Randhawa, 15 October 2014
3. Bryn Evans, *Air Battle for Burma*, Pen and Sword 2016, p84
4. Christopher Shores, *Air War for Burma*, Grub Street 2005, p92 (E-book)
5. NAO Air 27 1112-1
6. Bryn Evans, *Air Battle for Burma*, Pen and Sword 2016, p84-85
7. Christopher Shores, *Air War for Burma*, Grub Street 2005, p109
8. NAO Air 27 326-2
9. NAO Air 27 326-6
10. Graham Pitchfork, *Beaufighter Boys*, Grub Street 2019, p181
11. NAO Air 27 326-9
12. NAO Air 27 326-6
13. Christopher Shores, *Air War for Burma*, Grub Street 2005, p159
14. Ibid, p212
15. Atholl Sutherland Brown, *Silently into the Midst of Things*, Trafford Publishing 2001, p84-85
16. Christopher Shores, *Air War for Burma*, Grub Street 2005, p271-274
17. Christopher Shores, Clive Williams, *Aces High*, Grub Street 1992, p441

18, 19. NAO Air 27 1117-8
20. NAO Air 27 1117-14
21. Graham Pitchfork, *Beaufighter Boys*, Grub Street 2019, p184
22. www.211 Squadron.org/Bristol_beaufighter website
23. Graham Pitchfork, *Beaufighter Boys*, Grub Street 2019, p182
24. Ibid, p184.
25. Christopher Shores, *Air War for Burma*, Grub Street 2005, p254
26. Graham Pitchfork, *Beaufighter Boys*, Grub Street 2019, p165
27, 28. Robert Lyman, *A War of Empires*, Osprey 2021, p289-290
29. Ibid, p424
30. Atholl Sutherland Brown, *Silently into the Midst of Things*, Trafford Publishing 2001, p144-145
31. Christopher Shores, *Air War for Burma*, Grub Street 2005, p631-632
32. NAO Air 27 1303-35
33. Christopher Shores, *Air War for Burma*, Grub Street 2005, p743
34. Atholl Sutherland Brown, *Silently into the Midst of Things*, Trafford Publishing 2001, p205-206
35. www.211 Squadron.org/Bristol beaufighter website
36. Christopher Shores, *Air War for Burma*, Grub Street 2005, p683

Chapter 14 – Nightfighter Paradise

1. Graham Pitchfork, *Beaufighter Boys*, Grub Street 2019, p118-119
2. Shores, Massimello, Guest, Olynyk, Bock and Thomas, *A History of the Air War in the Mediterranean, 1940-1945, Volume 4: Sicily and Italy*, Grub Street, 2016, p70-118 (E-book). Count of recorded victories
3. Graham Pitchfork, *Beaufighter Boys*, Grub Street 2019, p115
4. NAO Air 27 1027-41
5. Shores, Massimello, Guest, Olynyk, Bock and Thomas, *A History of the Air War in the Mediterranean, 1940-1945, Volume 4: Sicily and Italy*, Grub Street, 2016, p192 (E-book).
6. RAF Boulmer website, www.raf.mod.uk/our-organisation/stations/raf-boulmer/news/1943-expeditionary-radar-surveillance-and-control-in-the-invasion-of-sicily
7. Shores, Massimello, Guest, Olynyk, Bock and Thomas, *A History of the Air War in the Mediterranean, 1940-1945, Volume 4: Sicily and Italy*, Grub Street, 2016, p363-5 (E-book)
8. Ibid, p378-380
9. Ibid, p434
10. Ibid, p443
11, 12. Graham Pitchfork, *Beaufighter Boys*, Grub Street 2019, p116-117
13. NAO Air 27 1518-59

14. Shores, Massimello, Guest, Olynyk, Bock and Thomas, *A History of the Air War in the Mediterranean, 1940-1945, Volume 4: Sicily and Italy*, Grub Street, 2016, p538-9 (E-book)
15. NAO Air 27 850-10
16. Shores, Massimello, Guest, Olynyk, Bock and Thomas, *A History of the Air War in the Mediterranean, 1940-1945, Volume 4: Sicily and Italy*, Grub Street, 2016, p577-8 (E-book)
17. Ibid, Count of Victories p253-569
18. Shoresl, Massimello, Guest, Olynyk, Bock and Thomas, *A History of the Air War in the Mediterranean, 1940-1945, Volume 4: Sicily and Italy*, Grub Street, 2016, p168 and 351 (E-book)

Chapter 15 – Strike wings

1,2,3. Roy Conyers Nesbit, *The Strike Wings*, Pen and Sword, new edition 2012, p31-39
4, 5. Ibid, p40-41
6. Ibid, p17
7. Andrew D. Bird, *A Separate Little War*, Grub Street, 2008, p11-12
8. Ibid, p11
9. Ibid, p9
10. Roy Conyers Nesbit, *The Strike Wings*, Pen and Sword, new edition 2012, p45-51
11, 12. Ibid, p57-58
13. Ibid, p63-64
14. Leo McKinstry, *Cinderella Boys*, John Murray, 2023, p191
15. Roy Conyers Nesbit, *The Strike Wings*, Pen and Sword, new edition 2012, p61-63
16. Leo McKinstry, *Cinderella Boys*, John Murray, 2023, p203
17. Ibid, p210-211
18. NAO Air 27 1786/44
19. Roy Conyers Nesbit, *The Strike Wings*, Pen and Sword, new edition 2012, p106-114
20. Ibid, p119-120
21. Ibid, p121-125
22. Ibid, p125 128
23. Ibid, p176-177
24. Ibid, p131-132
25. Ibid, p139-144, also Appendix III
26. Philip Brett quote, Discoursesonwargaming.blogspot.com/2018 (website) More on 144 Squadron
27. Andrew D. Bird, *A Separate Little War*, Grub Street, 2008, p16
28. Christopher Shores and Clive Williams, *Aces High vol 1*, Grub Street 1992, p93

29. Roy Conyers Nesbit, *The Strike Wings*, Pen and Sword, new edition 2012, p208-210
30. Ibid, Appendix III
31. Andrew D. Bird, *A Separate Little War*, Grub Street, 2008, p135
32, 33, 34. Roy Conyers Nesbit, *The Strike Wings*, Pen and Sword, new edition 2012, p217-235
35. Andrew D. Bird, *A Separate Little War*, Grub Street, 2008, p140-148
36. Ibid, p140-148
37. Roy Conyers Nesbit, *The Strike Wings*, Pen and Sword, new edition 2012, p244-245
38. Ibid, Appendix III (counting shipping losses and tonnage)
39. Ibid, p246

Chapter 16 – The Gates of Hell

1. Graham Pitchfork, *Beaufighter Boys*, Grub Street 1992, p145, quoting Harold Yorke
2. Roy Conyers Nesbit, *Armed Rovers*, Pen and Sword 2012 (E-book), p224
3. Christopher Shores and Clive Williams, *Aces High vol 1*, Grub Street 1992, p417
4, 5. NAO Air 27 1409-16
6, 7. Roy Conyers Nesbit, *Armed Rovers*, Pen and Sword 2012 (E-book), p223-228, count of losses
8. Ibid, p230
9. NAO Air 27 1508-47
10. NAO Air 27 1409-26
11. Roy Conyers Nesbit, *Armed Rovers*, Pen and Sword 2012 (E-book), p239
12. Ibid, p238
13. Leo McKinstry, *The Cinderella Boys*, John Murray 2023, p214
14, 15. Roy Conyers Nesbit, *Armed Rovers*, Pen and Sword 2012 (E-book), p 244-245
16. Ibid, p249
17. Ibid, p250-252
18. Ibid, p228-251, count of losses
19. NAO Air 27 464-32
20. Roy Conyers Nesbit, *Armed Rovers*, Pen and Sword 2012 (E-book), p265-266
21. Christopher Shores and Clive Williams, *Aces High vol 1*, Grub Street 1992, p156
22. Roy Conyers Nesbit, *Armed Rovers*, Pen and Sword 2012 (E-book), p266-267
23. Ibid, p268-269
24. Ibid, p270-272
25. Ibid, p272-273
26. Ibid, p276-277
27. Graham Pitchfork, *Beaufighter Boys*, Grub Street 1992, p148-151
28. NAO Air 27 461/18

29. Roy Conyers Nesbit, *Armed Rovers*, Pen and Sword 2012 (E-book), p279
30. Analysis based on various NAO Air 27 documents / Conyers Nesbit

Chapter 17 – Italian Denouement

1. Shores, Massimello, Guest, Olynyk, Bock and Thomas, *A History of the Air War in the Mediterranean, 1940-1945, Volume 4: Sicily and Italy*, Grub Street, 2016, p715 (E-book)
2. Ibid, p709-714
3, 4. www.raf.mod.uk/history/144 squadron (archived website)
5. Roy Conyers Nesbit, *Armed Rovers*, Pen and Sword 2012, p199
6, 7. Graham Pitchfork, *Beaufighter Boys*, Grub Street 1992, p110-114
8, 9. Shores, Massimello, Guest, Olynyk, Bock and Thomas, *A History of the Air War in the Mediterranean, 1940-1945, Volume 4: Sicily and Italy*, Grub Street, 2016, p776-7 (E-book)
10. Graham Pitchfork, *Beaufighter Boys*, Grub Street 1992, p124-125
11. Shores, Massimello, Guest, Olynyk, Bock and Thomas, *A History of the Air War in the Mediterranean, 1940-1945, Volume 4: Sicily and Italy*, Grub Street, 2016, p780-84 (E-book)
12, 13. Ibid, p694-695
14. NAO Air 2061-28
15. Shores, Massimello, Guest, Olynyk, Bock and Thomas, *A History of the Air War in the Mediterranean, 1940-1945, Volume 4: Sicily and Italy*, Grub Street, 2016, p745-61 (E-book)
16. NAO Air 27 1027-49
17. Shores, Massimello, Guest, Olynyk, Bock and Thomas, *A History of the Air War in the Mediterranean, 1940-1945, Volume 4: Sicily and Italy*, Grub Street, 2016, p884-8 (E-book)
18. Caitlin McHugh, *Unravelling the Secret of HMT Rohne*, Ezra's Archives, Cornell Historical Society 2011, p55-67
19. Shores, Massimello, Guest, Olynyk, Bock and Thomas, *A History of the Air War in the Mediterranean, 1940-1945, Volume 4: Sicily and Italy*, Grub Street, 2016, p772-897, (E-book), count of victories
20. James Holland, (2023), *The Savage Storm: The Battle for Italy 1943*, Bantam 2013, pp. 273, 310
21. US Naval Institute website, www.usni.org/magazines/proceedings/1967/september/bari-incident
22, 24. NAO Air 27 1518-70
23, 25. NAO Air 27 2061-34
26. Shores, Massimello, Guest, Olynyk, Bock and Thomas, *A History of the Air War in the Mediterranean, 1940-1945, Volume 4: Sicily and Italy*, Grub Street, 2016, p991-1021 (E-book)

27. NAO Air 27 2062-16
28. NAO Air 27 1519-02
29. Roy Conyers Nesbit, Armed Rovers, Pen and Sword 2012, p280
30. Christopher Shores and Clive Williams, *Aces High vol 1*, Grub Street 1992, p53 and p72
31. NAO Air 27 1519-02

Epilogue

1. C.J.M. Goulter, Air Power and Future Battlespace, *Aeronautical Journal*, vol 113, issue 1139, Jan 2009
2. C.H. Barnes, *Bristol Aircraft since 1910*, Putnam (1st edition 1964).
3. BAE Systems website, baesystems.com/en-uk/locations/Filton
4. See statistics, Appendices 1 to 4.

Index

Admin Box (Battle), 165
Advanced Air Striking Force, 21
Afrika Korps, 45, 48, 86
Agedabia (airfield, Libya), 55
Airborne Intercept radar (AI), 23–4
  AI Mark III, 24, 26
  AI Mark IV, 26, 59, 65, 70, 79, 138
  AI Mark VII, 71, 137–8
  AI Mark VIII, 71, 171
Air Gap, 146
Air Ministry, 7, 43, 61
Air Ministry spec F11/37, 11
Air Ministry spec F17/39, 15
Air Ministry spec F37/35, 11
Aitcherley, Flight Sergeant, 115
Aitken, Max, 186
Alam Halfa (Battle), 99
Albert Canal (Belgium), 21
Alexander, A.V., 36
Alexandria (port, Egypt), 59, 63
Allen, John Watson, 171
Allen, Maurice, 172
A.L.63 (anti-louse powder), 140
Antimachia (airfield, Dodeconnese), 193
Anzac strike wing, 181
Arab Revolt (Mandatory Palestine), 49
Arado Ar196, 147, 195, 197
Arakan (region, Burma), 159, 165
Argatala (airfield, India), 158
Ark Royal, HMS, 48
Armada Road (airfield, India), 157
Armidale, HMAS, 116
Armstrong-Whitworth FK-8, 4
  Whitley, 145–7
Ashfield, Glyn, 25
Australian Air Board, 102
Austri (Norwegian ferry), 188
Avro Anson, 36
Avro Lancaster, 19
Avro Manchester, 19, 69
Axum (Italian submarine), 97
Bader, Douglas, 6
Baedeker (Guide and bombing campaign), 73
Baldwin, Philip, 162
Ballyherbert (airfield, Northern Ireland), 142
Banff strike wing (Scotland), 186, 188–9
Barham, HMS, 48
Bari (air raid), 208–10
Barnett, Eric 'Basher', 116
Barnwell, David, 60
Barnwell, Frank, 3, 10–12, 60–1, 213
Barnwell, John, 25
Barnwell, Marjorie, 60
Bartlett, Maurice, 51, 53, 55–6
Bateman, Mark, 151
Bay of Biscay, 38, 145–50, 181
'Beaufort Fighter' 12–13, 15, 102
Becker, Ludwig, 77
Beer bottles (flak suppression technique), 92
Bell P-39 Airacobra, 207
Benghazi (port, Libya), 99
Benn, Michael Wedgewood, 170
Benn, R.J., 145
Bergamini, Carlos, 201
Bircham Newton, 36, 46
Birmingham (raid on), 75
Bismarck Sea (battle), 111–14
Bizerte (port, Tunisia), 126
Blackett, Patrick, 146
'Black Friday', 187–8
Blamey, Thomas, 109–10
Blohm und Voss Bv138, 181
Blohm und Voss Bv222, 126, 128–9
BMW 801 (engine), 74, 126
Boeing 247, 8
  B-17 Fortress, 131, 138
  B-29 Superfortress, 168
'Bomb Alley', 90, 95
Bomberai Peninsula (New Guinea), 114

Bone (port, Algeria), 138, 143
Bonifacio, Strait of (Corsica and Sardinia), 201
Bordeaux (airfield, France), 207
Borgo (airfield, Corsica), 211
Borneo, 119
Bougie (Béjaïa), Gulf of, 207
Boulton Paul Defiant, 25–6, 29, 32, 71, 79, 135, 141–2
Bounevialle, Cas de, 129
Bowen, Taffy, 24, 74
Braham, Jon 'Bob', 25, 29–31, 71, 214
Brest (port, France), 146, 182
Brett, Philip, 184–5
Bristol Aeroplane Company, 1, 213
Bristol Aquila (engine), 9
Boxkite, 3
F2B 'Fighter', 4–5
Jupiter (engine), 6
Beaufort (Type 152), 10, 16, 36, 42, 85–6, 89, 91–2, 98–9, 103–104, 132
Beaufighter (Type 156), 12, 15, 36
Mark IC, 37–43, 103, 155
Mark IF, 19, 59
Mark IIF, 19, 74, 135, 142
Mark V, 20
Mark VI, 19, 71, 100, 126–7, 155
Mark X, 19
Mark XI, 177
DAP Mark 21, 118–20
Bisley, 100
Blenheim (type 142M), 8, 21, 24–5, 36–8, 47–8, 52, 128, 157
Bludgeon (aka Bagshot), 6
Brabazon, 213
Brigand, 213
Britain First (Type 142), 8
Britannia, 214
Bulldog, 6
Centaurus (engine), 213
Filton (factory), 10, 37
Hercules (engine), 12–13, 15
Mercury (engine), 9
Pegasus (engine), 123
Scout, 3–4
Taurus (engine), 10, 85
Type 135, 8
British and Colonial Aeroplane Company, 2
British Fourteenth Army, 161–2
Brown, John, 138, 172
Brunel, Isambard Kingdom, 1
Bu Amud (airfield, Libya), 85, 171
Buchanan, John, 128–9, 132, 196
Budd, Graham, 31, 72
Buna, 107–108, 111
Burney, Dennistoun, 3
Burwell, Robin, 184
Butler, Roy, 199
Butterworth (airfield, Malaya), 157

Cairo (city), 59, 65, 86, 121
Cairo 'wastage pool', 87
Cairo, HMS, 97
Calcutta (raid), 154
Calgiari, 143
Campbell, Gillian Lorne 'Punch', 56
CANT Z1007, 49, 60, 65, 67, 172
CANT Z506, 128
Cape Pisarro (landing beach, Sicilly), 172
Cap Serrat (GCI station, Tunisia), 143-4
Cartridge, David, 39-40, 149, 153
Cassibile (airfield, Sicilly), 173
Catania (town, Sicilly), 169
Cat's Eye Fighters, 24–5, 31–3, 60
Cavity magnetron, 71, 79
Centimetric AI, 71, 79
Chadburn, Paul, 164
Chain Home (CH) radar stations, 23, 26
Chamberlain, Neville, 9, 11
Champs Elysee (raid), 44
Chandra Bose, Subhas, 155
Channel Dash, 41–2
Charinga (Burma), 167
Charybdis, HMS, 98
Chindits, 158, 165
Chindwin (river, Burma), 158, 161
Chin Hills (Burma), 159, 162
Chippendale, Malcolm 'Chips', 165
Chisholm, Rory, 27, 72, 83
Chivenor (airfield, Devon), 37, 147
Chocolate soldiers ('chockos'), 102, 105
'Churchill rations', 166
Churchill, Winston, 192
Clark, Francis B., 308

Clegg, Charles, 155, 164
Coate, Ern, 128
Colerne (airfield, Wiltshire), 59
Collishaw, Raymond, 48–9
Cologne (raid), 76–7
Colt-Browning 7.7mm machine guns, 20, 25
Coltishall (airfield, Norfolk), 177
Commonwealth Wirraway, 103, 106
Conder, Charles, 44
Coningham, Arthur 'Mary', 49, 208
Consolidated B24 Liberator, 87, 146, 150, 161–2
Control reversal, 6
Convoy HG53, 35
Convoy KMF26, 207
Convoy MW4, 90
Convoy MW11, 90
Convoy PQ18, 202
Coomalie Creek (airfield, Australia), 114
Coral Sea (Battle), 104
Cos (island, Dodeconnese), 192–3
Cosmos engines, 5
Coventry (raid), 27, 69
Coventry, HMS, 90
Cowper, Robert, 172
Cox, Neil, 204–205
Crawford, Hector 'Heck', 55, 88
Crete, 45, 47, 121, 123, 196
Crew, Edward, 29, 72
Crombie, Charles, 67, 156
Cunningham, John, 27, 29, 71–3, 214
Curtiss P-40 'Tomahawk, 56, 87, 102, 107, 121, 132

D-Day, 182–3
Dallachy strike wing (Scotland), 186–7, 189
Daniel, Edward, 62
Darwin (raid), 102, 116
Davidstow Moor (Cornwall), 183
Davison, Michael, 172, 175
Dawson, Grahame, 53
Decimomannu (Sardinian airfield), 95
de Havilland company, 7, 28
de Havilland, Geoffrey, 28
de Havilland Mosquito, 17, 75–6, 83, 167
  Mark NFII, 83
  Mark FBVI, 150, 186
  Mark XII, 171
  Mark XVIII 'Tsetse', 186
Demyansk (Soviet encirclement), 122–3, 129
Department of Aircraft Production (DAP), 118–19
Derna (airfield), 91, 121
Dick, George Turnbull, 114
Dingli Cliffs (Malta), 60
Distinguished Flying Cross, 56, 63
Distinguished Flying Medal, 56
Distinguished Service Order, 56, 100
Dixon, Lawrence, 141, 169
Djidelli (port, Algeria), 169
Dobodura (airstrip), 114
Dodeconnese campaign, 191–5
Dohazari (airfield, India), 159–60
Donitz, Karl, 151–2
Dornier Do17, 24–5, 31, 85
  Do24, 127, 199, 203
  Do217, 74, 153
  Do217K, 201–202, 206–207
Douglas, Sholto, 24, 32, 59, 73, 185, 193–4
Douglas A-20 Havoc (aka Boston), 29, 54, 72–3, 106–107, 112–13
  A-24 'Banshee', 106
  DC-1, 8
  DC-3, 151
Douhet, Guilio, 7, 154
Dowding, Lord Hugh 'Stuffy', 13, 23–4
Downing, Alwyn, 143–4, 206
Drem (airfield, Scotland), 186
'Drem system', 186
Dum Dum (airfield, India), 155
Düppel, 209
Dyce (airfield, Scotland), 36

E-boats, 97, 183–4
Edku (airfield, Egypt), 51, 53, 191
Edwards, Don, 167
Edwards, Henry, 64–5
El Alamein (Battle), 64, 66, 125
El Aouina (airfield), 127, 130, 144
Ellis, 'Handlebars', 103
Elmas (Sardinian airfield), 95
Embry, Basil, 49, 61
Eora Ridge (New Guinea), 110

Esmonde, Eugene, 42
Etherton, John, 138
Exeter, (raid), 74

Fairey Albacore, 52
Battle, 21
Fulmar, 45, 96
Swordfish, 10, 42, 45
Fedden, Roy, 5, 7–8, 11–12
Fell, L.F.R., 18–19
Ferrini, Renato, 97
Fiat BR20, 60, 62, 65
G50, 96
Fiesler Storch, 52
Filton works, 5, 11, 20
Fighter Interception Unit (FIU), 24–5
Fishermen's Bend (Melbourne), 119
Fleet Air Arm, 86–7, 96
Fletcher, Andrew, 47, 51–2
Focke-Wulf Fw190, 20, 42, 75, 139, 148–9, 152, 178–80, 187
Fw200 Condor, 35, 38, 130, 152
Foggia (airfields, Italy), 208
Fokker E.I. Eindecker, 3
Forrest, George, 56
Foster, Mike, 138
Frank, Hans-Dieter, 82
Fraser, Howard, 177
Fraser, Ian, 47
Free French Group de Chasse, 1–7, 207
Freeman, Wilfred, 13
Fresian Islands (Netherlands), 184
Freya (radar system), 77
Frise, Leslie, 4, 10–12, 43, 213
Fritz X (glider bomb), 201, 206
Froggatt, Pilot Officer, 207
Fumerton, Robert 'Moose', 63, 65

Gadd, Tony, 184, 186
Gambut (airfield, Libya), 190–1, 193
Garland, Donald 'Judy', 21
Gawith, Peter, 78
Gazala Line, 85, 89
Geddes, Keith, 29, 72
Gee (directional beam), 69
Geiger, August, 82
Gibbs, Patrick, 87, 89, 91–9, 101, 112, 125, 177
Gibraltar, 46, 90, 136, 206
Gloster Gladiator, 45
Gneisenau, 41–2, 64
Goebbels, Joseph, 27, 69
Goering, Herman, 33, 129–30, 132
Gona (New Guinea), 111
Gordon, Reginald Lloyd 'Butch', 118
Gottaglie (airfield, Italy), 208
Graham, Ray, 199
Gray-King, John, 172
Great Eastern steamship, 1
Great Western steamship, 1
Greaves, Douglas, 140
Green, Charles 'Paddy', 141, 169, 172–3, 175
Gregory, William 'Sticks', 80
Ground Control Intercept (GCI) stations, 27, 29, 60, 70
Grumman Wildcat, 96
Guedj, Max, 44
Gulf of Bothnia (Finland), 185
Gunn, Paul 'Pappy', 107, 112, 193

Hamburg (raids), 77, 80
Hammond, Derek, 52–3, 55–6
Hammond, Joseph, 5
Handley Page Halifax, 18, 69, 150
Hampden, 40, 69, 181, 202
Harrow, 32
Heyford, 12–13
Harding, Bob, 111
Harkness, Brian, 17
Harris, Arthur 'Bomber', 69
Hawker Hurricane, 25–6, 29, 32, 46–8, 58–60, 64, 72–3, 78, 155
Sea Hurricane, 96
Hurribomber, 161, 166
Hayton, Gil, 61–2
Heinkel He111, 24–5, 31, 40, 47, 67, 130, 138–9, 207
He115, 203
He177, 130, 153, 207–208, 211
He219, 82
Heho (airfield, Burma), 158
Heligoland (port, Germany), 202

Heliopolis (airfield, Egypt), 59, 61
Helmore, William, 72
Henschel Hs126, 52
  Hs293 (remote-control missile), 207
Heraklion (port, Crete), 198
'Hilo' system, 71
Himmelbett (radar stations), 77
Hispano Mark I 20mm cannon, 13, 20, 49
Hispano-Suiza, 20
Hitler, Adolf, 69–70, 73
Hodgkinson, Alan, 26, 72
Hoggarth, John, 88
Holly, 'Spike', 188
Homuth, Gerhard, 54
Honily (airfield, Warwickshire), 136
Horii, Tomito, 106
Horn, Ernest 'Bunny', 158–9
Horne, Angus, 210
Howard-Williams, Jeremy, 19, 28, 71
Howe, Jack, 203–204
Howes, Reg, 196
Howrah (district, India), 154
Hughes, Frederick Desmond 'Des', 141, 169, 173, 175
Hume, Jeffrey, 138
Hunt, Harold, 163

Illustrious, HMS, 45
Imphal (Battle), 166
Indomitable, HMS, 96, 173
Inniss, Aubrey, 149, 153
Interchangeable Power Plant Committee, 18
Irrawaddy (river, Burma), 158, 161
Italia (Italian battleship), 201

JAAF 98th Sentai, 154
JAAF 5th Hikodan, 156
Jagdgeschwader JG2, 148
Jagdgeschwader JG27, 91
Jagdgeschwader JG53, 91
Japanese 15th Army, 161–2, 165
Jeschonnek, Hans, 129
John Harvey, SS (US merchant ship), 208
Johnston, George, 108
Joll, Ian, 29
Joubert de la Ferte, Sir Philip (Head of Coastal Command), 42, 44, 178–9
Junkers Ju52, 47, 52, 54, 99, 121, 123–130, 143, 199, 204–206
  Ju87 (*Stuka*), 49, 52, 65, 90, 98
  Ju88, 24, 31, 46–8, 58, 61–2, 65, 67, 81, 89–90, 95, 141, 169, 170, 172, 174, 195, 199
  Ju88C-6 *Zerstorer*, 145–53, 175
  Ju188, 199
  Ju290, 127, 152

Kampfgeschwader KG40, 35, 207, 210
  V Gruppe, 146–153
KG100, 153, 210
  III Gruppe, 201, 206
Kancharpara (airfield, India), 158
Kawanishi H8K, 157
Kawasaki Ki-45 'Nick' (Toryu), 16, 118
  Ki-48 'Lily', 156
  Ki-61 'Tony', 159
Kelly, Dillon, 135, 140
Kelsey, Howard, 81
Kenney, George, 107
Kentucky, SS, 66
Kesselring, Albert, 32, 59, 61, 66
Kholm (Soviet Union), 122
Kiel (port, Germany), 179
King George V, HMS, 178
Kirkuk (oil fields, Iraq), 50
Klemm KL-35, 78
Kohima (Battle), 166
Kokoda (track, battle), 106–107, 111–112
Kraft, Georg, 82
Kuttelwascher, Karel, 78

Lae (New Guinea), 104, 111, 114
Lakatavia (airfield, Cyprus), 193
LAM (long aerial mines), 26
Lammer, Alfred, 134-5, 138–9, 174
Lander, John, 85
Landmark (GCI controller), 199
Langham (airfield, Norfolk), 182, 184
La Pallice (French U-boat base), 146
La Spezia (port, Italy), 201
Lashio (rail junction, Burma), 165

Lee, Norman, 53
Lee-Evans, Johnny, 194, 203
Leigh Lights, 146
Leigh Mallory, Trafford, 24
Lent, Helmut, 77, 79
Leros (island, Dodeconnese), 193–5
Leuchers (airfield, Scotland), 181
Leverette, William L., 194
LG10 (airfield, Libya), 51, 53, 88
Lichtenstein (AI radar), 77, 80
Lidda (airfield, Mandatory Palestine), 50
Limassol (airfield, Cyprus), 193
Linz, Rudi, 188
Littorio (Italian battleship), 90
Liverpool (raid), 32
Livingston (airfield, Scotland), 118
Lloyd, Hugh Pughe, 60, 64, 92, 126–7
Lockheed P38 Lightning, 87, 112, 132, 165, 194
Lockheed Hudson, 36, 42, 91, 106, 116, 146
London (raids), 23, 29, 32
Lorient (French U-boat base), 146, 152
Lübeck (raid), 69
Luftflotte II, 32, 125
Luftflotte III, 73
Luftflotte IV, 130
Luqa (airfield, Malta), 46, 85, 91
Lyons, John, 143–4

M3 (Lee-Grant) tank, 165
MacArthur, Douglas, 107, 110–11
Macchi C202, 60, 94
Mackenzie, Russell, 190
Mackie, Alex, 58
Maison Blanche (airfield, Algeria) 134–8
Majola, SS, 136, 138, 140
Maleme (airfield, Crete), 47
Maloy (raid, Norway), 40–1
Malta, 45, 58–66, 85–6, 92–7, 170–1, 173
Malta Night Fighting Unit (MNFU), 60
Maltzahn, Gunther von, 58
Mandalay (Burma), 159
Manning, Ralph, 101
Manston (airfield, Kent), 36
Mariet, William, 108
Marteban, Gulf of (raid), 166
Martin-Baker, 20
Martin Baltimore, 87, 201
Martin B-26 Marauder, 106
Martin Maryland, 47, 49, 87, 92, 124
Martinside Elephant, 157
Mason, John, 103
McKeever, Andrew, 4
Meagher, Patrick, 161
Meharg, Bryce, 198
Meiktila (Burma), 167
Meister, Dieter, 149
Mellersh, Francis, 172
Merrill's Marauders, 165
Messerschmitt Bf109, 20–1, 40, 42, 53, 58, 61, 79, 85, 89, 91, 94, 124, 128, 180, 194–5, 200
  Bf110, 14, 16, 38–9, 46, 81–2, 85, 89, 121, 124, 129
  Me323 '*Gigant*', 126–7, 130, 132, 204
Messina (Straits, Sicily and Italy), 175
Mia Moana (yacht), 119
Middlebrook, Garrett, 113
Milch, Erhard, 33
Miller, Reginald 'Dusty', 62
Milne Bay (New Guinea), 104, 111
Milson, Colin, 187
Ministry of Economic Warfare, 181
Mitchell, Henry, 64–5, 141
Mitsubishi A6M Zero / 'Zeke', 107, 117–19
Mitsubishi J4M 'Betty', 116
Mitsubishi Ki-21 'Sally', 154
Molins cannon, 186
Montague Brown, Anthony, 168
Montecorvino (airfield, Italy), 208
Moody, Flight Lieutenant, 115
Moran-Hilford, Des, 108
Morotai (airfield, Indonesia), 119
Morzik, Fritz, 122–3, 126
Mosby, William, 142
Moscow, 122
Mosquito panik, 83
Moss, C.W., 156
Mountbatten, Lord Louis, 40
Muller-Rowland, Eric, 203
Muller-Rowland, Stanley, 195
Munich crisis, 14, 36

Mussolini, Benito, 44
Mutaguchi, Renya, 161, 165
Myitkina, 162, 165

Nakajima A6M2N 'Rufe', 118
Nakajima Ki-43 'Oscar', 110, 160
Napier Sabre (engine), 12
Narvik (port, Norway), 179
Narvik class destroyer, 183
  Z24, 183
  Z32, 183
  Z33, 187
Nelson, Alf, 113
Nesbitt, Roy Conyers, 17
New Guinea, 104–10
Nicholas, Pilot Officer, 209
Nicholson, James, 161
Nicholson, Keith, 114
Nigeria, HMS, 97
Night intruder, 31–2
Noemfoor Island (New Guinea), 114, 119
North American B25 Mitchell, 106–107, 109, 112–13, 131, 166, 193, 204
North American P51 Mustang, 184, 186–7
North Coates strike wing, 178–81, 183–4
Nuremburg (raid on), 83

Ohio, SS, 66, 95
Okado, Seizo, 105
O'Neill, Tony, 155
Operation Accolade, 192–3
  Archery, 40–1
  Avalanche, 206
  Barbarossa, 48, 59–60
  Battleaxe, 48
  Compass, 45
  Corkscrew, 170
  Crusader, 52–7, 60, 124
  Flax, 132, 143
  Ha Go, 165
  Harpoon, 90–1
  Herakles, 61, 65
  Husky, 170
  Longcloth, 158
  Marita, 45
  Oboe, 119
  Pedestal, 66, 95–6, 147
  Seratte 79–80
  Steinbock, 76
  Torch, 125, 142
  U Go, 166
  Vigorous, 66, 90–1
Operational Research Group 146
Oran (port, Algeria), 169, 206
Orient (Finnish freighter), 185
Owen Stanley range (New Guinea), 109–10
Oxby, Doug, 67, 142–3

Pain, Derek, 63
Palermo (port, Sicily), 174
Palestine, 50–1
Palm Sunday Massacre, 132
Pantelleria (Island), 126, 170
Parade Middle East (newspaper), 164
Parer, Damien, 111, 113
Park, Keith, 4, 66, 93, 128
Passier, Hanny, 147
Pathfinders, 76
Peenemunde (raid), 82
Pemberton Billing, Neville, 3
Penfoei (airfield, Timor), 116
Peniakoff, Vladimir, 121
Phaphamau (airfield, India), 160
Phipps, Rodney, 205
Piaggio P108, 141
Piening route, 152
Pierse, Richard, 161
Pietro Orseolo (Italian blockade runner), 182
Pike, John, 44, 95
Pike, Thomas, 72
Pink's War, 157
Plagis, Johnny, 62
Player, John, 138–9, 174
Popski's Private Army, 121
Port Moresby (port, New Guinea), 104–105, 108, 110
Portal, Charles, 37
Portreath (airfield, Cornwall), 136
Powell-Sheddan, Colin, 60
Pratt & Whitney Twin Wasp (engines), 89
Predannack (airfield, Cornwall), 80, 150, 182
Pring, Maurice, 67, 155–6

Pringle, Flight Lieutenant, 197
Prinz Eugen, 41, 43
Protville 2 (airfield, Algeria), 203, 205

Quit India (nationalist campaign), 155

RAAF (Royal Australian Air Force), 102
No.30 Squadron, 103–14, 118–19
No.31 Squadron, 103, 114–19
No.455 Squadron, 181, 186–7
No.77 Wing, 118
RAF Armoured Car Corps, 50–1
Coastal Command, 35–7, 145–53, 177–83
3rd Tactical Air Force, 161
No.22 Squadron, 85, 89, 118, 166
No.23 Squadron, 78, 84, 206
No.25 Squadron, 26
No.27 'Flying Elephants' Squadron, 17, 157–61, 164–5
No.29 Squadron, 25–6
No.39 Squadron, 85–6, 92, 202, 204
No.45 Squadron, 167
No.46 Squadron, 63–4, 186, 193
No.47 Squadron, 166–7, 193–5, 202, 204
No.51 Squadron, 145
No.69 Squadron, 92
No.85 Squadron, 25, 84
No.86 Squadron, 93
No.89 Squadron, 59, 64, 138, 141, 155
C Flight, 64–5
100 Group, 82–3
No.108 Squadron, 172, 174
No.125 Squadron, 141
No.141 Squadron, 25, 79–84, 150
No.143 Squadron, 39, 143, 178, 180, 186
No.144 Squadron, 181, 183, 186–7, 202–204
No.153 Squadron, 142, 170, 206
No.176 Squadron, 155–6
No.177 Squadron, 160–1, 163
No.201 Group, 86, 126
No.211 Squadron, 161, 166–8
No.217 Squadron, 92, 166
No.219 Squadron, 26, 171
No.227 Squadron, 98, 127, 131, 191–2, 194, 196
No.235 Squadron, 36, 41, 92, 98, 147–8
No.236 Squadron, 36, 40, 177, 180, 186
No.248 Squadron, 36, 39–40, 42, 92, 95, 97–8, 147–9, 151, 153, 186
No.250 Squadron, 121
No.252 Squadron, 36–9, 46–7, 87–9, 95, 121, 191–2, 196
No.254 Squadron, 39, 177–8, 180–1
No.255 Squadron, 126, 135–40, 174–5, 206
No.256 Squadron, 142
No.264 Squadron, 25, 141
No.272 Squadron, 39, 46–7, 85, 87, 89–90, 124, 126–7, 131, 204
No.328 Wing, 202
No.420 Flight, 26
No.600 Squadron, 26, 31, 136, 141, 172, 206
No.603 Squadron, 194–6
No.604 Squadron, 27, 31
No.901 Wing, 161
No.1435 Flight, 60–1, 64
RCAF (Royal Canadian Air Force) 404 Squadron, 181, 187
RCAF No.406 Squadron, 63, 74
RNZAF (Royal New Zealand Air Force) 489 Squadron, 181, 186–7
Rabaul (airbase, New Guinea), 111–12
Rangoon (Burma), 162, 168
Rangoon jail, 168
Rawlings, 'Jimmy', 16, 28
Rayment, Kenneth, 142
Read, Charles, 115, 118
Read, James 'Jasper', 173
Reeves, Nevil, 64
Réghaïa (airfield, Algeria), 171
Regia Aeronautica, 51, 60, 86
Reichskommisar Schifffahrt, 179
Rhodes (Greek island), 192
Rhubarb (mission type), 158–9
Riley, Bill, 38, 47, 85, 89
Robert Rowan, SS (freighter), 172
Robinson, William Leefe, 4
Rocket projectile (3-inch), 180–1, 196
'Rockbeau', 150, 161, 167, 180–1, 196
Rodel, Gustav, 53
Rohna, SS, 207

Rolls-Royce engines, 5, 11, 214
Merlin, 18–19
Peregrine, 11
Vulture, 11, 19
Roma (Italian battleship), 201
Rommel, Erwin, 45, 99–101
Ross, J.M., 64
Rothermere, Lord, 8
Rotterdam (port, Netherlands), 179
Royal Aircraft Factory, 3–4
RE8, 4
Royal Aircraft Establishment, 3–4
Royal Marines, 136

SAAF (South African Air Force) No.12 Squadron, 124
SAAF No.21 Squadron, 124
SAAF No.24 Squadron, 54
Saint Nazaire (port, France), 146
Sakai, Saburo, 107
Salerno (allied landings), 206
Samos (island, Dodeconnese), 193, 198
San Andrea (freighter), 99
Savannah, USS, 206
Savoia-Marchetti SM79, 49, 90, 95
Savoia-Marchetti SM81, 47, 126
Savoia-Marchetti SM82, 126–8, 204
'Savoia Staffel', 204
Sayer, George, 108
Scharnhorst (German battlecruiser), 41–2
Schiff 50 (German flakship/carrier), 198
Schmidt, Dallas, 100, 128–9
Seizo, Okaido, 105, 109
Seratte radar box, 79
Setif (airfield, Algeria), 140
Sharman, Hank, 99–100
Shipard, Mervyn, 64–7, 142
Shore, Ross, 94, 98
Short Stirling, 18, 42, 69, 76
Short Sunderland, 36, 146–7, 151
Sidi Barrani (port, Egypt), 99
Siebel ferry, 193, 195
Simpson, Sturley, 187
Sinclair, Sir Archibald, 136
Singh, Harjinder, 156
Sirte (port, Libya), 88
Sittang River (Burma), 168
Skaergaard (Norway), 180
Skagerrak (strait, Denmark), 180
Skerki Bank (Tunisia), 95–6
Skip bombing, 112
Slapston Sands disaster, 182–3
Sleeve valves, 9, 159, 164
Slessor, Sir John, 146, 150, 181, 186
Slim, William, 111, 161
Smith, Percival, 188
Souk al Arab (airfield, Algeria), 138
Sparrow Force, 115
Spearey, Bill, 205
Special Air Service (L Detachment), 55
Spurgin, Arthur, 138
St Eval (airfield, Cornwall), 36
Stainforth, George, 7, 66
Stalingrad, 130–1, 133
Stephenson, Leslie, 170, 207
Sterling, Paddy, 165
Stevens, Richard, 78
Stolle, Bruno, 148
Strever, Ted, 94
Strubby (airfield, Lincolnshire), 185
Stumm, Gustav Brun von, 73
Suez Canal, 58–9
Sumburgh (airfield, Shetland Islands), 38, 41, 43
Supermarine, 3, 7
Supermarine S6, 7, 66
Supermarine Spitfire, 7, 31, 61, 66, 92, 94, 132, 134, 139, 175
Photo-reconnaissance Spitfires, 178
Free French squadrons, 206–207
Sutherland Brown, Atholl, 161, 166
Suthons, Harry, 112–13
Swedish iron ore, 179

Tahar (airfield, Algeria), 206
Taiman Kukugi Air Group, 107
Takali (airfield, Malta), 61–2, 64, 126
Taranto (port, Italy), 94
Taroona, SS (transport ship), 105
Tedder, Arthur, 47–9
Templeton's Crossing (New Guinea), 110
Thai-Burma railway, 162

Thazi (rail junction, Burma), 163
Thimble nose, 71
Timor, 115–18
Tizard, Henry, 23, 180
Tmimi (airfield, Libya), 52, 124
Tobruk (port, Libya), 55, 64, 89, 125
Topham, John, 72
'Torbeau', 43, 167, 178, 184, 193, 202
Toungoo (airfield, Burma), 158
Trento (cruiser), 91
Tunis (battle), 131–3, 143
Tunis (port), 126
Turbinlite, 24, 71–3
Turnbull, John, 172, 175
Type 95 *Ha Go* tank, 166

U-boats, 35–6, 38, 145–51
Udet, Ernst, 33
Ulster Queen, HMS (radar ship), 199
Ultra (intelligence), 98, 101
Unbroken, HMS, 98
Uren, Ron 'Torchy', 113
US 5th Air Force, 111–12
US 12th Air Force, 131–2, 193, 204
US 1st Fighter Group, 193
US 14th Fighter Group, 193
US 414th Nightfighter Squadron, 207, 210
Uwins, Cyril, 5, 15

Very flare, 94
Vian, Philip, 91
Vickers Warwick, 186
Vickers Wellesley, 128
Vickers Wellington, 7, 18, 42, 52, 62, 69, 128, 145, 161, 166
'Fishington' 100–101
Victorious, HMS, 96
Vildebeest, Vickers, 36
Vinke, Heinz, 82
Vittorio Veneto, 90
Vultee Vengeance, 161

Waddingham, John, 67
Wagga Wagga (airfield), 103
Walker, Brian 'Blackjack', 103
Waltersdorf, Helmut, 78
Warburton, Adrian, 92
Ward's Strip (airfield, New Guinea), 105, 114
Warspite, HMS, 206
Watson, Anthony, 127–8
Watson-Watt, Robert, 23
Waziri (tribesmen), 157
Westland Whirlwind, 11, 20
Westmacott, Innes, 61
Weston-super-Mare (Bristol shadow factory), 37
Wheeler, Neil, 178, 180
'Whispering death' (the myth), 164
White, Sir George, 1–3, 5
White, Harold, 81
White, Stanley, 5, 8
Whitehead, Ennis, 111
Whittle, Frank, 7
Wick strike wing, 181
Williams, 'Jock', 134
Wingate, Orde, 158
Woolton, Lord, 31
Wunderwaffe, 201
Wurzburg (radar stations), 77
Wyrill, Hugh, 134, 136

X-Great (radio beam), 27

Yaxley, Robert Gordon, 37, 47, 49, 55–6, 88, 124

Zodiac (French aircraft company), 2